PRO TOOLS
CLINIC

DEMYSTIFYING LE FOR **MACINTOSH** AND **PC**

MITCH GALLAGHER

SCHIRMER
TRADE
BOOKS

A Part of **The Music Sales Group**
New York/London/Paris/Sydney/Copenhagen/Berlin/Tokyo/Madrid

Schirmer Trade Books
A Division of Music Sales Corporation, New York

Exclusive Distributors:
Music Sales Corporation
257 Park Avenue South, New York, NY 10010 USA
Music Sales Limited
8/9 Firth Street, London W1D 3JB England
Music Sales Pty. Limited
120 Rothschild Street, Rosebery, Sydney, NSW 2018, Australia

Order No. SCH 10133
International Standard Book Number: 0-8256-7294-5

Cover Design: Phil Gambrill

Printed in the United States of America
By Vicks Lithograph and Printing Corporation

Library of Congress Cataloguing-in-Publication Data
Gallagher, Mitch.
 Pro Tools clinic : demystifying 6.1 for Macintosh and PC / by Mitch Gallagher.
   p. cm. -- (Clinic series)
 ISBN 0-8256-7294-5 (pbk. : alk. paper)
 1. Pro Tools. 2. Digital audio editors. I. Title. II. Series.
 ML74.4.P76G35 2004
 781.49'0285'536--dc22
                    2004025684

CONTENTS

ACKNOWLEDGMENTS

This book wouldn't have happened without the efforts of a number of wonderful people—too many to adequately thank here. My apologies to those I've inadvertently missed.

My good friend Craig Anderton is the man who made the connection between Omnibus Press/Schirmer Trade Books and myself. Without him, this book wouldn't exist—at least not with me as the author.

Andrea Rotondo, the managing editor for this project, was the driving force for making things happen. Without her extremely gentle prodding and gracious understanding of my schedule difficulties, this book probably would never have been finished, let alone been any fun to do.

Leonard Hospidor was the technical/development editor for *Pro Tools Clinic*; his Pro Tools knowledge and expertise are why the book is so complete and accurate.

Chandra Lynn at Digidesign is the magician responsible for getting me countless pieces of gear and software over the years for magazine reviews, as well as the person who arranged for the loan of a Digi 002 system while I worked on this book.

Thanks to Rob McGaughey, my studio partner-in-crime through many sessions. Together we spent countless hours learning our way around Pro Tools. No one has been a more staunch supporter for me in all I've done through the years.

How can I thank my family for all they've done for me? To my parents, thank you so much for all your support and love through many years in this crazy music business. Grandma Lorraine, I swear I'll have a finished CD of my guitar music for you soon….

Finally, this book is dedicated to my wife Felicia, who makes it all worthwhile. I love you.

Mitch Gallagher hails originally from Jamestown, North Dakota, the home of the World's Largest Buffalo. He was introduced to recording music in 1982, when the manager of the rock band he was in loaned the group a 4-track cassette recorder. His background includes studies in electrical engineering and computer science, and a Bachelor of Arts degree in music from Moorhead State University, in Moorhead, Minnesota (now known as Minnesota State University, Moorhead). His graduate studies in composition, electronic music composition, and classical guitar took him to the University of Missouri, Kansas City.

As a guitarist, he toured the Midwest for several years playing rock and country music. He has performed with big bands, jazz-rock fusion groups, experimental music groups, in small ensembles, and as a classical and steel-string guitar soloist. He has taught countless guitar lessons, both private and in university classrooms.

As a composer, he has worked in both the commercial and classical realms. *Prophecy #1: At First Glance*, his experimental work for percussion ensemble and synthesizers, received a NARAS (Grammy) award.

He began building his first project studio in 1983—with a Commodore 64 computer, primitive MIDI software, a low-end drum machine, and a small Radio Shack PA for monitoring. Eventually his studio evolved into MAG Media Productions, which provides a full range of recording, mixing, editing, mastering, and radio and multimedia production services, as well as freelance writing and editing services.

In addition to years spent in pro-audio retail and as a freelance recording and live sound engineer, Gallagher has taught university-level recording and electronic music classes and labs, countless seminars on recording, MIDI, and live sound, and lectured on music-technology topics throughout the United States and in Europe.

He was named senior technical editor of *Keyboard* magazine in 1998. In January 2000, Gallagher assumed the editor's chair at *EQ* magazine. He has published hundreds of product reviews and articles on music technology and recording in magazines such as *EQ*, *Keyboard*, *Pro Sound News*, *Guitar Player*, *Government Video*, *Extreme Groove*, *Music Technology Buyer's Guide*, *Videography*, *Microphones & Monitors*, as well as in magazines in Japan, Australia, and throughout Europe. His first book, *Make Music Now!* was released in 2002.

He currently resides with his wife Felicia and their Yorkie Paddington in the Atlanta, Georgia area. When he has time, he works on a CD of his fingerstyle acoustic guitar instrumentals. At the rate he's going, it will be released in 2015.

FOREWORD

With the computer revolution firing on all cylinders, the world of audio has hitched a ride on falling hard disk, memory, and computer prices to revolutionize the way we record music. In less than a decade and a half, computer-based hard-disk recording has gone from an esoteric system of audio recording available only to the wealthy, to the most common method of recording music. We now have the means to not only record performances, but to edit, mix, backup, and process them with repeatable, pinpoint precision.

No other system has evangelized the cause of hard-disk recording as much as Digidesign's Pro Tools. The history of Digidesign reads like the paradigm of Silicon Valley's go-go gestalt: Two guys start a business in their garage, selling replacement sound chips for a popular drum machine. Then, dissatisfied with the Mac's ability to process audio, they came up with a hardware booster based on digital signal processing. From there it was a short trip to editing stereo signals, and from there, to multitrack recording...and Pro Tools was born.

Over the years, Pro Tools has evolved into an ever more complex and creative system, while forming a tight and symbiotic relationship with the Macintosh and Windows platforms. And that brings us to this book, which will help you sort out the technical complexities so you can move forward with the important part: Creating music.

Author Mitch Gallagher is no mere Pro Tools jockey, but an accomplished, award-winning musician and prominent figure in the music industry who is currently editor of *EQ* magazine. More importantly, he's a straightforward, no-nonsense kind of guy, and that vibe translates into his writing. He's not here to impress you with his knowledge, but to help increase yours. Reading this book is like having a knowledgeable, patient instructor at your side who can guide you through the maze of today's recording technology.

The more you know about Pro Tools, the more you'll find that using it becomes second nature. When it does, you'll stop thinking about the technology, and just flow with the music. So sit down with your Pro Tools system, start reading, and practice your new "instrument." Once you get good at it—and this book will certainly help you accomplish that goal—I predict you'll be delighted with what you can accomplish.

Craig Anderton

INTRODUCTION

I always get a kick out of those books and articles that say something like, "We live in an amazing time, technology has made everything so affordable, and we can do things now that we never even dreamed of just a few short years ago." I have to laugh (though I also have to admit I've been guilty of writing such things more than once!), because just a few short years from now we'll be saying, "What the heck were we thinking? The technology was so *stone-age* back then...look at all we can do with what we have *now,* and how *cheap* it is."

But with regard to recording studio technology, the former statement is certainly true (as, of course, is the latter). The gear we have access to today *is* so affordable and so powerful, it's simply amazing. Case in point: Digidesign Pro Tools. I started using Digidesign systems back in the dark ages of hard-disk recording, around 1992. (Is it already that long ago?) In those days, it was Sound Tools, a mono/two-track recording/editing system. I still remember what a revelation it was when Dino, my friendly neighborhood Digi rep, gave me my first demo of this new multitrack hard-disk recording system, Pro Tools. Back then, Pro Tools consisted of two pieces of software, one for mixing and one for editing, rather than the single streamlined application it comprises these days. Plug-ins and other forms of computer-based processing weren't even distant dreams in the minds of software developers. Looking back, it sure seems primitive now, but I (and most everyone else) thought it was a technological marvel...coming from

a background of recording on tape through a big hardware mixing console, the idea of doing everything inside a computer seemed completely mind-boggling. And as each updated software version of Pro Tools was released, as each piece of new, improved hardware came out, my amazement was renewed.

These days, Pro Tools is considered the industry standard—the hard-disk recording system that all the others are chasing. It's in use in virtually every type of studio, from commercial music facilities to major film studios, from computer game developer stations to multimedia production suites, from school music labs to project studios. This isn't because Pro Tools is the most feature-laden of the current crop of hard-disk recording systems—it's not (although it certainly has way more features than most of us will ever use). But it *is* arguably the most targeted toward getting things done in the studio. It's this approach, along with a design that makes it feel familiar to those experienced in recording studios, that has led to its adoption by myriad studios of every type around the globe.

The release of Pro Tools LE extended the reach of Pro Tools even further, into the world of home studios and smaller project studios. Other versions of Pro Tools were decidedly high-end; only the most well-heeled project and home-studio owners could afford (or justify) the expense. (Of course, even high-end Pro Tools systems seemed cheap compared to the $100,000+ you could drop on other early digital recording systems!) But Pro Tools LE systems bring the power of Pro Tools to a price-point that's affordable for many, without compromising the attractive capabilities offered by high-end systems—at least not enough compromise that it matters to those not doing large production sessions for hire.

To paraphrase what was said earlier: With a Pro Tools LE system in your studio, you have recording power that was unheard of just a few years ago, at a price that doesn't destroy your pocketbook. The technology is there to realize your musical dreams and visions, we just have to learn to harness, control, and use it to best effect.

That's what this book is all about: Learning the ins and outs of Pro Tools, how to get the most from your system, and most important, learning the things you need to know to get down to making music. Whether you want to lay down simple songwriter demos, sketch out musical ideas, compose and record a full CD with your band, or put together MP3s of your compositions to post on your Website, Pro Tools LE can do it for you.

So what are we waiting for? Let's dive in and use Pro Tools to make some music!

HOW TO USE THIS BOOK

I'm a flexible kind of guy, so I've put this book together in such a way that you can use it however you like. If you're looking for a beginning-to-end Pro Tools course, one that will take you from raw beginner to seasoned expert, start on page one and read your way through to the end. I've arranged the materials so that, especially if you work through the examples included on the CD-ROM, you'll learn all the Pro Tools techniques and information you need to know in order to record, edit, process, and mix your projects from initial creative spark to completely finished Grammy-award caliber tracks.

If you already have a handle on some aspects of Pro Tools, but want to expand your knowledge and perfect your techniques, feel free to jump around to the parts that interest you. I've arranged things into seven sections, each addressing an important aspect of Pro Tools.

- **Part One** will give you some background on Digidesign Pro Tools, what Pro Tools can do for us, and a bit of information on how hard disk recording and digital audio works.

- **Part Two** covers Pro Tools hardware, computer requirements, and installation in your PC or Mac. We'll also talk about how to connect your Pro Tools system to the rest of your studio equipment, as well as how to hook up instruments such as guitars, basses, and keyboards.

- **Part Three** is where the real fun begins: We'll launch Pro Tools for the first time, take tours of the Mix and Edit windows, create our first Pro Tools Session, and learn how to route sound into and out of our Pro Tools hardware.

- **Part Four** gets us to the nitty-gritty: We'll record our first audio tracks, overdub additional parts, nail down some basic audio file issues, and learn how to transfer audio from CD into Pro Tools.

- **Part Five** contains everything you need to know about editing your tracks; the various editing modes, cutting/copying/pasting audio, fades and crossfades, AudioSuite plug-in processing, and deep editing commands.

- **Part Six** is all about mixing—taking your audio tracks from raw recordings to finished songs. This is where we'll get into applying plug-ins and effects, using automation to control everything, and creating final files ready to be burned to CD or converted to MP3.

- **Part Seven** is where we'll dive deep into MIDI. We'll learn more about sequencing and using MIDI controllers, we'll get into quantizing and more advanced MIDI event editing, and we'll have some fun using software synthesizers with Pro Tools.

Whichever way you choose to use this book, make sure to take a few minutes to read through the Pro Tools manuals. Yeah, everyone hates manuals. That's why you're reading this book, right? Still, Digidesign has done a good job on the Pro Tools manuals, and they'll serve as a handy reference as you begin your Pro Tools journey.

DECIPHERING THE CODE

Look in any bookstore: There's a ton of manuals and after-market books out there on every conceivable computer and software package. Those scholarly tomes have laid the groundwork for how commands and menu selections are notated in text. So I'm not going to waste my (or your) time or energy trying to fix something that's not broken. Just in case you haven't seen these conventions:

- **Click**—click with the mouse button (just testing, you probably knew that one....)

- **Alt-click**—hold the Alt key down and click with the mouse button. Other examples similar to this include **Ctrl+click, Option+ click, Command+click,** etc. In each case, hold down the computer keyboard modifier key specified and click with the mouse button.

- **↑-click**—the "↑" symbol refers to the shift key, so this would indicate that you should hold the shift key and click the mouse button.

- **Ctrl+Tab**—hold down the Ctrl key and press the tab key. Similar examples include **Option+8, Alt+S, +=,** and so on. In all these cases, hold down the indicated computer keyboard modifier key(s) and press the indicated key on the computer keyboard.

- **File◆Open Session...**—click on the File menu at the upper left of the computer screen, pull the mouse down to choose "Open Session..."

MAC VERSUS WINDOWS

Pro Tools started out as a Mac-only product, but a version for the Windows platform has also been available for some time. There are few differences between the two platforms, and those fall primarily among the computer keyboard commands. For reference, the Mac "command" key (the one with the Apple logo—(and ⌘ on it) and the Windows "Ctrl" key do the same thing, as do the Mac "Option" key and the Windows "Alt" key. The Mac "Return" and Windows "Enter" keys are the same. When commands differ between the two platforms, I'll list the one for Mac first, then the Windows equivalent in parenthesis like this: ⌘+↑+**N** (Ctrl+↑+N)

MOUSE GAMES

The Macintosh mouse generally has one button, while most Windows mice have (at least) two buttons. For Windows users, **Click** refers to the left mouse button, while **Right-click** refers to, well, clicking with the right mouse button.

OPERATING SYSTEMS, VERSIONS, AND UPDATES

One thing is for certain whenever you're dealing with computer-based software and hardware: Nothing stays the same for very long. Computer operating systems are upgraded constantly, and new versions of software are released at an almost alarmingly fast pace. Given this fact, there's no way a book like this can be absolutely up-to-the-minute with the latest software revision—by the time the text and graphics for the book get put together, printed, and shipped to your favorite bookstore, there's certain to be a new version of Pro Tools available. (By the way, check *www.digidesign.com* often for downloadable updates and information on new versions.)

Fortunately, the overwhelming majority of what we'll be talking about here remains relevant regardless of what version of Pro Tools you're using (even if you're using an older version than we discuss here). A few details may change in a new version and some new features may be implemented, but once you have the program sussed, figuring out the new stuff shouldn't be a problem. So take heart and don't worry too much about the details of the latest and greatest...we're building a foundation here that's going to serve you well as Pro Tools evolves into the future.

Having said all that, this book focuses on Pro Tools LE version 6.1, which runs on Windows XP and Mac OS X (up to OS X 10.2.8). If you're using a newer or older version of Pro Tools LE, no worries, almost everything we cover here will still be completely valid. Likewise, most of the screenshots and graphics are taken from a Macintosh running OS X; there will only be minor differences for Windows users or users of Mac OS 9.x.

SPINNING THE CD

Enclosed with this book is a CD-ROM containing audio and Pro Tools session examples for use as you're working your way through the text. You'll get best results if you create a folder on your hard drive and copy the contents of the CD to it.

PART ONE

Pro Tools Explained

one

WHAT IS PRO TOOLS?

Who wants to be a millionaire? All that's required is to answer the following question: What is Digidesign Pro Tools?

A. A handy belt-clippable multi-tool
B. Tools for Digidesign professionals
C. A computer-based DAW
D. Professional tools used for designing Digidesigns

If you answered, "C. A computer-based DAW," you're correct! Unfortunately, I lied about the million dollars. But you can rest secure in the fact that knowledge is its own reward. If you missed the question, no worries...you've come to the right place for the answer. (And I promise, this is the last time I'll lie to you....)

So Digidesign Pro Tools is a computer-based DAW. Let's examine that statement a bit more closely. The first part, "computer-based," is fairly self-explanatory: Digidesign Pro Tools is a software and hardware package that operates in conjunction with a computer, running either Windows or Macintosh operating systems. The last part, "DAW," is an acronym—an abbreviation for "Digital Audio Workstation."

Clear? Or maybe not...what the heck is a digital audio workstation? The short answer is that it's a virtual (computer) re-creation of a recording studio; software and hardware that lets you record, edit,

process, mix, and master audio signals.

THE OLD WAY

In a "traditional" analog studio, several large, expensive pieces of electronic gear are required to create recordings. Pro Tools gathers the capabilities to those pieces of gear into one software application. Let's take a closer look.

Analog

In older-style "hardware" studios, sound is represented using electrical voltage; the voltage is a direct representation (or "analog") of the sound wave. A microphone, for example, "hears" or responds to the sound waves by sending out a tiny electrical signal. The tiny signal is amplified, or increased in level, and sent to a recorder, where the electrical signal is converted to magnetic impulses that are stored on tape. When the tape is played back, the magnetism is converted back to electrical signals, which are amplified to a high enough level that they can move a speaker cone, creating sound waves our ears can hear.

In a "hardware" studio, there is a mixing console, or mixer. A mixer accepts numerous external signals, routes, and combines them. As an example, if the studio were recording a rock band, there might be microphones on lead vocal, harmony vocal, two guitars, electric bass, and six mics on a drum kit—one on kick drum, one on snare, two on toms, and two as overheads to capture cymbals. The mixer accepts each of those microphones into an input channel, one channel per mic. Each input channel provides the ability to adjust the tone and volume, among other things, for each microphone.

The mixer routes each microphone out, to be recorded on to a tape recorder. But we're not talking about a stereo recorder, like the cassette recorder on your stereo. A studio uses a "multitrack" recorder, where each signal from the mixer can be recorded as a separate, discrete track. Continuing our example, the lead vocal gets a track on the recorder, the harmony vocal another, there's one for each guitar, and so on.

In a "traditional" studio, each microphone feeds into the mixing console, which routes each microphone input to a separate output that feeds an input on the multitrack tape recorder. The mixer also sends feeds out to headphones for the musicians to listen to and to studio speakers (monitors) so the recording engineer can hear what's going on as the tracks are recorded.

mixer. The tone of each channel can be adjusted, as can its volume. Processing can also be added; special effects and so on. These effects are provided by external hardware processing boxes. One box might provide reverb, another echo, another compression (which controls the dynamics of a signal), etc. Signals are sent out from the mixer, through the processing boxes, then returned back into the mixer to be combined with the input channels coming from the multitrack recorder.

All those input channels, along with the signals coming from the processing boxes are combined, or mixed, usually to stereo, although if the project will be used for video, DVD, or games, the signals might be mixed to 5.1 or other surround-sound format.

Each track on the multitrack tape recorder has its own output, which feeds into the mixing console. Signals are sent out of the mixer to various processors, then returned into the mixer. All those inputs are combined by the mixer to create the final stereo (or surround sound) mix. A stereo feed is also sent to the monitors, so the engineer can hear what's happening as he mixes.

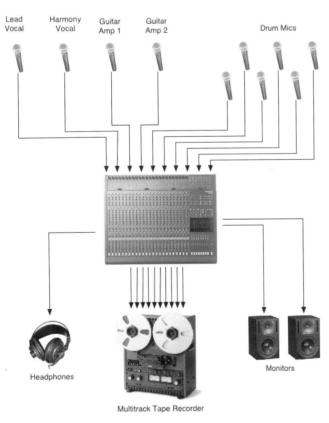

Figure 1-1

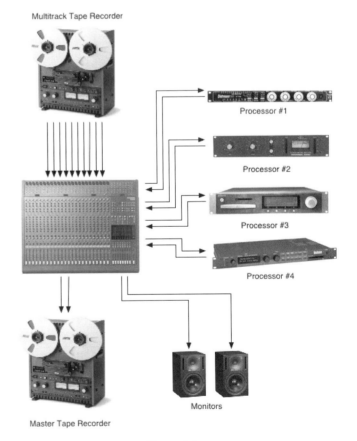

Figure 1-2

When the recording is finished, the tracks from the multitrack recorder get routed back through the mixer, to be combined to stereo so that they can be played from a cassette, CD, or through the radio. As with the original microphone signals, each track from the multitrack recorder gets its own channel on the

Additional processing might be applied to the final stereo signal as it is being recorded to yet another recorder, referred to as the master recorder.

Compression might be added, overall tone adjustments made, and so on.

THE PRO TOOLS WAY

All that hardware cost a lot of money, took up a lot of space, and generated a lot of heat! Fortunately for us, modern technology offers an alternative: The virtual world and digital processing. Pro Tools duplicates the functionality of the studio hardware in one software program. There's a software mixer that accepts incoming signals. The mixer can route those incoming signals to virtual multitrack "tape" tracks. Once the tracks are recorded, they're routed back through the mixer, and can have their tone and volume adjusted. Processing can be applied, either using external hardware boxes, or, more likely, using little virtual software processors called "plug-ins." Signals are sent to the plug-ins, then the processed signal is returned back into the mixer. All of the above takes place inside the computer.

As with hardware, the Pro Tools channels, along with signals from the processors, are mixed to stereo or to a multi-channel surround-sound format. Overall processing can be added on the final signal: Dynamics, tone control (a.k.a. equalization or EQ), and special effects.

But Pro Tools has other tricks up its virtual sleeves. Because everything Pro Tools does is in the digital computer world, all the signals are digital data. This gives Pro Tools power never available in the hardware world: Audio can be edited—cut, copied, and pasted—just like text with a word processor. If there's an unwanted noise in a track, say, a vocalist sneezes, it's no problem at all to go in and quickly cut out the offending olfactory blast without disturbing any other tracks. In a hardware-based studio, you would have had to carefully erase the sound, manually hit a mute button, or try to use a razor blade to cut a sneeze out of the tape—any of which might prove a difficult task!

With Pro Tools LE, pretty much everything lives inside the computer. In this example, the signals from the mics feed the Digi 002 interface, which connects to the computer and software. The Digi 002 and Pro Tools software also send sound out to headphones and monitors so the engineer can hear what's happening. Everything else—all processing, mixing, and final stereo master recording—takes place inside the computer using the Pro Tools software (of course, you can still use

external hardware if you prefer).

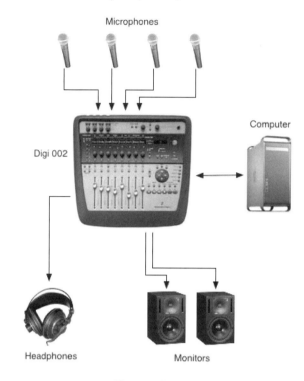

Figure 1-3

Digital

In Pro Tools (or any other digital studio gear or software), sounds are converted to, and stored as, digital information; a series of ones and zeros. Computers (and any digital equipment by definition includes a computer) can understand and manipulate those ones and zeros with ease. In order to hear the sound, it's converted from digital form back into an electrical voltage that can be amplified and used to move a speaker cone, just like in an analog studio.

In Pro Tools, you can reverse sounds and words, even entire passages. You can record the chorus of a song once, then copy and paste it to create a new arrangement...all in seconds. A single drum hit copied and pasted and combined with inspired editing, might be all you need (along with a bit of time, imagination, and savvy mouse work) to create a complete rhythm part. And because everything in Pro Tools consists of digital data, if you decide you don't like an edit or change, just hit the undo button and you're back where you started—try that in an analog hardware studio.

Software processing also provides unprecedented power, from tuning a flat note to copying and transposing an entire vocal passage to create a perfect harmony part. Plug-ins can bend, mutilate, warp, and otherwise transform pristine acoustic sounds into completely new sounds never heard before.

Where an analog studio usually required a second "master" recorder that the final stereo mix was recorded to, Pro Tools can serve as its own master recorder. You can either record your mix back onto unused tracks (which, to be fair, you can also do with an analog multitrack recorder), or you can "bounce" the finished mix straight onto the computer's hard drive without ever sending it out to the outside world at all.

In the old days of analog studios, the signals were always subject to degradation. Tape hiss was a common problem. Brightness or treble could be lost as the magnetic tape cycled back and forth. Simply storing the recorded tape in a closet could introduce distortion or unwanted noise because the magnetism on the tape could "print through" from one layer on the tape reel to another. None of these problems exist in the digital world.

That's not to say that the digital world is perfect. It isn't. In fact it creates some new problems! But it has allowed for new techniques and sounds, the reduction or elimination of many of analog's inherent problems, and has reduced the price of admission to the recording world to the point where it is affordable to nearly all.

So what is Pro Tools? It's a recording studio in a computer: A mixer, multitrack recorder, processor, editor, and much more. It's a tool that, along with a few items, such as a microphone or two and some speakers or headphones, can turn your desktop or laptop computer into a full-blown recording studio with pristine digital sound quality and amazing flexibility and power.

I'm not going to use the tired old "the possibilities are endless" cliché, since that's pushing things a bit. But I will say that by using Pro Tools, the limitations are going to be your talent, imagination, skill, and knowledge of how to use the program to its fullest extent. The first three are beyond the scope of this guidebook; the last one I can help you with! Let's dive in and learn how to get the most from your "recording studio in a computer."

two

AUDIO 101

In this chapter, we'll be getting an introduction to some audio-related concepts and terms we'll be using throughout this book—things will be theoretical and explanatory in nature for a bit here, but I promise we'll get more practical and hands-on with Pro Tools as soon as possible.

This isn't a book on the physics of sound, but picking up a few key audio/sound terms and concepts will help us to carry on our Pro Tools conversation a bit more easily.

SOUND

Here's a news alert: All recordings start with sound. It might be the sound of a voice, a trumpet, or a drum—or maybe it's an electronic representation of a sound as in an electric guitar, sampler, or synthesizer.

Sound travels in waves (cleverly called "sound waves")—similar to the waves you see in a lake or in the ocean. Vibration of a sound source creates wave motion in the air. The *frequency*, or how fast the wave vibrates, determines the pitch of the sound. A common example is "*A*-440," often used as a tuning reference for instruments. Basically, *A*-440 means that the note *A* has a frequency of 440Hz ("Hz" stands for "Hertz," named for one of the guys who figured this stuff out), which means 440 cycles, or wave vibrations, per second. The higher the note, the higher the frequency. A low note on a bass guitar

might be at 45Hz. Something like the shimmer on a crash cymbal might have a much higher frequency, up in the 6,000, 7,000, or even 10,000Hz range. (Large numbers like these are generally represented by "kiloHertz," or "kHz." A kiloHertz is a thousand Hertz, so 6,000Hz is written as 6kHz, 10,000Hz is abbreviated 10kHz, 7,500Hz becomes 7.5kHz, and so on.) Doubling the frequency of a note moves it up an octave in musical terms. So an *A* at 880Hz is an octave above *A*-440.

In Figure 2-1 we see two tones, one at 20Hz, the other at 40Hz. Note that the wave cycles for the 40Hz tone occur twice as fast—it has double the frequency of the 20Hz tone. In musical terms, it sounds one octave higher.

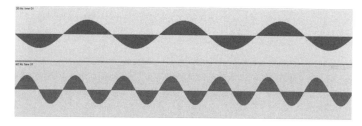

Figure 2-1

Human hearing is generally accepted to extend from around 20Hz to 20kHz. As you work with sound, your ears will start to dial in on and recognize various frequencies. This will be a big help when you want to adjust the tone of a signal. Below is Chart 2-1, I find it useful for breaking down the human range of hearing.

Frequency response is the range of frequencies a piece of audio equipment can deal with; for example, a microphone might handle from 20 to 15,000Hz (or 20Hz to 15kHz). *Bandwidth* is the width of a range of frequencies, for example, the range of frequencies affected by an equalizer (tone) control—the midrange control on an EQ might affect a band from 250Hz to 4kHz.

The volume or "level" of a sound is measured using *decibels,* or "dB," named for Alexander Graham Bell. Not to get *too* mathematical on you, but because the range of sound levels we work with is so wide, the decibel scale is logarithmic to keep things manageable. A very quiet professional recording studio might have 30dB to 40dB in background noise, where getting up close and personal with a jet airplane engine might measure 140dB. Comfortable music listening (except for those into heavy metal) might be in the 70dB to 90dB range, while a rock concert often hits 120dB to 130dB. What this logarithmic scale means for us is that you don't need to make much of a change dB-wise to hear a relatively large change in the volume or tone of a signal; 3dB of increase or decrease is quite a bit.

The shape of a sound wave is called its *waveform,* which determines what it will sound like. Almost no sound consists of a single frequency. (One exception is a "sine wave," which by definition contains only one frequency—but sine waves aren't found in nature; they're produced by synthesizers and electronic equipment.) Rather each sound can be represented as a series of "harmonics" or overtones—higher frequencies the combination of which give it a

THE RANGE OF HUMAN HEARING

Frequency	What's There
10–80Hz	This is what I call the lower bass range. Rumble, richness—low-end *thump* lives here. Many small speakers can't play much below 60 to 80Hz, so be careful of loading this area up with too much sound.
80–200Hz	This is the upper bass zone. The body of bass instruments resides here, and much of the power of the rhythm section will be found here. Too much, and the sound will turn to mud. Too little, and it will be wimpy and lack impact.
200–500Hz	This area—the lower midrange—determines the fullness of rhythm and accompaniment instruments, as well as the bottom end of many voices and solo instruments. Too much here, and things will get puffy and bloated. Too little, and the sounds will be thin.
500Hz–2.5kHz	This is the ever-popular midrange, where you'll find violin, the middle range of the piano, and solo instruments such as guitar. Most vocal sounds dwell in the midrange.
2.5–5kHz	Right here in the upper midrange is where we have harmonics and overtones—a big part of what determines the timbre of a sound. You'll also find brightness and clarity here. Too much, and things will get brittle and harsh.
5–10kHz	Lower treble is the part of the spectrum where hiss, presence, and shimmer are found. Not enough and the sound will be dull and lose clarity. Too much and the tone will be edgy and strident enough to erode metal.
10–20kHz	Way up in the stratosphere we find the upper treble range. There's not a lot of actual musical information here, but in the top octave is where characteristics such as sheen, liveness, and the ever-elusive "air" make their homes. Too much up here and the sounds will sizzle uncomfortably. Too little and the sound will be lifeless and one-dimensional.

Chart 2-1

particular tone or *timbre*. The overtones in the sound (among other things) are what make the same pitch played on a flute sound different than on a clarinet, for example. In Pro Tools, we can actually see a representation of the waveform of each sound we record—very useful when we start editing our tracks.

Here's what a flute note waveform looks like in Pro Tools.

Figure 2-2

This, on the other hand, is how a kick drum note appears.

Figure 2-3

Dynamic range is a key concept for us. It's the difference between the loudest and softest signals an audio device can handle or the loudest and softest volume levels an acoustic instrument or sound source can produce. If the dynamic range of an acoustic source is too wide for an audio device to handle, there will be problems! If the acoustic sound is too soft, it will be lost in the noise floor of the recording electronics, or will sound "hissy" (like an old cassette recording). If the signal is too loud, it will "clip" or be distorted—a nasty sound, and one to be avoided.

This sound has been recorded at a good level. It's not so soft that it could get lost in hiss or electronic noise, and it's not so loud that it's distorted.

Figure 2-4

This is the same sound recorded at too high of a level—it's been distorted or clipped. It's actually the same waveform shown in the Figure 2-4, but its volume has been boosted until Pro Tools can't handle it—the tops and bottoms of the waveform have literally been cut off, or "clipped."

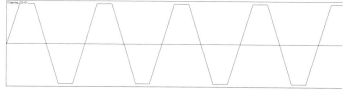

Figure 2-5

HARD-DISK RECORDING

Recording to a hard disk-based system is very different from working with an analog tape recorder. On a tape recorder, sound waves are captured and turned into voltage. The signal (voltage) is recorded onto the tape recorder as magnetism.

With an analog system, the sound waves entering the microphone are converted to voltage, then recorded as voltage on the tape recorder. *See Figure 2-6.*

On a hard-disk system, sound is captured and turned into voltage, just like with an analog system. But before it can be recorded to the hard disk, the signal must be digitized—converted to digital data. This is done using an analog-to-digital converter (a.k.a., A/D or ADC). The A/D can be incorporated into the system's audio interface, as it is for the analog inputs on Digidesign's interfaces, or it can be an external box connected to a digital input on the interface.

With a digital system, sound waves entering the microphone are converted to voltage. But before the computer can deal with them, they must be converted to digital data. This is done using an analog-to-digital converter (ADC), like those built into Digidesign Pro Tools hardware interfaces. *See Figure 2-7.*

On the way out of the hard-disk system, the process is reversed. A digital-to-analog converter (D/A or DAC) changes the digital ones and zeros into an analog voltage.

LINEAR VERSUS NON-LINEAR

A traditional tape recorder is a linear device, where a hard-disk system is *non-linear*. In order to get from place to place in a song on a tape recorder, you have to fast-forward or rewind, which takes time. You can't jump from location to location. You have to linearly wind through the tape. With a hard disk-based system, however, the opposite is true. All the audio is simply stored data on the hard drive—as far as the computer and hard drive are concerned, it's just ones and zeros—so jumping from the end of your song to the beginning is instantaneous; the hard drive just reads a different chunk of data. Likewise, in Pro Tools you can mark locations on a timeline, say, the beginning of each verse and chorus. By simply clicking a button, Pro Tools jumps instantly to that spot. Some tape recorders can automatically wind to specific points on the tape, but it sure isn't instantaneous!

On the Eve of Destruction

Another great feature of hard-disk recording in DAWs (digital audio workstations) like Pro Tools is that it's non-destructive. This means that you can make changes, chop up the audio, apply processing—pretty much anything you want to do to wreck things—and you can use the Undo command to get right back where you started. Be careful of relying too much on undo, however. You can box yourself into a corner using certain types of destructive edits and processing.

DIGITAL AUDIO BASICS

Digital audio recording works sort of like filming a movie: The movie camera records the action in front of it. What's actually on the film is a series of frames, each containing a single image from the action. When the film plays back, the images are projected in

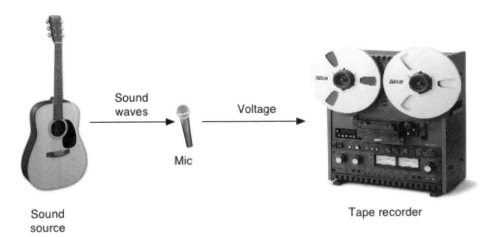

Figure 2-6

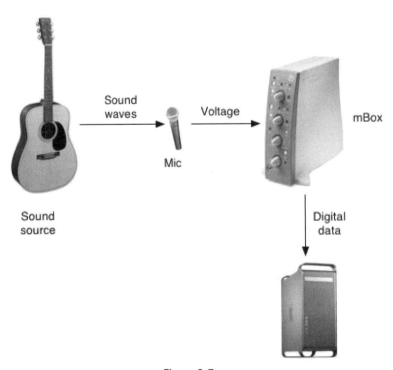

Figure 2-7

a stream, which our eyes perceive as continuous motion.

Digital audio recording works in a similar fashion. The A/D converter takes a series of "samples" of the audio signal. Each sample contains a "snapshot" of the sound—a digital measurement of what's happening at that point. When the samples are played back in a stream, we hear continuous sound—just like a sonic movie!

SAMPLE RATE

With movies, taking a series of snapshots is one thing; our eyes are pretty easily fooled into seeing continuous motion, so films can get by with as few as 24 frames per second while still appearing continuous. Our shrewd ears, however, are much less easily fooled. To be able to record and re-create audio digitally, you have to take and store a near-continuous stream of measurements.

The *sample rate* is how fast the A/D converter takes snapshots; the number of samples per second. This is expressed in kHz. A compact disc, for example, has a sample rate of 44,100 samples per second or 44.1kHz. DVDs can have higher sample rates: 48kHz, 96kHz, or even 192kHz. In audio terms, the sample rate determines the highest frequency that can be recorded. Due to something called the *Nyquist Theory,* the highest frequency that can be sampled is about half the sample rate. So the previously mentioned CD, sampled at 44.1kHz, has a frequency range up to 22.05kHz. (In the real world, it ends up being closer to 20kHz.) Pro Tools LE systems (depending on which hardware you use) support sample rates up to 96kHz, and can record frequencies up to 48kHz or so.

So if, as we discovered earlier, humans can only hear up to 20kHz, why would we want to record at a 96kHz sample rate, with a top frequency of 48kHz? There are a number of reasons; lower sample rates require steep filters in the signal path, for example, which can change the sound. There are theories that say humans can sense frequencies over 20kHz, and others say that the interaction of frequencies over 20kHz can produce audible artifacts in the human hearing range. Still others (those of a more cynical bent) say that high sample rates are an excuse for manufacturers to sell more equipment—we all want bigger, better, higher, and faster, right?

Choose whichever explanation you like—no one knows for sure right now. But, that won't stop us from arriving at a final answer to our question: Why record at high sample rates? For the answer, use your ears. If it sounds better to you to record at high rates, use them! Otherwise don't, as higher sample rates require more computer horsepower and generate larger audio files that eat up hard-drive space faster.

RESOLUTION

Resolution is the accuracy with which the audio is measured in each sample. This is measured in bits. Increasing the number of bits of resolution is like adding finer divisions to a ruler. A 1-bit recording might be like a ruler divided into feet—you're not going to get very accurate measurements with it. A 2-bit recording might divide the ruler into 6-inch steps. A 3-bit recording might be a ruler with 1-inch divisions, and so on.

A waveform like this is known as a "sine wave." It's the simplest waveform, and therefore seems like it should be the easiest to convert to digital form, right? Unfortunately, "simple" doesn't mean "easy" in this case.

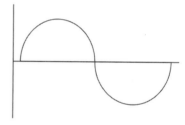

Figure 2-8

Let's take some samples (digital measurements) of the waveform. The resolution divisions are shown on the vertical axis, samples fall across the horizontal. We'll use a medium sample rate and a fairly low resolution. For simplicity sake, let's say the sample value only changes when the waveform crosses exactly at a sample/bit division cross-point.

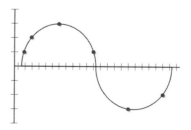

Figure 2-9

These are the samples that result from measuring

the waveform. This is what's actually stored during digital recording—just the measurements.

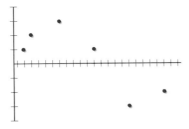

Figure 2-10

On the way out of the digital recorder—when we're playing back and listening to the sine wave we recorded—the digital-to-analog converter will attempt to reconstruct the waveform using the sample points we measured. Hmmm, doesn't look too much like the original does it?

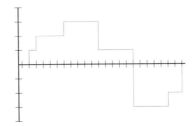

Figure 2-11

Not literally, of course. In computer terms, each bit can have one of two values, a 1 and a 0, so with a 1-bit system, there are two "divisions" for measuring the audio. Each additional bit doubles the number of possible values. A 2-bit system has four possible values, a 3-bit division has eight possible values, and so on. The first commercially available digital audio gear used 8-bit resolution, with 256 values. A 16-bit system (like a compact disc) has 65,536 possible values. Modern digital gear often has 24-bit resolution, with 16,777,216 possible values. Inside the computer, some software can represent signals with 56-bit resolution (way too many divisions for my calculator to figure out).

In audio terms, each bit translates into approximately 6dB of dynamic range. So older 8-bit gear has 48dB of dynamic range—less than a cassette tape. A CD has 96dB. A 24-bit system has a theoretic dynamic range of 144dB, though for tweaky technical reasons, the real-world limit to electronic dynamic range is more like 120dB to 130dB.

In general, the higher the resolution, the better.

Higher resolution does require more hard-drive storage space, but the trade-off is noticeably better sound. Most ears agree that, all other things being equal, the difference in going from a lower resolution to a higher resolution is more audible than going from a low sample rate to a higher one.

Here's our old friend, the sine wave. Let's take a look at what happens when we record digitally at a higher resolution. We'll keep the sample rate the same as before.

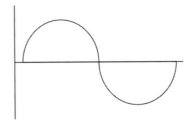

Figure 2-12

With higher resolution (more bits) there's more divisions available. This will result in more measurement changes than in our previous example.

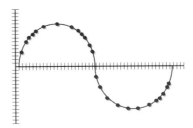

Figure 2-13

These are the samples that result from our higher resolution recording. Quite a few more than when we used low resolution, aren't there?

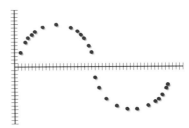

Figure 2-14

Here's the waveform the digital-to-analog converter will produce when we play back our digital recording. Still not perfect, but quite a bit closer than before. As you increase the resolution, the output of the DAC will get closer and closer to our original sine wave.

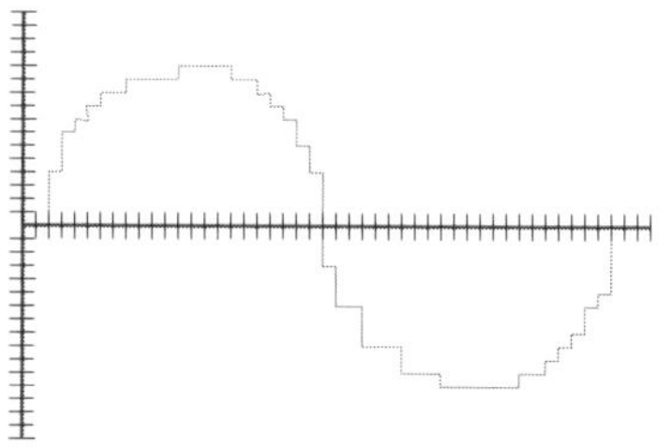

Figure 2-15

File Formats and Sizes

All those samples create a lot of data, and can chew up a lot of hard-drive space. At standard compact-disc resolution and sample rate (16-bit, 44.1kHz) you'll need about 5MB (megabytes) per minute of audio, per track. So a stereo (2-track) recording will eat about 10MB per minute. Sixteen tracks will take 80MB per minute. A 5-minute, 16-track song will consume 400MB on your hard drive!

Increase the resolution and sample rates, and the data requirements are even higher. A minute of 24-bit/96kHz audio needs 17.2MB per track of storage space. So our 5-minute, 16-track example would require 1,376MB (or almost 1.4 gigabytes) of space. The old saying goes, "You can never be too rich...." But in computer-based digital recording circles we say, "You can never have too much hard-drive space!"

There are a number of different file formats in use for storing that data on your hard drive. Pro Tools uses SDII (Sound Designer II, developed by Digidesign), AIFF (Audio Interchange File Format, developed by Apple), and WAV, (developed for Microsoft Windows) as its "native" formats—those are the ones you'll see most often in Pro Tools. There are many other common formats, including MP3, RealAudio, AAC, Quicktime, and others, although we won't be using them much in Pro Tools.

Once upon a time, the file format you chose might have been a consideration, but these days, it's no longer really an issue. Any of the three "native" Pro Tools formats, SDII, AIFF, and WAV, are broadly compatible. Many users choose to work with WAV files, especially if projects may go back and forth between Macintosh and Windows systems.

three

PRO TOOLS LE VERSUS PRO TOOLS TDM

Okay, it's time to start figuring out this whole Pro Tools business. Let's start by laying some groundwork.

NATIVE VERSUS TDM

Pro Tools systems come in two varieties: LE and TDM. All LE systems are "native" systems, meaning that they run on the host computer—all the audio processing, recording, playback—everything is handled by the computer's processor. TDM systems, on the other hand, utilize DSP (Digital Signal Processing) cards to handle audio recording and processing. There are advantages to each. TDM (which stands for Time Division Multiplexing) systems offer "power on demand"; the DSP cards have signal-processing chips sitting there at the ready, anxiously waiting to be called into action. Since those chips aren't used for any other purpose by the computer, you always know exactly how much processing power you have available. And if you find you need more power, just pop another DSP card in your computer.

Assuming you have the dollars floating around to purchase one, that is—and they're expensive. Which brings us to one of the big advantages of native systems: They're *way* cheaper. Since native systems run solely on the computer itself, you don't have to spring the big bucks to pay for DSP cards. But therein lies one of the limitations of native systems: The power available to you is determined by how much power your computer has available. And the amount can change, depending on what else your computer

is being called on to do at any given time.

Sounds bad, doesn't it? Like a native system is going to be seriously wimpy compared to a TDM rig? Take heart, the situation isn't grim. In fact, with today's computers, Pro Tools LE users are sitting pretty! A modern Mac or Windows machine can crank out an amazing amount of power. I run both a large TDM and a native Pro Tools LE rig in my studio, and except for in very large sessions, I rarely feel deprived when running LE.

Of course, you do get other benefits when you lay down all those dollars for a TDM system. You can add multiple interfaces for more simultaneous inputs and outputs. You can also run a lot more tracks (up to 128 playing at once) and can work at sample rates up to 192kHz. You can do other things, such as record and mix in surround sound. There are few other differences as well (see Chart 3.1; for more information on these items, visit the Pro Tools Reference Guide), but many of them only apply to certain situations that won't come up for most users.

All is well: In almost every case, you'll be able to do whatever you want when using Pro Tools LE on your computer.

PLUG ME IN

A big difference between native and TDM systems is the plug-ins they run. Plug-ins are small, "helper" pieces of software that perform specific processing tasks. (We'll get up close and personal with plug-ins in Chapter 21.) Pro Tools LE supports two formats:

AudioSuite, a non-real-time format and RTAS (Real-Time AudioSuite), a real-time format.

Get Real

What's all this business about real-time versus non-real-time (also known as "offline") plug-ins? Basically it comes down to when you can use the plug-ins. A "real-time" plug-in can be used while Pro Tools is playing. For example, while an audio track is playing, you could send part of its signal through an echo plug-in. You could then hear both the original track and the output of the echo plug-in live, as the song is playing back.

	Pro Tools LE	Pro Tools TDM
Audio inputs and outputs	2 or 18	16 to 96
Sample rates	up to 96kHz	up to 192kHz
Mono audio tracks	up to 128 (32 voiceable)	up to 256 (128 voiceable)
Internal mix busses	16	64
Plug-in formats	AudioSuite, RTAS	AudioSuite, RTAS, TDM, HTDM
Surround support	No	up to 8-channel
Universe window	No	Yes
QuickPunch and Auto Voice	No	Yes
Discontiguous region select	No	Yes
Shuttle mode (numeric keypad)	No	Yes
Track voice assignment	No	Yes
Dynamic voice allocation	No	Yes
Mute frees assigned voice	No	Yes
Bounce with mute frees voice	No	Yes
System memory allocation	No	Yes
MachineControl	No	Yes
Find matching tracks	No	Yes
Session data to import	No	Yes
Track playlist options	No	Yes
Export session as text	No	Yes
Calibration mode	No	Yes
Timecode support	with DV Toolkit	Yes
Continuous scroll during playback/with playhead	No	Yes
Object to timeline selection	No	Yes
Multiple trimmer modes	No	Yes
Replace region command	No	Yes
Repeat paste to fill selection	No	Yes
Compress/expand edit to fit timeline	No	Yes
Fade/crossfade preferences	No	Yes
Autofade	No	Yes
Beat Detective	No	Yes
Copy track settings to sends	No	Yes
ProControl support	No	Yes
Automation trim mode	No	Yes
Copy track automation to sends	No	Yes
Write automation to start, end, or all of a selection	No	Yes
Snapshot automation	No	Yes
Digibase	Yes	Digibase Pro
Import Digidesign Pre settings	No	Yes

Chart 3-1

"Non-real-time" plug-ins, on the other hand, can't be used while Pro Tools is recording or playing. You have to stop Pro Tools, choose the track or section of a track that you want to process, apply the plug-in, wait for it to process, then play Pro Tools to hear what the plug-in has done.

Real-time plug-ins (and other processes) have the advantage of letting you hear exactly what's being done, while it's happening. If there's a problem, you can make adjustments to settings while listening to playback—just as you'd reach over and turn up the volume on your stereo if it was too quiet while you were listening to a song.

Non-real-time processing provides less immediate feedback as to results, but it's still quite useful. To continue our analogy, non-real-time is like having to stop your stereo, turn down the volume if it's too loud, then start your stereo playing again. Certain processes, such as time-stretching and time-compressing (changing the length of a piece of audio without changing its pitch), require a lot of processing, and are usually done offline. If your computer is struggling to keep up with all the plug-ins you want to use, non-real-time AudioSuite plug-ins provide a solution: Take some of the plug-ins offline, and ease the load on your Mac or PC.

Pro Tools TDM systems support both AudioSuite and RTAS, as well as TDM (real-time) and HTDM (Host Time Division Multiplexing, along with RTAS, a second variety of Pro Tools real-time native-based processing). TDM tends to have more plug-in options available, but they're way more expensive. Besides, in the past few years, the number of RTAS plug-ins has come on strong. In fact, there are now a number of plug-ins out there that run only on RTAS, with no equivalent versions for TDM or HTDM.

Plug-ins such as this 4-band equalizer from Digidesign that comes free with Pro Tools LE can take the place of expensive hardware processors.

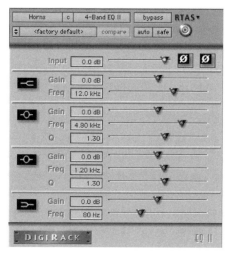

Figure 3-1

Whether you'll be able to run more plug-ins using

Pro Tools LE or Pro Tools TDM depends on a number of factors. Some of these include how powerful your computer is, how many DSP cards the TDM system has, which plug-ins are being run, and what else is happening in your computer and Pro Tools at the time. It might seem as if an LE system would always be lagging behind since it's so much less expensive, but that's simply not true. Pro Tools LE on a modern computer has plenty of power to create large productions. In one case with a Mac dual-G5 computer, using RTAS in Pro Tools LE, I was able to open up 273 separate 4-band EQ plug-ins. *Way* more than *anyone* will ever need.

LATENCY

There's another important issue regarding native and TDM systems: *Latency.* Latency is the amount of time it takes for a signal to enter the Pro Tools hardware, pass through the computer and software, and come back out of the Pro Tools hardware again. This is important when recording signals. If the latency time is high, a performer trying to play or singer trying to sing will hear and feel the delay, which can make it difficult to record in time with background music. All native systems have at least a bit of latency; TDM systems have no latency issues. But don't get overly concerned, there are some simple work arounds for curing latency in Pro Tools LE. Current Pro Tools LE hardware also has built-in features for defeating the latency problem. (We'll talk more about latency in Chapter 13.)

The time it takes for a signal to pass through the Digidesign interface, into the computer, through the Pro Tools software, out of the computer, and back out through the interface to headphones or speakers is called "latency." *See Figure 3-2.*

START YOUR ENGINES

The part of the Pro Tools LE software that actually handles the audio is called the DAE (or Digidesign Audio Engine). DAE is the ground upon which Pro Tools operates; it's the power plant behind recording audio to, and playing it back from the hard disk, and it handles the digital signal processing necessary for audio mixing and processing, as well as powering most other things that go on in the software. DAE has a Playback Buffer, a certain amount of computer memory dedicated to ensuring the flow of digital audio data off the hard drive. Setting the buffer for the correct amount of memory is important for optimizing system performance.

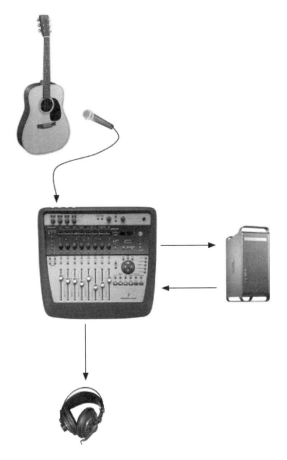

Figure 3-2

The Playback Engine dialog is where you set the DAW Playback Buffer. This is also where you set the maximum amount of your computer's power that Pro Tools can use, and the H/W Buffer, which affects latency and processing power.

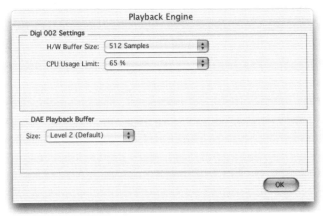

Figure 3-3

The DAW Playback Buffer is set in the Playback Engine dialog. If you got Pro Tools open, **Setups → Playback Engine...** will open the dialog if you want to check it out. The Playback Engine dialog is also

where you set the amount of your computer's power Pro Tools can claim for itself (the CPU Usage Limit), and the H/W Buffer Size, which can affect latency and the number of RTAS plug-ins you can run. For now, leave all the settings at their defaults (the way they were when you first opened Pro Tools). If necessary, we'll optimize them later.

CHANNELS

The word "channel" is used in a variety of ways in the audio world. In Pro Tools, the first thing to think of is that a channel is a hardware input or output through the Pro Tools interface. For example, the Mbox interface has two ¼-inch analog inputs and two ¼-inch analog outputs, so it's a 2-channel interface—each input/output is a channel. The number of channels determines how many signals you can get in and out of your Pro Tools system at the same time. Note that the number of channels on your interface doesn't in any way correspond to the number of tracks recorded and playing back inside Pro Tools. (See below for more on tracks.)

Inside the Pro Tools software, we can manage and configure inputs and outputs using what are called "paths." A Pro Tools path is a memorized routing to the outside world, giving you instant access to Pro Tools' hardware inputs and outputs when you're recording tracks and hooking up external devices. (Look for more on paths in Chapters 11, Session File, and 12, On the Right Track.)

The word "channel" is also used with regard to the Pro Tools mixer, which is divided into channel strips, although things will be more clear if you think of these as tracks. And we'll encounter the term "MIDI channel" when we delve into the mysteries of MIDI.

SESSIONS AND TRACKS

When you start a new project in Pro Tools, the over-all master document that's created is called a *session*. A Pro Tools session contains all the information about the project; the settings, sample rate, bit depth, any changes or edits you make—basically anything having to do with your project is part of the session. (We'll learn more about sessions in Chapter 11, Session File.) The digital audio recordings themselves are saved as separate files on your hard drive, as are a few other file types that the session uses to build your project.

This is what a Pro Tools Session icon looks like under OS X.

Figure 3-4

Here's how a Pro Tools audio file looks on your hard drive in OS X.

Figure 3-5

Two audio tracks in Pro Tools LE, as seen in the Edit window. On the left are the track controls, on the right are the waveforms for the audio signals that have been recorded.

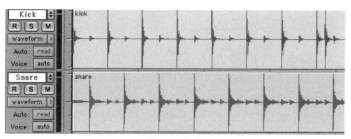

Figure 3-6

Each Pro Tools session can contain a number of different types of tracks. You can think of a *track* as a container for digital data that runs from the beginning to the end of a song or piece of music—where audio, MIDI, and automation data is recorded. Track types include audio, used to record audio data, and MIDI, used to record MIDI data. A third type, Auxiliary Input, doesn't record data, but can be used to bring audio sources into Pro Tools or for a variety of routing, processing, monitoring, and other tasks. Master Fader tracks are overall controls for outputs. An audio track in Pro Tools LE—whether audio, Auxiliary Input, or Master Fader—can be either mono (single channel) or stereo (2-channel).

REGIONS AND PLAYLISTS

Regions are created from the audio or MIDI data associated with a track. A *region* might cover an entire track, or it might be a super-small section of an audio or MIDI file on the hard drive. Regions can be moved around, copied, pasted, deleted, and arranged however you like on a track. Each audio and MIDI track has a *playlist,* which remembers the arrangement of regions on that track. You can create a number of different playlists for each track, which allows you to try out different edit possibilities and arrangements.

A region in Pro Tools is a chunk of audio or MIDI data in a track. A region can range from an entire track down to a tiny slice of audio.

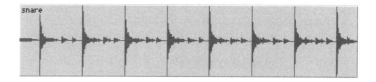

Figure 3-7

When you click the little up/down arrows beside a track name...

...a menu opens up that let's you create, delete, and select among playlists.

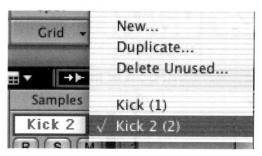

Figure 3-8

This is a playlist for a kick-drum track with several regions.

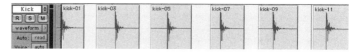

Figure 3-9

This is another playlist for the same kick-drum track. Note the different arrangement of regions. Playlists are powerful tools for trying out different song arrangements and edits.

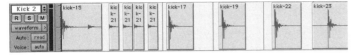

Figure 3-10

VOICES AND TRACKS

If you play an instrument or even if you sing, then you understand the concept of polyphony—the number of notes an instrument can play simultaneously. A wind instrument such as flute or trumpet has one voice of polyphony; it can play one note at a time. Likewise, the human voice is capable of one note of polyphony—not many of us can sing in chords by ourselves (although Tuvan throat singing is practiced in Mongolia and elsewhere)! A 6-string guitar has six voices of polyphony—it can play up to six notes at once. An acoustic grand piano has 88-voice or 88-note polyphony—if you had enough fingers (or invited eight 10-fingered friends to join you), you could play all 88 keys at once, and each note would sound in a glorious dissonant sonic mass.

Pro Tools is similar: It has a maximum number of voices it can play at once. In Pro Tools LE, this number was 32. A mono audio track requires one voice, while a stereo audio track requires two voices. (Only audio tracks require voices, not MIDI, Auxiliary, or Master Fader tracks.) So you can play up to 32 mono tracks or 16 stereo tracks, or some combination thereof totaling 32 voices, such as 14 mono tracks (14 voices) and nine stereo tracks (18 voices).

But as of version 6.1 and higher, Pro Tools LE is no longer limited to 32 audio tracks per session. In these newer versions, Pro Tools LE can have up to 128 tracks, with 32 of them "voiceable," or playable, at the same time. This means that 32 of the 128 tracks will play. The remaining 96 won't; they'll be set for "voice off," otherwise known as *inactive*. You can choose which 32 of the 128 tracks will play using a selector in Pro Tools.

One situation where having access to inactive tracks works out well is when you have old tracks that you're no longer using in a session. You don't want to delete them in case you need to go back later and change something. But make a track inactive, and it's basically out of the picture as far as Pro Tools is concerned—it becomes invisible, although it retains all its settings. And with a couple of mouse clicks, you can turn an inactive track back on (make it playable) and use it in the session again. Much easier than deleting or clearing a track, then needing to import

or re-create it from scratch later.

You can make a Pro Tools track inactive by setting its voice to "off." This makes it invisible to Pro Tools, but the track still remembers all its settings. You can turn it back on and pick up working on it right where you left off.

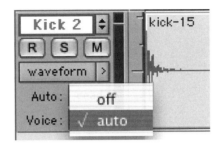

Figure 3-11

By the way, other things in Pro Tools can also be set to inactive, such as plug-ins. With plug-ins, the cool thing is that if you set one to inactive, the computer resources it eats up are made available for Pro Tools to use in other ways—but you don't lose the inactive plug-in's settings. This is great if you're bumping up against the limits of your computer's processing power, and don't want to resort to offline plug-ins.

MIDI

The Musical Instrument Digital Interface (MIDI) is a communication standard developed in the early 1980s for connecting together electronic instruments and devices. Regardless of manufacturer or device type, as long as a piece of gear is MIDI-compatible, it can talk to any other MIDI-compatible device. MIDI interface boxes are available that allow Mac and Windows computers to speak MIDI, as well.

At its most basic, MIDI can be thought of as a glorified remote-control system. In this basic example, if you play a key on the keyboard on the left, the same note will play on the keyboard on the right (assuming everything is set up correctly!). One use for this might be to layer together an orchestra sound playing on one keyboard with a grand piano playing on the other. *See Figure 3-12.*

MIDI allows for 16 channels of communication so you can independently control 16 different devices simultaneously. Some computer MIDI interfaces have multiple MIDI ports, each of which can handle 16 separate MIDI channels—this allows for the assembly of large, complex MIDI systems.

A MIDI system can become complex and very

powerful. In this case, we have a master MIDI keyboard connected to a MIDI interface, which allows the computer to record, playback, edit, and process MIDI information. The MIDI interface has multiple outputs, so it can simultaneously control a number of other keyboards and sound modules. If desired, it can also control effects boxes, tape machines, and any other piece of gear with a MIDI input connection. *See Figure 3-13.*

Mbox users will have to use a separate MIDI interface (or a keyboard with a built-in USB MIDI interface) to access MIDI gear using their computer.

But users of the Digi 002 and Digi 002 Rack will be pleased to learn that their Digidesign audio interface has a bonus built-in computer MIDI interface with one input and two independent outputs. *See Figure 3-14.*

There are a variety of MIDI message types, which represent the keys on a synthesizer or keyboard being pressed (and how hard they're pressed), movement of pitchbend and modulation wheels, patch/preset changes, and other control changes. MIDI can also be used to synchronize or lock different boxes, such as drum machines, to each other so that they play in time.

Figure 3-12

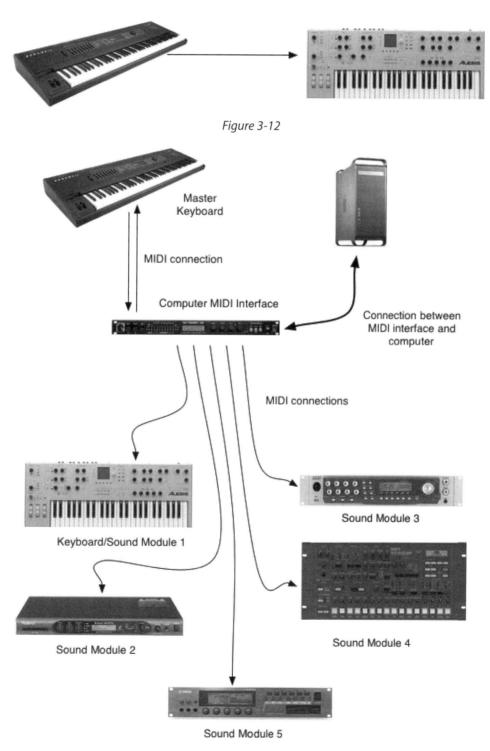

Master Keyboard

MIDI connection

Computer MIDI Interface

Connection between MIDI interface and computer

MIDI connections

Keyboard/Sound Module 1

Sound Module 3

Sound Module 2

Sound Module 4

Sound Module 5

Figure 3-13

Figure 3-14

MIDI information can be recorded and played back by a sequencer on a computer or in a synthesizer or sampler. Fortunately for those of us into using MIDI, Pro Tools contains a powerful MIDI sequencer. But having a performance recorded into Pro Tools as MIDI data allows us to do much more than just play back: We can change the pitch of notes, mess with their timing (give them more or less "groove" or "swing"), and easily input or delete notes using the mouse. We can add pitchbend or vibrato to a note, or fix errors in a performance. Since all that's recorded via MIDI is performance information—not the actual audio— we can even change the sound that's playing a part. You might play in a MIDI performance using a keyboard, but then assign that MIDI track to play using a string, guitar, drum, or totally synthetic sound.

A Pro Tools MIDI track with notes in it looks sort of like a player-piano roll—and works in a similar fashion, as well. A MIDI note isn't actually a note of music or piece of audio, rather it's the instructions for playing a note of music on a synthesizer or sampler.

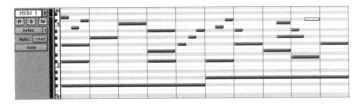

Figure 3-15

MIDI offers a broad range of possibilities, and Pro Tools ships with powerful MIDI tools to help us take advantage of those possibilities. We'll talk much more about Pro Tools and MIDI in Chapter 24, MIDI Tracks and 25, MIDI Editing.

BACKING UP AND SAVING

There are two final Pro Tools-related topics that we must discuss before we move on. We're going to be mentioning the first one throughout the book, but let's go ahead and introduce it now: Backing up. Backing up is the process of archiving your Pro Tools data off to a hard drive other than the main one you work on, to CD-R or DVD-R, or to some other storage solution. (Most computers these days come with a built-in CD or DVD burner—perfect for backing up your Pro Tools projects.) Backing up is *vital,* because every computer, every software program, every hard drive *will* hiccup, burp, or completely fail at some point. Trust me on this one. If you haven't backed up your files, they're gone—do not pass go, do not collect $200—gone forever.

Backup often. Pros do it after every session. If I'm not working with "critical" material, I do it every time I've created something that I wouldn't want to—or more likely wouldn't be able to—re-create. Backing up follows a corollary to one of the infamous Murphy's Laws: The corollary goes like this: "If you back up, you'll never have a hard-drive crash. If you don't back up, expect your hard drive to crash at any second."

Saving your data as you work is just as important. Save your files every time you make a significant change to them; that way your work is written to the hard drive rather than just living in the computer's memory. If there is a power glitch, your computer freezes, or a piece of software crashes, your data is safe and sound on the disk...and that's a comforting feeling. Saving is easy in Pro Tools; just hit ⌘+s (ctrl+s). For safety's sake, consider occasionally using Pro Tools' "Save As" command, which allows you to save the Session under a new name, without erasing any older versions.

PART TWO

2

The Pro Tools Studio

four

PRO TOOLS LE CONFIGURATION

Pro Tools systems always have two components: Hardware and software. In order to use the Pro Tools LE software, you have to have compatible Digidesign hardware. The opposite isn't necessarily true; you can sometimes use Digidesign hardware for input and output using other manufacturers' software. (It's beyond the scope of this book to cover all the possible permutations of Digidesign hardware and third-party software. Consult the software manufacturer for further information on your particular combination.) For this book, we're going to focus on Pro Tools LE software using Digidesign hardware.

Digidesign currently offers three hardware/software packages featuring the Pro Tools LE software. These packages cover a range of prices, and differ in their number of inputs and outputs, as well as other capabilities. Note that the processing capability of Pro Tools LE isn't dependent on which Digidesign hardware you're using. Rather (as we'll see later), your computer's horsepower is what determines how much you can do.

SOFTWARE

No matter what Pro Tools LE system you purchase, the software is the same—Pro Tools LE. What changes is the hardware and what the hardware can do as far as control capabilities and connections for getting sound in and out of the computer. Since the software is a constant across all the packages, let's start there first.

The Pro Tools LE software has features that fall into several areas; taken together the software is extremely powerful, yet remains easy to use—once you learn your way around! The current Pro Tools LE software supports up to 128 audio tracks, with 32 of those tracks playing back simultaneously. You can also record up to 32 tracks at once. How many of those track inputs can simultaneously come from external sources (outside the computer) depends on which hardware audio interface you're using. In addition to the audio tracks, Pro Tools LE supports up to 128 Auxiliary tracks (also known as Auxiliary Inputs). These can come from external audio sources, buses in the Pro Tools mixer, software synthesizers, and other sources. There are 16 internal mix buses, five inserts, and five sends per track. On the MIDI front, Pro Tools LE contains a sequencer that supports up to 256 MIDI tracks. (Note: Don't worry if you aren't completely familiar with all the terms and specs above; things will become clear as we make our way through this book.)

Keep in mind that the above capabilities are dependent on how much power your computer has. You should have no trouble hitting those marks if you have one of the latest fire-breathing Macs or PCs. However, if you're using an older machine, you may find yourself limited in the number of tracks, number of plug-in processors, and number of software synthesizers you can run at the same time.

Likewise, if you're running an older version of Pro Tools, the limitations stack up differently. In version

5.2 (or earlier) of Pro Tools LE, for example, the maximum number of simultaneous mono tracks that can play back is 24.

And, the audio interface you're using may limit things. With the Audiomedia III card in the Digi Toolbox system, for example, analog resolution is limited to 18 bits. (The Audiomedia III card does support 24-bit operation via its digital inputs and outputs.)

HARDWARE

So, the Pro Tools LE software stays the same no matter what system you choose. But the Pro Tools hardware interface you buy determines a lot about how you'll be working with your system. As you're selecting your system, a number of questions should be considered. Here are just a few examples:

- Do you require maximum portability?
- Do you want your Pro Tools rig to be the centerpiece of your studio, or will you use a hardware mixer with it?
- How many hardware inputs and outputs do you need at once?
- How many mic preamps do you need?
- Do you need a built-in physical control surface?
- What other gear do you have in your studio?
- How much space do you have?
- How much money do you have to spend?

Each hardware interface has its own set of features and capabilities. Let's take a look at what each one has to offer.

Mbox—The most affordable Pro Tools LE package is the tiny Mbox, a two-in/two-out unit that connects to the host computer via USB. The Mbox doesn't even require an AC power cable; it draws the juice it needs from the USB connection to the computer. This makes it ideal for situations where portability is required. With a laptop computer, an Mbox, and a set of headphones, you're all set to work on your tracks wherever you might be.

Digidesign's Mbox is the smallest and most affordable Pro Tools interface. *See Figure 4-1.*

The Mbox has two analog inputs, which feature built-in microphone preamps designed by high-end preamp manufacturer Focusrite, each with 48v phantom power. Its "combo" analog connectors can accept either XLR cables from microphones or ¼-inch cables from line-level sources such as synthesizers, external effects processors, etc., or high-impedance instruments such as guitar and bass. Two ¼-inch insert jacks allow you to connect external hardware processors during the tracking phase of recording— insert a hardware compressor in the signal path while you're tracking vocals, for example. Two ¼-inch analog outputs are provided. There's also stereo (two-channel) S/PDIF digital in and out. The Mbox has two headphone outputs; an ⅛-inch jack on the front panel, and a ¼-inch jack on the back panel. You can't use both headphone outs at once. If you plug into the rear-panel jack, the front-panel output is disabled.

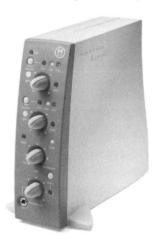

Figure 4-1

The back panel of the Mbox has "combo" input connectors that can accept either XLR or ¼-inch plugs. This allows it to handle microphone, line-level, and high-impedance instrument level signals.

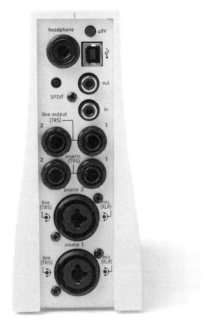

Figure 4-2

The Mbox supports zero-latency monitoring during recording, which means that you won't hear a delay when adding parts to tracks that are already recorded in Pro Tools (more on this in later chapters). Resolutions up to 24-bit and 44.1 and 48kHz sample rates are supported.

USB Versus FireWire

USB (Universal System Bus) and FireWire (also known as IEEE1394) are two different communication bus standards used in computers. They allow external hardware peripherals to interface with Macs and PCs. USB and FireWire share some features: Plug-n-play flexibility (no need to fool with device IDs, etc.), standard connectors, automatic configuration as devices are added, hot swapping (plugging and unplugging devices with the power on and without re-booting the computer), on-bus power (power carried through the USB or FireWire cable), and support for multiple devices.

But there are some major differences between the two. There are currently two flavors of USB: USB 1.1 and USB 2.0. Both support 127 devices per bus and cables up to five meters (over 16 feet) long. USB 1.1 can transfer at up to 12 Mbps, while USB 2.0 can do 480Mbps (40 times faster!).

FireWire also currently has two flavors: FireWire 400 and FireWire 800. Both support up to 63 devices per bus. FireWire 400 operates at up to 400Mbps, with cables up to 4.5 meters (around 15 feet) long. FireWire 800 can transfer twice as fast, at up to 800Mbps (fast enough to send a CD's worth of data in 10 seconds), on cables up to 100 meters (330 feet) long. FireWire 400 is far more common; at this writing FireWire 800 devices were just starting to hit the market. In most cases, when you see something referred to as "FireWire," it means FireWire 400.

Firewire and USB both have their place. USB is commonly used for connecting computer mice, keyboards, digital cameras, and other low-bandwidth devices. It has plenty of speed for Digidesign's Mbox, which has two simultaneous inputs and outputs. USB 2.0, with its far faster transfer speeds, has yet to make much of an in-road in the audio world, although it is becoming more common on hard drives and other storage devices.

FireWire is ideal for applications that require transferring lots of data. It's commonly found on digital video cameras, hard drives, and—most important to us—on many digital audio interfaces such as the Digidesign Digi 002 and Digi 002 Rack.

Digi 002 Rack—Stepping up from the Mbox in Digidesign's interface pantheon, we come to the Digi 002 Rack. The 002 Rack is a two-space rackmountable unit. (Not to state the completely obvious...you probably figured out the "rackmountable" part from its name.) It connects to your computer using FireWire, which means that it can input and output a great deal more simultaneous channels than the USB-format Mbox. In fact, the 002 Rack can handle up to 18 channels of input and output simultaneously along with tons of MIDI information.

The Digi 002 Rack connects to either Mac or Windows computers using FireWire. It supports 18 simultaneous inputs and outputs.

Figure 4-3

The 002 Rack has enough input and output firepower to be able to serve as the hub for your entire studio. It has eight ¼-inch analog inputs; the first four analog inputs also have XLR jacks with built-in microphone preamps with 48v phantom power. Eight ¼-inch analog outputs are provided; outputs 1 and 2 are duplicated with an extra set of ¼-inch jacks for connection to studio monitors (speakers). There's eight-channel ADAT optical digital input and output, and stereo (two-channel) S/PDIF digital connections. On the MIDI side, the Digi 002 Rack has one MIDI input and two independent MIDI outputs (supporting up to 32 MIDI channels).

There's tons of connectivity to be found on the back of the Digi 002 Rack. It has analog as well as optical and coaxial (RCA) digital inputs and outputs. In addition, there's one MIDI in and two MIDI outs.

Figure 4-4

The 002 Rack also has a couple of convenient hardware features: The front panel has a headphone jack. Around back is a footswitch, which can be assigned to control several things in the Pro Tools LE software. An extra FireWire port allows you to daisy chain hard drives off the 002 Rack. There's a set of "Alternate Source" RCA input jacks; these can be switched to take the place of the ¼-inch channel 7 and 8 inputs. One application for this is to use the "Alt

Src" RCA jacks to connect a CD player or other reference source.

The Digi 002 Rack supports resolutions up to 24-bit, and sample rates up to 96kHz.

Digi 002—For hands-on control of your Pro Tools LE system, you can't beat the Digi 002. The 002 has the same inputs, outputs, mic preamps, and Firewire connections as the Digi 002 Rack, but it packages them in an entirely different form. The 002 is a tabletop unit that combines input and output connections with a control surface—essentially it's a fancy remote control for Pro Tools LE. There are eight touch-sensitive motorized faders, and eight rotary encoders (fancy term for "knobs"); these are assigned to "remote control" the channel controls in the Pro Tools LE software. There are also tape recorder-style transport controls; play, stop, record, fast-forward, rewind, etc. Hardware buttons are provided that let you access other controls in the LE software—the idea is to give you physical control over the virtual world of Pro Tools, and it works. It's especially effective for those who have experience working with more "traditional" studio hardware. But even if the 002 is the first piece of studio gear you've ever seen, you'll find that putting your hands on the hardware makes using it more intuitive and enjoyable.

Want to take charge of the Pro Tools software? The Digi 002 allows you to physically grab hardware knobs and faders that correspond to Pro Tools' software controls. As a bonus, it can serve as a stand-alone digital mixer.

Figure 4-5

The Digi 002 has another trick up its sleeve, one that ups the value quotient radically. Press a switch on the front panel and the 002 is disconnected from your computer and serves as a stand-alone digital mixer with eight inputs, two outputs, two external effects sends, two internal effects processors, and snapshot automation. Perfect for miscellaneous mixing jobs in the studio, and for the occasional small live-performance gig.

"LEGACY" SYSTEMS

Digidesign also offered two PCI card-based Pro Tools LE systems, both of which had been discontinued at this writing. Although they've been discontinued, if you own one of these packages (or are looking to purchase one used), they're still supported. You can use either with Pro Tools LE version 6.1 under Mac OS 9 and X with most PCI-slot-equipped Macs through G4s, but neither will support G5s. Both will work with Pro Tools LE version 6.1 under Windows XP. Don't look for either system to work with future versions of Pro Tools, though.

If you're running an older computer that doesn't have a USB or FireWire port on it, then one of these systems may be just what you need. However, note that both require that you open your computer up and install a PCI expansion card in an open slot—some people are a bit squeamish about that sort of thing.

Digi Toolbox—This system used the Audiomedia III PCI card, which had two analog inputs and outputs, and stereo S/PDIF digital input and output. This allowed for potentially four channels in and four channels out at the same time. (Audiomedia III cards with serial numbers below BK16376, manufactured before 3/18/97, and pre-revision "E," may not be compatible with newer Macs and operating systems. Some of these cards can, however be updated; contact Digidesign for more information.)

The Audiomedia III card was part of Digidesign's Toolbox, which bundled it with Pro Tools LE software. The card's format required that you open your computer and install it in a free PCI slot. The Audiomedia III featured stereo analog in and out as well as stereo digital in and out. *See Figure 4-6.*

Digi 001—The Digi 001 system featured an external rackmount hardware box that connected to a PCI card, which went into a slot in the computer. The Digi 001 hardware box featured eight analog inputs and outputs, eight channels of ADAT lightpipe (optical) digital input and output, and stereo s/PDIF digital in and out for a total of 18 simultaneous channels of input and output. The Digi 001 offered other features as well: Two built-in microphone preamps, MIDI in and out, and a stereo headphone output.

Digidesign's 001 hardware was a combination of a PCI expansion card that mounted in the computer, and an external "breakout" box that had most of the audio connections.

Figure 4-6

Figure 4-7

Digidesign Hardware Interface Comparison

	Toolbox	Digi 001	Mbox	Digi 002	Digi 002 Rack
Analog inputs	2 RCA	eight ¼″	two ¼″	eight ¼″	eight ¼″
Analog outputs	2 RCA	eight ¼″	two ¼″	eight ¼″	eight ¼″
Monitor outputs	0	two ¼″	0	two ¼″	two ¼″
Microphone preamps	0	2	2	4	4
Headphone outputs	0	1	1 front, 1 back	1	1
Other analog connections	0	0	2 inserts	2 RCA Alternate Source	2 RCA Alternate Source
Digital inputs	2-channel S/PDIF (RCA)	8-channel ADAT or 2-channel S/PDIF (optical), 2-channel S/PDIF (RCA)	2-channel S/PDIF (RCA)	8-channel ADAT (optical), 2-channel S/PDIF (RCA)	8-channel ADAT (optical), 2-channel S/PDIF (RCA)
Digital outputs	2-channel S/PDIF (RCA)	8-channel ADAT or 2-channel S/PDIF (optical), 2-channel S/PDIF (RCA)	2-channel S/PDIF (RCA)	8-channel ADAT (optical), 2-channel	8-channel ADAT (optical), 2-channel S/PDIF (RCA)
Analog resolution	18-bit	24-bit	24-bit	24-bit	24-bit
Digital resolution	24-bit	24-bit	24-bit	24-bit	24-bit
Sample rates	44.1, 48kHz	44.1, 48kHz	44.1, 48kHz	44.1, 48, 88.1, 96kHz	44.1, 48, 88.2, 96kHz
MIDI inputs	0	1	0	1	1
MIDI outputs	0	1	0	2	2
Control connections	0	1 footswitch	0	1 footswitch	1 footswitch
Max simultaneous inputs and outputs	4 (2 analog, 2 digital)	16 (8 analog, 8 digital)	2 (analog or digital)	18 (8 analog, 10 digital)	18 (8 analog, 10 digital)
Special features	—	Monitor mode	Zero-latency monitoring	Low-latency monitoring, 8-fader hardware control surface, stand-alone mixer mode with two built-in digital effects	Low-latency monitoring

five

POWER PLANT

As we learned way back in Chapter Three, Basic Pro Tools Concepts, with Pro Tools LE everything comes down to your computer. Your computer system—its processor speed, amount of memory, hard drives, and so on—is what determines how far you'll be able to take your Pro Tools rig and the productions you do with it. If your system isn't up to the task, you'll be limited in the number of tracks you can record and play simultaneously, the number of plug-ins you can use at once, how many software synthesizers and samplers you can run, and so on.

Fortunately, with today's Macintosh and Windows computers, we have a *ton* of power at our disposal—and future generations will only get more powerful. Let's take a look at the minimum requirements for running Pro Tools LE, as well as some recommended additions that will crank the furnace up to the next level.

DUELING PLATFORMS

Here's a question: Should you use a Macintosh or Windows PC computer for running Pro Tools LE? On second thought, nope, not gonna touch that one! Each platform has its respective users, fans, disciples, loyal followers, and even fanatical zealots. If a computer platform war is what you want, they're available in spades in chat rooms and forums on the Internet.

But is there a difference between the platforms, as far as the Pro Tools hardware and software is concerned? In the Pro Tools software, there are only a few minor differences. For example, with the Mac version, you can import audio from a CD directly into Pro Tools; with Windows you can't (but there are other ways to do this on Windows). On Windows, you can access your Pro Tools hardware using third-party software and Digidesign's ASIO driver. On the Macintosh running OS X, you can access Pro Tools hardware using Core Audio drivers. A few other little things pop up here and there, but for the most part, the software is cross-platform equivalent.

However, there is still one area where I feel the Mac is ahead on software: Plug-ins. The number and variety of RTAS plug-ins available on the Mac is still larger, although it looks as though the list of Windows plug-ins is well on the way to catching up.

On the hardware side, there's little difference if you're using an Mbox with either Mac or Windows computers. USB ports are standard equipment on both Macs and PCs these days. With FireWire, the last few generations of Macs have pretty much all had FireWire connectors—both desktop/towers and laptops. So it's no problem to plug in a Digi 002 or 002 Rack. On the Windows side, some machines now come equipped with FireWire. If your desktop or tower PC doesn't have built-in FireWire, you can add a PCI expansion card that will provide one or more FireWire ports. (You can also use some of these expansion cards with Macs to provide more FireWire ports for connecting additional drives, CD/DVD burners, etc.) On a laptop Windows machine, adding

FireWire ports will likely require the addition of a card-slot expander.

In the end, the choice really comes down to personal preference: Do you already own one computer platform or the other? Which platform are you most experienced and comfortable with? Which one runs the other programs that you need to use professionally or personally? Do other people you'll be working with use a Macintosh, or does everyone you know use Windows?

The answers to these questions can help you choose the computer platform you want to work with. Once you've made that decision, then it should be fairly obvious which platform you want Pro Tools LE to run on!

MINIMUMS SPECS

Digidesign publishes minimum specifications for computers and operating systems that will support Pro Tools LE software and Pro Tools hardware. These specs are always changing as computer hardware evolves and operating systems are updated. At the time of this writing, the following specs had been published for running Pro Tools LE version 6.1. Before you purchase a new computer or install an operating system, be sure to pay a visit to Digidesign's Website to verify the latest compatibility and minimum requirements specifications. Consider it a given that the minimum specs will probably never decrease, and that they really are the *minimum* required. For best performance, you'll want a more powerful computer than one that just meets the bare minimums.

WINDOWS MINIMUMS

On the Windows platform, to run Pro Tools LE 6.1, you'll need a computer that meets at least the following:

Minimum Windows Requirements for 002 and 002 Rack

CPU models and requirements	Intel Pentium 4 or Xeon at 2.0GHz, AMD AthlonXP 2000+, desktop or laptop
Chipset	*Pentium 4:* Intel 850/850e, Intel 845/845e/845pe, Intel 865pe/875p; *AthlonXP:* VIA KT266A, NVIDIA nForce
Operating system	Windows XP Professional or Home, with Service Pack 1
Ports	FireWire (internal, PCI, or Cardbus)
Total system RAM	384MB, 512MB recommended
Monitor	color, 1024x768 resolution
Hard-drive speed	7,200 RPM
Hard-drive seek time	less than 10.0ms

Minimum Windows Requirements for Mbox

CPU models and requirements	Intel Pentium 4 or Xeon at 1.3GHz, Intel Pentium III at 500MHz, AMD AthlonXP (all speeds), Athlon Thunderbird (all speeds), desktop or laptop
Chipset	Intel for Intel processors, VIA or NVIDIA nForce for Athlon
Motherboard	ATX
Ports	USB
Operating system	Windows XP Professional or Home, with Service Pack 1
Total system RAM	384MB, 512MB recommended
Monitor	color, 1024x768 resolution
Hard drive speed	7,200 RPM
Hard drive seek time	less than 10.0ms

MACINTOSH MINIMUMS

On the Macintosh platform, to run Pro Tools LE 6.1, you'll need at least the following:

Minimum Macintosh OS X Requirements for 002 and 002 Rack

CPU models and requirements	dual-processor PowerMac G4 at 800MHz with AGP graphics, single-processor PowerMac G4 at 733MHz with AGP graphics, Powerbook G4 at 800MHz, or iMac G4 "Flatpanel" at 1GHz
Operating system	Mac OS X 10.2.6 or 10.2.8
Total system RAM	384MB, 512MB recommended
Monitor	color, 1024x768 resolution
Video	Apple QuickTime 6.1
Hard drive speed	7,200 RPM
Hard drive seek time	less than 10.0ms

Minimum Macintosh OS X Requirements for Mbox

CPU models and requirements	single- or dual-processor PowerMac G4 with AGP graphics, Powerbook G4, iBook G3 ("Ice White" dual USB models), or iMac G4 "Flatpanel"
Operating system	Mac OS X 10.2.6 or 10.2.8
Total system RAM	384MB, 512MB recommended
Monitor	color, 1024x768 resolution
Video	Apple QuickTime 6.1
Hard drive speed	7,200 RPM
Hard drive seek time	less than 10.0ms

I'm going to emphasize it one more time: These are the *minimum* requirements. You'll get better results with a faster machine, and certainly with more RAM (see below). In fact, Pro Tools LE *may* run on machines that don't meet these requirements; it's just that Digidesign doesn't officially support them and won't make any promises as to the performance that you'll receive or problems that you may encounter.

Other things may also be required, depending on what you're doing. For example, if you're using Windows and you'll be working with putting music or audio to video, you'll need to have Apple's QuickTime installed on your computer. There are other things as well; Digidesign's Website does a fine job of listing all the most current system requirements and settings. Check there first if you have any questions.

PROCESSOR SPEED

The faster your computer's CPU (Central Processing Unit), the better. A faster CPU means more tracks and more DSP power for running plug-ins in Pro Tools LE. What matters is the class of your computer's processor (Pentium 4, G4, G5) and how fast it operates (how many MHz or GHz). Pro Tools LE will run on multi-processor machines, but on Windows it doesn't take advantage of the additional processors (it does on the Mac). However, other programs, such as software synths and samplers, might take advantage of the extra processor, as may your mundane (non-audio/non-music) software.

DISPLAYS

The display or monitor screen you use with your computer doesn't matter all that much to Pro Tools, but it will matter to you! You're going to be spending a lot of hours staring at that screen, so make it a good one. Consider getting a large screen; most Pro Tools users find a 17-inch screen to be the bare minimum, an 18-, 19-, 20-inch, or larger screen is even better. A bigger screen allows you to view more of what's happening in Pro Tools at a glance, without clicking on, opening, or closing windows. You can see more of your tracks for editing, more of your mixer channel strips when mixing, open more plug-in windows simultaneously, and so on.

In fact, Pro Tools LE power users frequently have more than one screen connected to their computer. Having two monitors, for example, lets you view the mixer and editing windows at the same time, each on their own screen, so nothing is covered up. When mixing, you can have the mixer on one screen, and have some plug-in windows (such as meters and spectrum analyzers) always open, and so on, in the other screen.

Some computers, such as current Macintoshes, support two independent monitor screens out of the box. For computers that don't, you can add a second video display card, or better yet, buy a dual-head video display card for driving two screens.

In general, LCD, or flat panel, displays are easier to look at for long periods of time than CRT (Cathode Ray Tube) or television-type monitors. They also take up less space, give off less heat, and don't cause as many hum and buzz problems with guitar and other instruments with pickups. Plus, they look really high-tech and cool! Unfortunately, they're still more expensive than CRT monitors, though prices are dropping quickly.

More RAM

Pro Tools LE relies on the memory in your computer for a variety of things. As with processor speed, the more RAM (Random Access Memory) you have installed, the better! The amount of RAM will affect the number of plug-ins you can run to a certain extent. But the available RAM will also be an issue if you want to run software synthesizers, and even more so, software samplers, at the same time as you are running Pro Tools LE.

Luckily for us, RAM is an inexpensive commodity these days. Load up your machine with more than you think you'll ever possibly need. In 25 years of working with computers, I've never encountered a single person who said, "I wish I had less memory in this machine." I currently have 2GB (gigabytes) of RAM in my main Pro Tools computer. That may be overkill, but I figure Pro Tools can use the elbowroom.

Hard Drives

All computers come from the factory with a hard drive installed. This disk is sometimes referred to as the "system" or "boot" drive, since the operating system and all the programs are installed and run from there. While you can record audio to this drive from Pro Tools LE, you're much better off having a second drive that's dedicated to audio.

Recording and playing back as many as 32 tracks of audio at once can be demanding on a hard disk.

And the load on the drive increases significantly when you start editing the audio in your session—cutting, pasting, copying regions—since the drive has to do a lot more bouncing around to find and play from all those edit points. Sometimes system drives are too slow, and in other cases, your computer might need to access the system drive while you're recording or playing music—not a good thing. For these reasons, and others, it makes sense to have a second drive available for dedicating to recording and playing your Pro Tools audio files.

With hard drives, capacity is always an issue. You want a big enough drive to hold all the music you're working on—and as we saw earlier in this book, it can take a lot of space to store audio. In case you've forgotten (I know I have) at the lowest 16-bit/44.1kHz resolution, we're using 5MB of disk space per track for each minute. For a 5-minute song, this means 25MB for a single 5-minute track, 200MB for eight tracks, and 800MB for 32 tracks. And that's assuming we aren't doing any extra takes, overdubs, bouncing, or anything else requiring more tracks. At 24 bits, the requirements are 50% higher. Use a higher sample rate and the requirements will more than double again! At Pro Tools' highest resolution and sample rate, you could easily eat up 2GB of hard drive space for a single 32-track, 5-minute song. Multiply that by 10 to 15 songs on a CD and you're talking quite a bit of space required to record, store, and mix the average album project.

Fortunately, hard-drive prices have dropped—and continue to drop—rapidly. Get a good-size drive, but my recommendation is not to get too carried away. A super-large drive is hard to back up and archive. These days I prefer hard drives that are in the 80 to 100GB range. They're big enough for several large projects, but not so big that there's tons of old stuff taking up space—plus you don't lose everything if you have a hard-drive crash. Whatever size drive you choose, don't let it get too full. There can be weird problems when a hard drive gets close to filling up with stored data. Allow your audio files plenty of breathing room.

When you search for a second hard drive to add to your computer, you can go with an internal drive using ATA, S-ATA, or one of the flavors of SCSI (assuming your computer supports SCSI or you have a SCSI expansion card installed). You can also go with an external FireWire drive if you need portability, or. if you want to be able to easily unplug one drive and plug in another (nice for quickly swapping between projects). USB drives, however, generally aren't fast enough for multitrack audio work, so avoid those. USB drives can be used for backup, although they're often very slow. For laptops, internal drives are usually too slow to record and/or play very many tracks. Plus, it's tough to find a laptop that will allow you to install a second drive internally—go with a FireWire drive if your laptop supports it (or add a FireWire CardBus expander to the laptop).

Look for a drive that has a fast rotation speed (10,000 to 15,000rpm drives are common these days). Another important specification is "seek time": The time it takes for the drive to rotate around and find a particular chunk of audio data. The lower the seek time, the better.

Fortunately, most drives on the market today will easily be able to handle 32 tracks and a large amount of edits. Go for the fastest one you can find (and afford) and you'll be just fine—and remember to back up and archive regularly!

OTHER STUFF

All the other computer add-ons—printers, scanners, memory card readers, etc., etc.—are nice to have, but will rarely be used with Pro Tools LE. If you need them for other things you do with your computer, great. If not, don't bother spending money on them—save that hard-earned cash for more RAM or another hard drive.

MORE POWER

There are some things you can do to improve your system's performance a bit. The difference won't be night and day, but every extra bit of processing power helps.

1. Even though you can run other types of programs at the same time as Pro Tools LE, that doesn't mean that you should. Remember that even if programs are running in the background, they're taking up precious CPU power and RAM space.

2. Strip out anything unnecessary from your system. This means turning off any utilities Pro Tools doesn't need, shutting down disk optimizers, calendars, virus protection (turn it back on before getting on the Web, receiving e-mail, or installing a new program!) and so on.

3. Some USB devices can be a computer power-drain, even when they're just sitting there idling along. I always turn off any USB equipment that isn't essential for Pro Tools LE.

4. Digidesign recommends turning on bus mastering for any video display cards that support it. This is usually done using a control panel supplied by the card's manufacturer.

5. The fine folks at Digidesign also recommend disabling network cards, although I haven't found this to make a huge difference with my own machines. At the same time, I don't make my Pro Tools machines active on my network unless I need to transfer files or something.

The idea is to turn off anything that isn't required in order to maximize the power available to Pro Tools LE. *Warning and disclaimer:* If you aren't absolutely sure what you're doing, be cautious of disabling bits of software in your system—you could find yourself in a painful time-devouring struggle to get your computer working correctly again. If you have any doubt, leave things the way the factory has them set up. One utility that can help prevent problems caused by random (and not-so-random) fiddling around with your system is Norton Ghost, which memorizes your system's configuration and allows you to revert to the original state should you mess something up beyond easy recovery.

six

INSTALLATION

ongratulations—you're a Pro Tools owner! Let's get that shiny CD of new software into your computer and on the way to recording music. Installing the software is pretty easy...all you have to do is start the process and follow the onscreen directions. First up, we'll get the Windows XP users happening, then we'll get you Mac folks installed. (See page 45.)

WINDOWS XP

There are several steps involved in installing Pro Tools LE on a Windows XP computer. First, we have to take care of a few Digidesign-recommended system-setting changes.

System Settings

Turn On DMA—Setting DMA (Direct Memory Access) for your hard drives is an important step, as it eases the load on your computer. That means more power is available for recording and processing audio.

1. Click Start, then right-click My Computer, and select Manage.

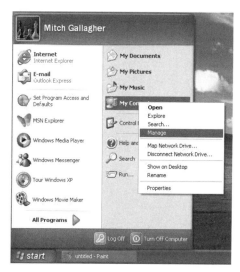

Figure 6-1

2. Double-click System Tools.

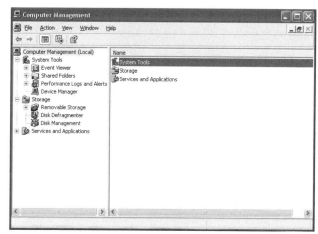

Figure 6-2

3. Double-click Device Manager.

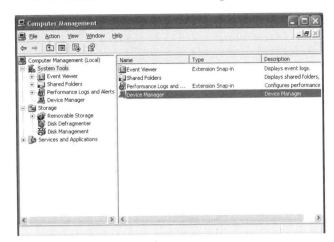

Figure 6-3

4. Double-click IDE ATA/ATAPI controllers.

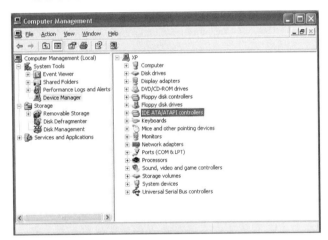

Figure 6-4

5. Double-click Primary IDE Channel.

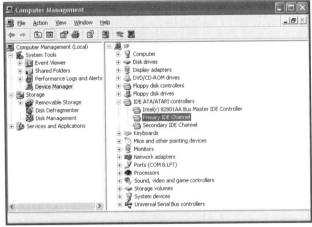

Figure 6-5

6. Click the Advanced Settings tab. For each device, pull down the Transfer Mode menu and select "DMA if available." (Actually, we're just double-checking; normally Windows XP will automatically choose the correct setting.) Click OK.

Figure 6-6

7. Repeat steps 5 and 6 for any additional IDE channels. Then close all open windows.

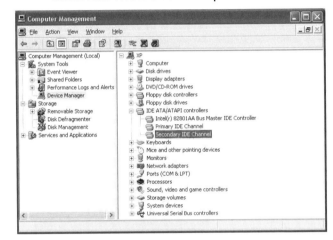

Figure 6-7

Turn Off Font Smoothing—Pro Tools won't work if the "Clear Type" setting is turned on.

1. Click Start, then click Control Panel.

Figure 6-8

2. Click Appearance and Theme.

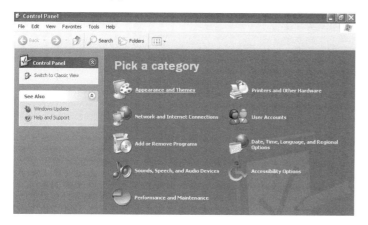

Figure 6-9

3. Click Display.

Figure 6-10

4. Click the Appearance tab.

Figure 6-11

5. Click Effects, then uncheck "Use the following method to smooth edges of screen fonts." Click OK, then close all open windows.

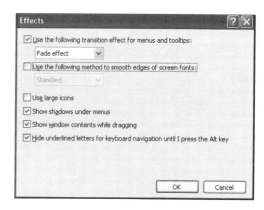

Figure 6-12

Turn Off System Standby and Power Management
Windows XP has features for automatically putting the computer to sleep if there's no activity for a certain period of time. This can be a real problem if you happen to be recording at the time! To prevent this (and other power management mishaps) we'll turn off these features.

1. Click Start, then click Control Panel.

Figure 6-13

2. Click Performance and Maintenance.

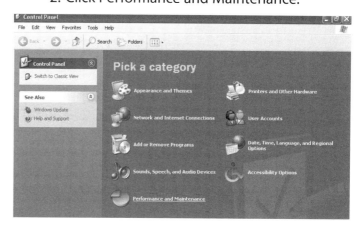

Figure 6-14

3. Click Power Options.

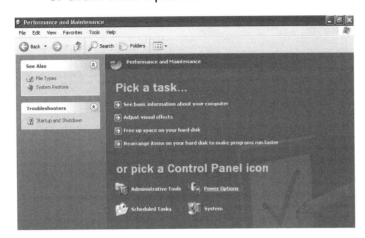

Figure 6-15

4. Click the Power Schemes tab, then pull down the Power Schemes menu and select "Always On." Click OK, then close all open windows.

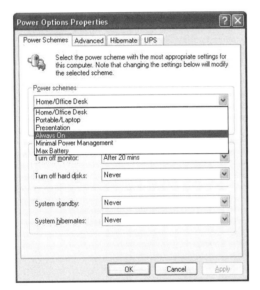

Figure 6-16

That's all we need to do with the system settings. Let's move on to the real action: Installing Pro Tools LE.

Install Pro Tools LE

1. Pop the Pro Tools LE CD-ROM into your computer's drive. It should launch automatically and open to the location of the installer (labeled "Setup"). If the disc doesn't open automatically, click Start, click My Computer, then double-click the CD-ROM drive, which will be labeled as the Pro Tools disc. Double-click the installer application.

Figure 6-17

2. A splash screen will appear.

3. When the installation wizard window opens, click Next.

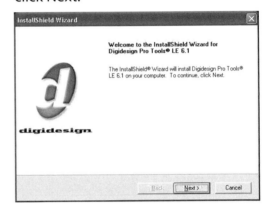

Figure 6-18

4. Read the license agreement (after all, the lawyers spent a lot of time writing it), and assuming you can live with it, click Yes. (If you choose No, the installer will quit, and you'll have no software to record with...guess the lawyers have us on this one.)

5. Select where you want Pro Tools LE to be installed. In most cases, the default location will be fine.

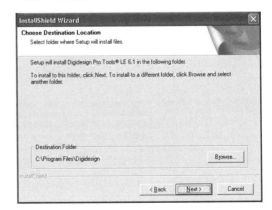

Figure 6-19

6. Choose the components you want to install. In most cases, this will be Pro Tools LE and the Digidesign ASIO Driver (which is used by any other ASIO-compatible software you might have. If you don't have any ASIO-compatible software, install it anyway...someday you probably will).

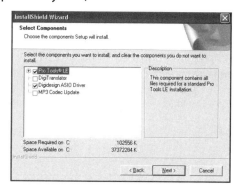

Figure 6-20

7. The progress bar will tell you what's happening with the installation.

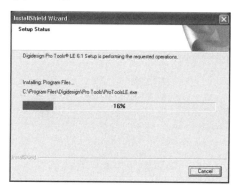

Figure 6-21

8. Digidesign recommends installing QuickTime separately from Pro Tools. Click No, we'll come back and take care of QuickTime later.

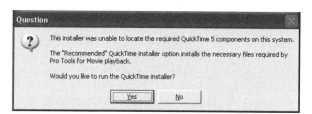

Figure 6-22

9. The Windows Media Format 9 installer opens next. Click Yes to install it.

Figure 6-23

10. Another one of those pesky license agreements...read and click Yes.

11. Once the Windows Media Format 9 installer is finished, click OK

12. The Digidesign installer wizard will reappear. Make sure "Yes, I want to restart my computer" is selected, remove the Pro Tools LE installer CD, then click Finish. Your computer will automatically reboot.

Figure 6-24

13. When your computer is finished restarting, a shortcut to Pro Tools LE will be on the desktop.

Figure 6-25

Now that we've got the Pro Tools LE software installed and our computers re-started, let's go back and install the QuickTime software.

Install QuickTime

1. Click Start, then click My Computer.

Figure 6-26

2. Double-click the Pro Tools LE CD-ROM icon.

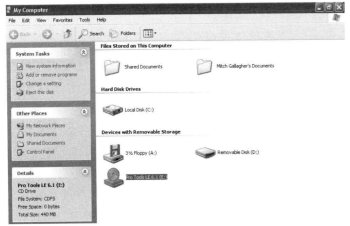

Figure 6-27

3. Double-click the Additional Files folder.

Figure 6-28

4. Double-click the QuickTime Installers folder.

Figure 6-29

5. Double-click the English folder (unless you prefer to use Japanese).

Figure 6-30

6. Double-click the QuickTime Installer application.

Figure 6-31

7. A progress bar will show you what's happening with the installation.

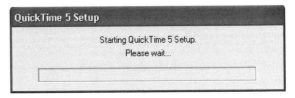

Figure 6-32

8. Read the blurb, then click Next.

Figure 6-33

9. Another blurb, another Next.

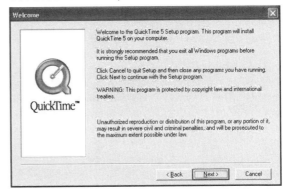

Figure 6-34

10. You didn't think we'd get away without a license agreement did you? Read, nod vigorously in assent, and click Agree.

11. Choose where you want QuickTime installed. The default location normally works fine.

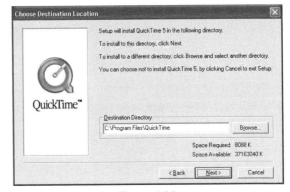

Figure 6-35

12. Unless you have some specific reason for doing otherwise, make sure Recommended is selected, and click Next.

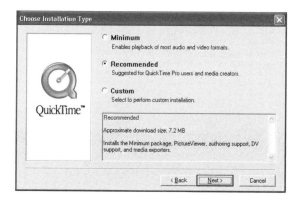

Figure 6-36

13. If you have a problem with "QuickTime" being the name of the QuickTime folder, change it. Otherwise, click Next.

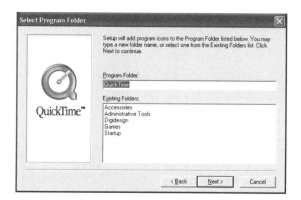

Figure 6-37

14. This screen will install QuickTime into your Internet browser. Click Next.

Figure 6-38

15. If you have purchased QuickTime Pro, you can enter the number, etc., now. If not (which will be most of us) just click Next—QuickTime will work fine without this information.

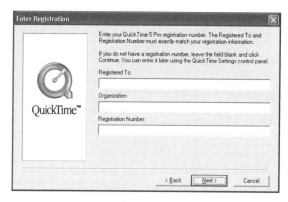

Figure 6-39

16. This progress bar tells you what's happening with the QuickTime install.

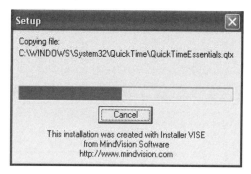

Figure 6-40

17. This screen allows you to configure QuickTime. You can always do this later if necessary. Don't click Next, close the window instead.

Figure 6-41

18. Don't do anything, the installer will close this window for you automatically. Or, if you want to prove that you don't have to rely on any machine to close your windows, you can do it manually.

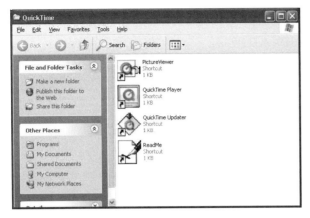

Figure 6-42

19. Uncheck "Yes, I want to view the QuickTime Read Me file" and "Yes, I want to launch QuickTime Player. You can look at those things some other time if you feel the need. Click Close, and you're done.

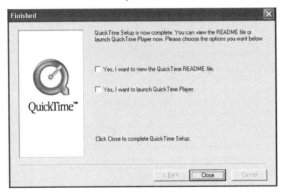

Figure 6-43

So we've got our computers set up, Pro Tools installed, and the QuickTime software loaded in. There's also a demonstration song on the Pro Tools installer CD. Let's load it on our computers. We'll use it later on.

Install the Demo Session

1. Click Start, then click My Computer.

Figure 6-44

2. Double-click the Pro Tools LE CD-ROM icon.

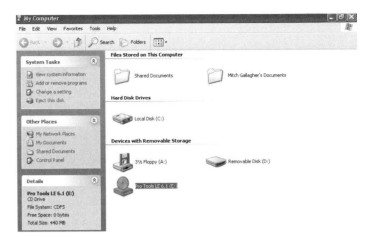

Figure 6-45

3. Double-click the Additional Files folder.

Figure 6-46

4. Double-click the Pro Tools LE Demo Session Installer folder.

Figure 6-47

5. Double-click the Pro Tools LE Demo Setup icon.

Figure 6-48

6. The installer will gather together the files it needs on the CD. This progress bar will show

you where it's at in the process.

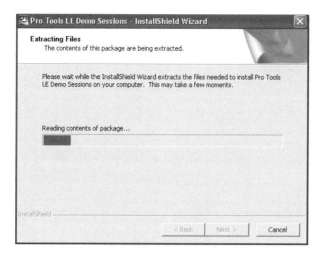

Figure 6-49

7. Once the installer is ready, the installer wizard will open. Click Next.

Figure 6-50

8. Choose where you want the demo installed. The default is for it to go in the Digidesign folder where Pro Tools lives.

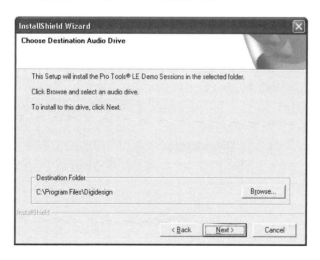

Figure 6-51

9. Choose what you want to install. The default is to install all three options. Click Next.

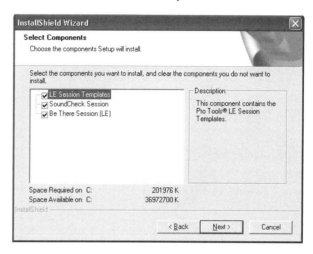

Figure 6-52

10. This progress bar shows how far the installer is in the installation process.

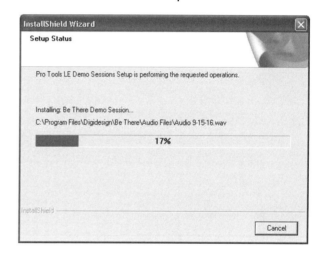

Figure 6-53

11. When the wizard is finished, click Finish to complete the installation.

MACINTOSH OS X

Okay Mac-oids, let's begin by making sure that our Macs are set up correctly. There are a few things that you need to change in the system settings for Pro Tools to work its best.

System Settings

1. Go to the Apple Menu. Click the System Preferences icon.

Figure 6-54

2. On the Hardware panel, click Energy Saver.

Figure 6-55

3. Slide the "Put the computer to sleep when it is inactive for:" slider to the "Never" position. Make sure the checkboxes for "Use separate time to put the display to sleep" and "Put the hard disk to sleep when possible" are not selected. This will prevent the computer from automatically going to sleep during a critical recording take.

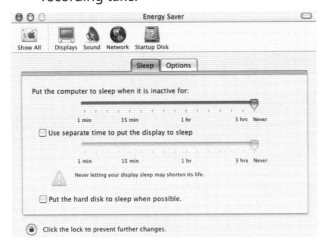

Figure 6-56

4. Click Show All at the upper left of the window to return to the System Preferences window.

Figure 6-57

5. In the System panel, select Software Update.

Figure 6-58

6. Deselect the checkbox for "Automatically check for updates when you have a network connection." This prevents the Mac from wanting to update itself whenever new versions of the OS software are posted on the Net. Not that updates are bad, but it's best to wait for Digidesign to approve them as compatible before you install them. Always check *www.digidesign.com* before installing any OS updates.

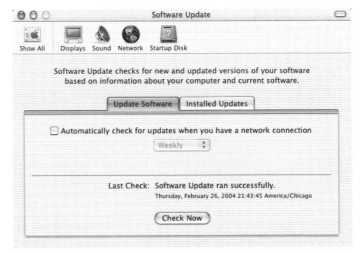

Figure 6-59

7. Close the Software update window.

Now that our Macs are configured properly, let's get the Pro Tools LE software installed.

Install Pro Tools LE

1. Drop the Pro Tools LE CD-ROM into your Mac's CD-ROM drive. The CD icon should appear on your computer's desktop.

Figure 6-60

2. Double-click the CD icon to open the installer CD window.

Figure 6-61

3. Double-click the Install Pro Tools LE icon. Enter your passphrase or password, if you have one. Click OK.

Figure 6-62

4. When the Digidesign splash screen appears, click Continue.

5. Read the license terms—c'mon, wading through legalese is fun—then click Accept.

6. Select your Pro Tools hardware. (I've checked the box for Digi 002, since that's my hardware.) Choose where to install your Pro Tools software—the default location is usually fine. Click Install.

Figure 6-63

7. If the "No other applications can be running during this installation...." dialog appears, click Continue.

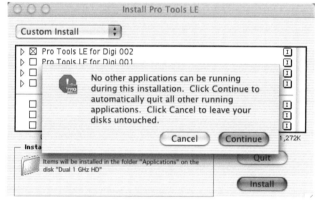

Figure 6-64

8. Wait until the installer installs all the required components. Don't click stop unless you want the installer to abort the process.

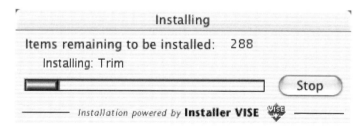

Figure 6-65

9. When the installer is finished, this dialog will appear. Click Restart to restart your computer.

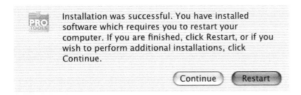

Figure 6-66

Now that we've got the software installed, you can go digging through your computer's hard drive looking for Pro Tools every time you want to use it, or you can make life easy by putting an alias—a shortcut—to it on your desktop. Whenever you want to run Pro Tools LE, just double-click the alias.

Make an Alias

1. Locate the icon for the Pro Tools LE application

Figure 6-67

2. Go File → Make Alias or type ⌘+**L**

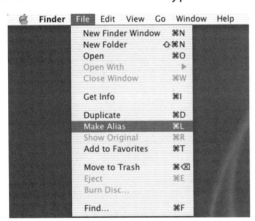

Figure 6-68

3. The alias icon will appear offset from the original icon. Drag the alias icon to wherever you want it to be. I leave a copy on my computer desktop, ready for immediate access. The installer also places a Pro Tools icon in the OS X dock, if you prefer to access it from there.

Figure 6-69

That's it, Pro Tools is installed! One more thing: Digidesign thoughtfully provided a demo song on the installer CD-ROM. Let's go ahead and copy it over to our hard drives—we'll use it later on.

Install the Demo Session

1. If the Pro Tools LE CD-ROM isn't in your Mac's CD-ROM drive, insert it. The CD icon should appear on your computer's desktop.

Figure 6-70

2. Double-click the CD icon to open the installer CD window.

Figure 6-71

3. Double-click the Install LE Demo Session icon. Read the license terms, then click Accept.

4. Select your Pro Tools hardware. (I've checked the box for Digi 001/002, since that's my hardware). Choose where to install the demo session. Click Install.

Figure 6-72

5. Wait until the installer installs all the required components. Don't click stop unless you want the installer to abort the process.

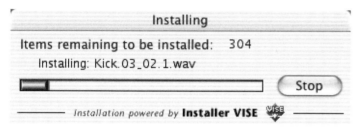

Figure 6-73

6. When the installer is finished, it will present this dialog. Click Quit to exit the installer.

Figure 6-74

That's it! Whether you're running Windows or Mac OS, if you followed the instructions in this chapter, Pro Tools LE is now installed on your hard drive. Onwards and upwards!

seven

MAKING CONNECTIONS

S o you've installed your Pro Tools LE software in your computer. Congratulations, the hard part is done! (And it wasn't all that hard, now was it?) Now you're ready to hook up your Pro Tools hardware of choice and to connect it to the rest of the gear in your studio.

CONNECTING PRO TOOLS HARDWARE TO YOUR COMPUTER

The days of having to open up your computer to install Pro Tools LE hardware are over! Today's interfaces, the Mbox, Digi 002, and Digi 002 Rack, plug right into connectors on the back of the computer using a single USB or FireWire cable. It doesn't get much easier than that!

With an Mbox, simply connect the included USB cable to the matching jacks on the back of the Mbox and on the computer.

Figure 7-1

To connect a Digi 002 or 002 Rack to your computer, hook the FireWire cable that came in the box to the matching jacks on the back of the 002 and on the computer.

Figure 7-2

That's all there is to it. With the software installed, and the hardware connected, you're read to roll with your Pro Tools LE system. Now let's get started hooking up the rest of your gear.

HOOKING UP MICROPHONES

In order to record acoustic sounds, we need to get those sounds converted into electrical signals that we can convert into digital data Pro Tools can deal with. The first stage of this is the microphone or "mic," for short. Most microphones connect using 3-pin XLR cables.

A mic puts out a very tiny amount of electrical current. To raise this tiny signal up to a level where we can work with it, a preamp is needed. Microphone preamps are found built into mixers, as stand-alone units, and—thanks Digidesign—built in on some of the analog inputs of Pro Tools LE interfaces. The Mbox has two mic preamps, while the Digi 002 and 002 Rack have four microphone preamps each.

When you want to use microphones with the Mbox, connect them, using XLR cables, to the Source 1 or Source 2 jacks on the back panel. With the Digi 002 or Digi 002 Rack, plug the mics into Mic 1, Mic 2, Mic 3, or Mic 4. In both cases, there are knobs on the front panel for adjusting the mic preamp gain.

The Mbox has two built-in mic preamps, so you can connect two microphones at a time to it using XLR cables.

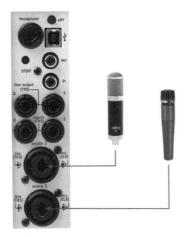

Figure 7-3

You can run up to four microphones at a time into the 002 or 002 Rack.

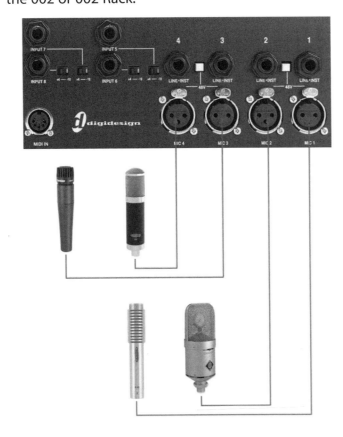

Figure 7-4

Phantom Power

Condenser microphones, a type commonly used in recording studios, require electrical power in order to operate—dynamic and ribbon mics don't require any power. A few condenser models can operate off batteries, but the vast majority requires "phantom power." Phantom power is a method for carrying electrical power over three-conductor microphone cables.

The most common variety of phantom power is 48 volt. The power is supplied via the microphone's connection to the microphone preamp, over its XLR cable. It's a pretty transparent situation; about all you have to do is turn on phantom power when using a condenser mic. But be careful when doing so: Activating phantom power can sometimes result in a loud thump from the audio system. Turn your speakers down first!

The Digidesign Mbox, Digi 002, and Digi 002 Rack all feature built-in phantom power on their analog mic-level inputs and can be used with condenser microphones. Check your mic's specs to see if it needs phantom power or not.

Hooking Up Guitars and Basses

Instruments with pickups such as guitars and basses require special inputs that have very high impedance. On the Mbox, the same XLR connectors that are used for microphones have a center section that doubles as an input for ¼-inch connectors. These can be switched from line-level operation for use with synthesizers and other sources to instrument level for use with guitars, basses, and other pickup-equipped instruments.

On the 002 and 002 Rack, four of the ¼-inch inputs on the back panel are labeled LINE•INST. Using a front-panel button, these four inputs can switched from line-level to instrument-level operation.

With either the Mbox or 002/002 Rack, use a shielded unbalanced (2-conductor) ¼-inch cable to hook the guitar or bass straight into the interface.

The two "Source" jacks on the Mbox can also accept instrument level—meaning electric guitar and bass—signals. *See Figure 7-5.*

The 002 and 002 Rack have four ¼-inch jacks that can switch from line to instrument level. Use the INST setting when plugging guitars or basses straight in. *See Figure 7-6.*

Hooking Up Synthesizers and Samplers

Synthesizer and sampler keyboards and sound modules connect to the Mbox and 002/002 Rack in the same fashion as guitars and basses, using shielded unbalanced ¼-inch cables. In fact, the same input jacks are used. The difference is that the corresponding buttons are set to LINE instead of INST. This allows them to accept the higher levels sent out by synths and samplers without overloading and distorting. In addition to the first four inputs on the Digi 002 and 002 Rack, you can also use inputs 5 through 8, which are ¼-inch balanced. These four jacks can be switched from -10dBv to +4dBu operating level to match the operating level of the gear you're using. In general, for keyboards, you'll want the switches set for -10. (Check the specs or contact the manufacturer of your gear to find out the correct setting for the switches with your equipment.)

Figure 7-5

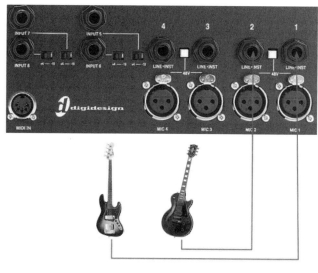

Figure 7-6

Those multi-purpose "Source" jacks on the back of the Mbox can also accept line-level signals such as those from keyboards and other studio devices. *See Figure 7-7.*

There are eight ¼-inch input jacks on the 002 and 002 Rack that can accept line-level signals from keyboards. Use the LINE setting on the first four

inputs. With most keyboards, the last four inputs should be switched to "-10" operating level. *See Figure 7-8.*

Figure 7-7

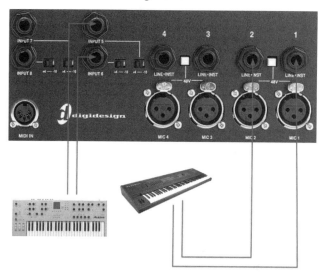

Figure 7-8

A second type of connection may be required with keyboards, samplers, and sound modules: MIDI. If you're going to use MIDI with Pro Tools LE and the Mbox, you'll need a separate MIDI interface for your computer. The 002 and 002 Rack have built-in MIDI interface capabilities, so no external MIDI interface is required.

MIDI cables have five pins and are used to carry information about musical performances—no actual sound is carried on a MIDI cable—as well as other types of control information.

Figure 7-9

Hook the MIDI output of your keyboard to the MIDI input of your interface or the 002/002 Rack MIDI input. In order for Pro Tools to control your keyboard or sound source, you'll also need to run a cable from the MIDI output of your interface or 002/002 Rack to the MIDI input of the instrument.

The 002 and 002 Rack have one MIDI input and two MIDI outputs. If you have more than two MIDI keyboards or sound modules, you can "daisy-chain" the additional devices using their MIDI Thru jacks.

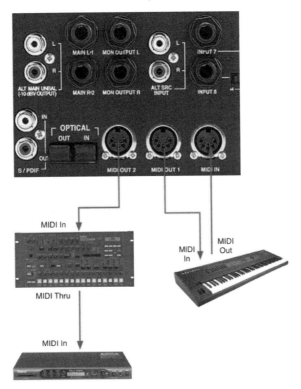

Figure 7-10

The 002 and 002 Rack have two independent MIDI outputs so they can control two MIDI instruments with up to 32 MIDI channels at the same time. If you need to connect more instruments, you can connect the keyboard's MIDI Thru jack, which sends out a copy of what arrives at the instrument's input, to the input of the next keyboard or module. If you have more gear to MIDI-fy, continue this process, daisy-chain fashion (MIDI Thru connected to MIDI In), until all of your synths, samplers, and other devices are MIDI'd up.

Analog I/O Flavors

Pro Tools systems can send and receive audio signals either through analog or digital connections. There are three types of analog connectors used on Pro Tools LE interfaces:

- RCA (the kind found on most home stereo equipment)

RCA jacks are unbalanced and operate at -10dBv when used with analog audio signals. RCA connectors can also be used for carrying S/PDIF digital audio signals.

Figure 7-11

Home and "semi-pro" audio equipment often uses RCA plugs for carrying analog audio signals.

Figure 7-12

- ¼-inch (the kind found on most music gear, such as guitars and amps, synthesizers, and effects)

¼-inch jacks can be balanced or unbalanced and operate at instrument (guitar) or -10dBv or +4dBu line level.

Figure 7-13

Guitars, keyboards, and other audio gear use unbalanced ¼-inch plugs. You can tell the plug in this photo is unbalanced by the two sections on its metal shaft—the "tip" and the "sleeve."

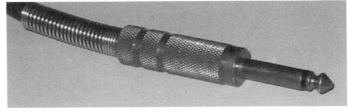

Figure 7-14

Balanced ¼-inch plugs are used on some professional audio equipment. This plug tells you it's balanced because it has three sections on its metal shaft: The "tip," the "ring," and the "sleeve."

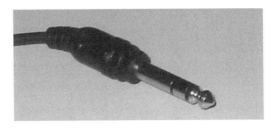

Figure 7-15

- XLR (found on microphones and "profes-sional" audio equipment).

XLR jacks are used for microphones and +4dBu balanced pro-audio equipment.

Figure 7-16

Mic cables use 3-conductor XLR cables. The same cables are also used for connecting professional audio equipment with XLR jacks.

Figure 7-17

Each type of connector operates slightly differently. RCA connectors are unbalanced (meaning two conductors), and usually operate at -10dBv level. Quarter-inch connectors can operate at instrument (guitar), -10dBv, or +4dBu level. Some ¼-inch connectors are balanced (three conductors, which helps reduce noise) and some are unbalanced. XLR connectors are balanced and run at +4dBu. The important thing is to match up inputs and outputs so that they're hooked into the same type, whether balanced or unbalanced, and at which level.

Of course, as a last resort you can always use adapters to go from one kind of connector to another: An RCA to unbalanced ¼-inch, or a balanced ¼-inch to XLR adapter or adapter cable, for example. In general, things will stay cleaner if you use the proper type of connectors and cables wherever possible.

One other thing: For lowest noise, all audio cables (except speaker cables) should be shielded to reduce pickup of buzz and hum.

HOOKING UP EXTERNAL PROCESSORS

Pro Tools LE has very powerful software processing plug-ins available, but there are some times when you'll want to use hardware processors—compressors during recording, external hardware reverbs, and the like.

The Mbox provides an analog insert loop—a "send," which routes signal to your processor, and a return, which brings the signal back into Pro Tools. Since the loop is in the analog domain, it can only be used during the tracking phase of your projects, so

generally you'd use it for patching in a hardware compressor or limiter when recording. The Mbox's inserts use TRS (Tip-Ring-Sleeve) ¼-inch connectors, the same kind as are used for balanced ¼-inch connections. But the connections aren't actually balanced. Rather, a special "Y" cable (called an "insert cable") is used, where one side of the Y cable is the send from Pro Tools, the other side is the return.

With the 002/002 Rack, you can send signal out of any of the outputs—analog or digital—through a processor and bring it back in on any of the inputs, analog or digital. For analog connections, use balanced ¼-inch outputs 3 to 8 to feed your processor, then use the eight ¼-inch input jacks to bring the signal from your processor back into Pro Tools LE. Make sure to set the level correctly for the input jacks.

Digitally you can use the RCA S/PDIF jacks on either the Mbox or the 002/002 Rack as a send and return. And, if your processor supports it, you can connect it to the 002/002 Rack optical digital output and input. Using either the S/PDIF or optical connections allows you to keep the signal entirely in the digital domain, avoiding extra conversion to and from analog. This helps maintain the best sound quality.

The Mbox has special insert jacks that let you connect analog processors while recording signals. Each of the two single insert jacks uses a type of "Y" cable called an "insert cable." One side of the "Y" carries signal out of the Mbox, the other side brings it back. *See Figure 7-18.*

You can hook up hardware processors to the 002 and 002 Rack using either analog or digital connections. For analog connections, come out of outputs 3 to 8 (outs 1 and 2 carry the main stereo mix, don't use them to feed effects) into your processor. Next connect the outputs of your processor to inputs 1-8—make sure to set the operating level switches beside the input jacks to the correct setting. You can also connect processors digitally using S/PDIF and/or optical. *See Figure 7-19.*

HOOKING UP EXTERNAL RECORDERS AND PLAYERS

There are some instances where you'll want to play an external device such as a CD or DVD player into Pro Tools. If the player has analog outs, you can use the regular line-level inputs on either the Mbox or 002/002 Rack to bring it into Pro Tools. The 002/002 Rack has an additional option: The "Alt Src Input" (Alternate Source Input) connections, which are on

RCA jacks. Hit one of the Alt Src buttons on the front panel and the input will be routed to either Pro Tools inputs 7 and 8, or directly to the monitor outs. This feature works great when you want to compare a commercial CD to a mix you're working on in Pro Tools LE.

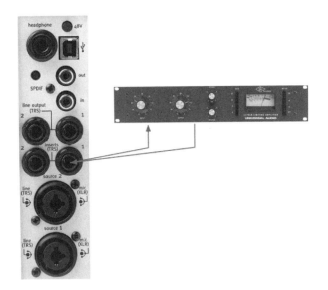

Figure 7-18

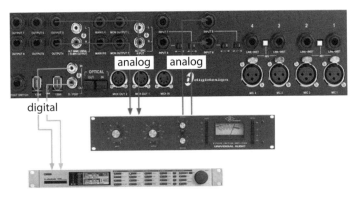

Figure 7-19

There may also be times when you want to record out of Pro Tools into an external recorder such as an analog 2-track or a DAT machine. On the Mbox, you can send out of Pro Tools LE using the two Line Out connectors, which use balanced ¼-inch connectors.

If you have a digital recorder such as a DAT machine or a stand-alone CD recorder, you can connect it digitally to the Mbox using the S/PDIF connections. Analog recorders, such as cassette recorders, can be hooked up to the Line Outs and Source 1 and 2. *See Figure 7-20.*

Note: Sharp-eyed readers will have spotted a problem with this diagram: There's no place to connect speakers. One solution is to connect your speakers to the output of the cassette recorder—

hopefully it has an output volume knob—which will also prevent feedback problems. You could also plug headphones into the cassette machine or Mbox and listen from there.

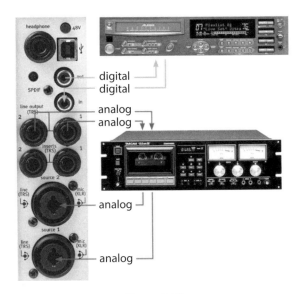

Figure 7-20

There are a number of ways to connect external players and recorders to the 002 and 002 Rack. You can bring CD players into the Alt Src Input. An analog machine can connect to the Main Outs and a pair of analog inputs. (You could also use the Alt Main Unbal connections to feed your analog recorder.) Digital recorders can be connected using either S/PDIF or optical format. *See Figure 7-21.*

Any of the eight analog outputs on the 002/002 Rack can be used to feed an external recorder. However, you'll generally send mixes out to an external recorder using the Main Outs (Outs 1 and 2), which are ¼-inch balanced. These Main Outs are also duplicated on RCA jacks labeled "Alt Main Unbal." Whatever appears on the Main Outs also appears on the Alt Main Unbal outs. If you have two recorders, this lets you make multiple copies simultaneously.

Digitally, you can send out of the Mbox in S/PDIF format using an RCA connector. The 002/002 Rack also has a S/PDIF output on RCA, but it has the additional option of optical outputs. *See Figure 7-21.*

The Golden Rule of Gear Hookup

There's one mantra that you can repeat to yourself as you're hooking up equipment in your studio: Outputs always go to inputs. As long as you keep this rule in mind, it will be easy to hook up gear in a logical fashion. And if there is a problem due to improper connections, you'll be able to troubleshoot: If two outs are connected together, or two ins are hooked up, no sound will pass. In order for audio to work, it must come out of an output, and go into an input.

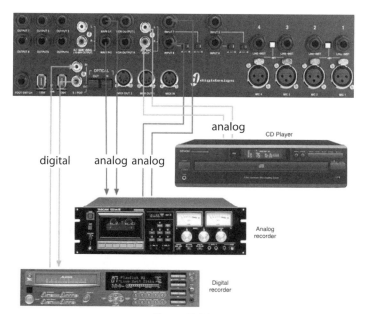

analog

digital   analog analog

Figure 7-21

HOOKING UP DIGITAL GEAR

There is a little bit more to hooking digital gear together than just connecting the cables. Digital audio must be clocked so that all the data arrives at the correct time. Each piece of digital gear has its own internal clock that it uses when playing by itself—if you're not making digital connections, there's nothing to worry about. But when a piece of digital gear is hooked up digitally to another piece of digital gear, the clocks in the two items must be synced together. If you don't sync the clocks, you'll get clicks and pops in the audio.

Don't worry, it's easy. The piece of gear that's sending out digital data is the master. The receiving piece of gear is the slave, and must be set to sync to incoming or external clock. How you do this varies from device to device, so consult your owner's manuals.

Digital I/O Formats

Pro Tools LE systems feature two digital-interconnect formats: S/PDIF and ADAT. S/PDIF (Sony/Philips Digital Interface) is a stereo (2-channel) format that is generally carried via RCA connectors, although it is sometimes carried on optical connectors, as on the now-discontinued Digi 001 interface.

On the 002 and 002 Rack, there are RCA S/PDIF digital in and out, as well as ADAT-format optical in and out connectors. The Mbox has RCA S/PDIF digital ins and outs. *See Figure 7-22.*

Alesis developed the adat format for use on their groundbreaking 8-track digital-tape recorder. It's an optical format, carried on fiber-optic cables. Eight channels can be carried per cable. Many types of audio gear have adat optical connectors, not just the afore-

mentioned digital tape recorders. Many current effect processors, microphone preamps, synthesizers, and other devices can be hooked up using optical connections.

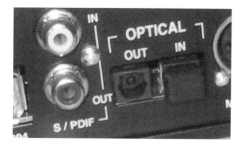

Figure 7-22

ADAT-format optical cables can carry up to eight channels of digital audio information.

Figure 7-23

Digital connections have a few advantages: You're not making unnecessary conversions from digital to analog and back, which helps maintain sound quality. And with digital connections, you don't have problems with hum, buzz, and other types of noise being picked up by the cables.

HOOKING UP MONITORS AND HEADPHONES

Now that we've got all that gear hooked up to our audio interface, we need to hear what we're doing. And that means hooking up either headphones or speakers. The Mbox has two headphone jacks, one is a ⅛-inch, on the front panel, and the other is a ¼-inch on the back. If you plug into the back-panel headphone jack, you'll disconnect the front jack. The 002 and 002 Rack have a single front-panel mounted ¼-inch headphone jack. The Mbox, 002, and 002 Rack all feature a dedicated front-panel knob for controlling the volume in the headphones. You'll probably be using headphones whenever you're recording sounds using microphones. Many engineers also use headphones when mixing, to double-check what they're hearing from their speakers.

Speakers—usually referred to in the studio world as "monitors"—are, needless to say, a vital part of the studio world. You can use either "normal" passive monitors, which require a separate power amplifier (as you would have with a home stereo system), or you can use powered (a.k.a. "active") monitors, which have the amplifier built right into the speaker cabinet.

Connect your monitors to the Mbox's line outputs. The playback knob on the front panel will control the volume. You can connect headphones to either the front- or back-panel headphone jacks.

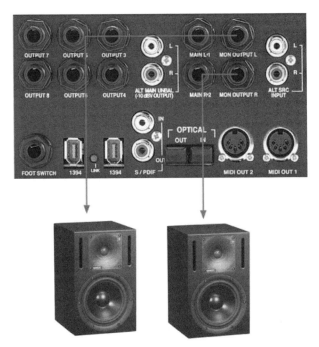

Figure 7-25

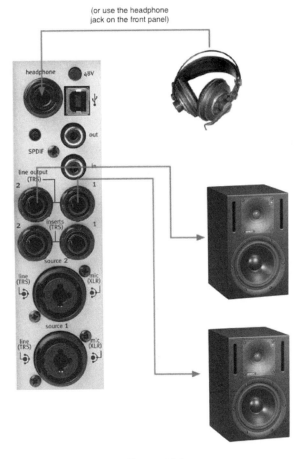

Figure 7-24

The 002 and 002 Rack have dedicated monitor outputs for connecting your monitors. A front-panel knob provides control over monitor volume. The 002/002 Rack headphone jack is around front with its own volume knob. *See Figure 7-25.*

The 002 and 002 Rack have dedicated ¼-inch balanced monitor outputs, which have a volume control knob on the front panel. For monitoring with the 002/002 Rack you can use a set of passive speakers with a power amplifier, or you can connect a set of powered monitors directly to the 002/002 Rack monitor outs.

Using speakers with the Mbox isn't quite as straight-ahead, mainly because there's no volume control for the outputs. In order to effectively use speakers with your Mbox, you'll probably want a small mixer or power amplifier with a volume control of its own.

Monitor Placement

Setting up your monitors correctly will make all the difference in hearing your music accurately. Most studio monitors these days (at least those used in home and project studios) are "nearfield" designs, meaning that they're relatively small speakers intended to be placed close (in the "nearfield," as opposed to the "midfield" or "farfield") to the listener, usually within three to six feet or so.

Placement of the monitors is crucial for accurate playback of music—and we need accuracy when making critical mixing, editing, and processing decisions. The speakers should be placed on stands or other solid surfaces so that their high-frequency drivers (tweeters) are at or maybe slightly above ear level. The two speakers should form an equilateral (equal-sided) triangle with the listener's head, meaning that the two speakers should be spaced as far apart as they are from the listener. So, if the speakers are each a distance of four feet from the listener, the speakers should be placed four feet apart from each other.

For best results, studio monitors should be at ear level and form an equal-sided triangle with the listener's head. *See Figure 7-26.*

A few more monitor placement tips: Try to place the speakers on a surface that doesn't vibrate or resonate when the speakers play. You can increase the physical isolation of the monitors by placing a pad between the speakers and whatever they're resting on. You can use commercially available foam isolators (one company that supplies these is Auralex, *www.auralex.com*) or for a down-and-dirty solution, I use dense foam mouse pads. Try to place the monitors away from nearby surfaces such as walls, and never put them in corners. This will cut down on problematic room reflections and help the speakers play low frequencies with greater accuracy.

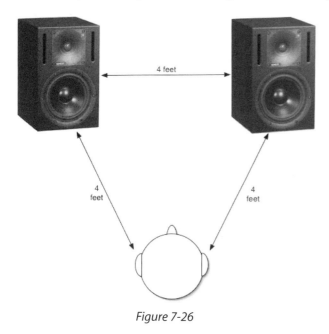

Figure 7-26

WHAT ABOUT A MIXER?

In many situations, all you'll need will be your Pro Tools LE audio interface to keep your studio humming along. Plus, the software mixer in Pro Tools can duplicate the functions of a hardware mixer extremely well. But if you have more gear than you have connections on your interface, you may be thinking that you need an external hardware mixer.

When might you want a mixer for your studio? The list of reasons could be long, but here are four:

- You have a lot of instruments that you need to blend together before recording them in Pro Tools.

- You need more mic preamps than you have available on your Pro Tools interface.

- You need to connect a lot of external hardware effects processors.

- You have other uses for a mixer, such as for PA use with a band.

The Mbox doesn't provide a ton of inputs and outputs, which isn't a problem if you usually record one or two tracks at a time, or if you don't use much hardware processing gear. But if you have a lot of gear, a mixer will almost certainly be a useful addition to your rig.

With the 002/002 Rack, there's more input and output possibilities in the interface itself, so the need for a mixer may be reduced. This is particularly true with the Digi 002, which has its own control surface features and can also serve as a stand-alone mixer when you're not using it with Pro Tools.

Okay, now that all your gear is hooked up, you're ready to move on and launch Pro Tools LE! Please proceed to Chapter Eight, Launch.

PART THREE

Getting Started

eight

LAUNCH!

It's time to launch Pro Tools and start learning our way around—I know, I know, you thought we'd never get here. In this chapter, we're going to get some music playing in Pro Tools, and in the process, take a very brief tour of the Transport window.

LAUNCHING PRO TOOLS FOR THE FIRST TIME

Let's begin by starting the Pro Tools LE software. Begin by making sure that your audio interface is connected properly and is powered up.

In order to get rolling, we need to find Pro Tools. There are several ways to do this: Locate the Pro Tools LE application on your hard drive. You can find the application itself inside the Pro Tools folder.

Figure 8-1

Or, on Windows XP look for the shortcut on your computer desktop (automatically created during installation).

Figure 8-2

With OS X, find the alias I suggested you create on the desktop after installation . . .

Figure 8-3

. . . or you can look for the Pro Tools icon the installer created on the OS X dock.

Figure 8-4

Double-click the Pro Tools LE icon (or shortcut or alias). A splash screen will appear that shows the progress of Pro Tools as it is preparing to bring you musical joy.

The first time you run Pro Tools, you'll need to authorize the software by entering the code found on the inside cover of the Pro Tools LE *Getting Started Guide*. Type in the code exactly as it appears, being careful to match the upper- and lower-case letters. When you're finished, click Validate.

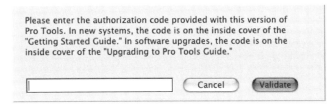

Figure 8-5

Once Pro Tools LE is finished loading, you'll see the Pro Tools menu bar across the top of your screen, but that's it—you won't see anything else until you either open an existing Session or create a new one.

Figure 8-6

WANNA HEAR SOME MUSIC?

Let's open the demo session we loaded on our computers when we installed Pro Tools LE. (Remember that a "Session" is the master file Pro Tools uses to contain all the audio, MIDI, processing, and other data for a song or audio production.) Before you begin, make sure that your monitor or headphone volume isn't cranked up too far—there's nothing worse than getting inadvertently volume-blasted by screaming speakers or headphones! Just crack the volume open for now; you can turn it up later once you know how loud things are going to be.

The following process will be the same whenever you want to open an existing Session file. In Pro Tools, when you want to open an existing Session file, go **File → Open Session...** or type ⌘+O (Ctrl+O).

Figure 8-7

In the window that opens, navigate to the location on your hard drive where you put the demo when you installed it. On the Mac, you'll see something

similar to this, depending on how you have the OS X view set up. Double-click the icon for the demo session.

Figure 8-8

In XP, the window will look something like this, depending on how you're viewing things:

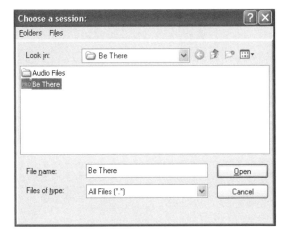

Figure 8-9

Depending on which hardware you're using with your system, you may see a dialog similar to this one—Pro Tools is telling you that you're using a different audio interface than the person who created the session file. For our purposes now, it's not a big deal. All we want to do is listen to what's in this existing demo song, so go ahead and click Yes. If you don't see this dialog, no worries!

Figure 8-10

Pro Tools will begin loading the demo session. This dialog will show the progress as the various tracks, plug-ins, and settings are loaded. If you want to stop the Session from loading, click the Cancel button.

Figure 8-11

The first time you open the demo or any song that was originally created on a Pro Tools system other than your own, you may see this dialog. What Pro Tools is saying with this dialog is that the files used in the Session are in a different place than they were the last time the demo was opened—which is true, you've copied the demo session and all its accompanying audio and other files onto your computer! Click No to proceed. Once again, if you don't see this dialog, no worries.

Figure 8-12

Depending on your Pro Tools hardware, you may also see this dialog, which is Pro Tools telling you that you're using an audio interface with a different input/output configuration than the demo was created on. Yep, true again…boy, Pro Tools is pretty smart. Click OK. And again, if you don't see this dialog, no worries!

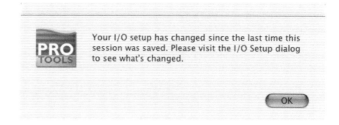

Figure 8-13

At last! The demo session is open. That wasn't so hard, now was it? This is roughly what the Mac demo will look like: *See Figure 8-14.*

In Pro Tools on XP, you'll see something that looks like this: *See Figure 8-15.*

Wow, lots of "stuff" there—and it may look completely alien to you. No worries, we'll figure everything out as we go along!

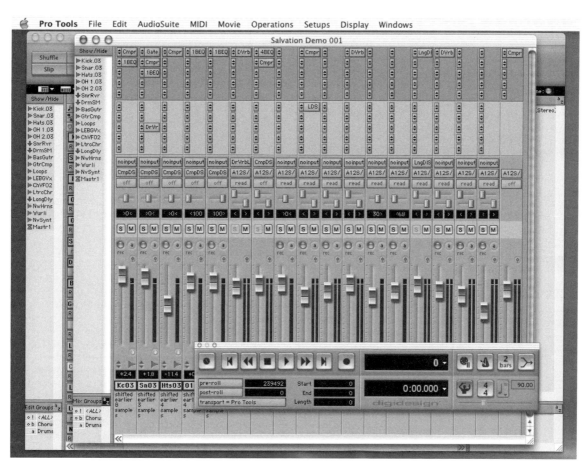

Figure 8-14

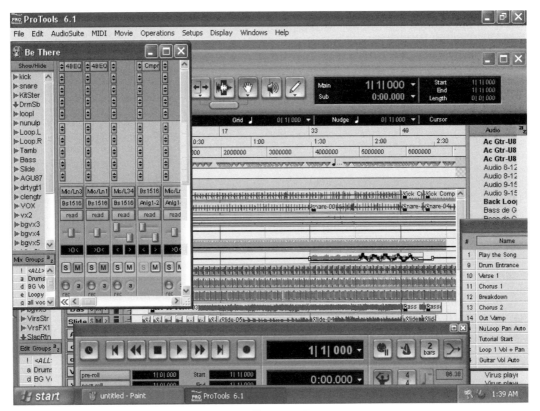

Figure 8-15

To listen to the demo, click the play button on the Transport window (the one with the right-facing triangle). The button will turn blue, and the counter will begin running, indicating Pro Tools is playing. If your hardware is hooked up correctly, the volume is at a reasonable level, and your speakers are turned on, you should hear the demo play. Wahoo! We've got Pro Tools working!

Figure 8-16

Space To Breathe

Start Pro Tools playing by simply hitting the space bar. To stop playback, hit the space bar again.

Silence Isn't Golden

If you've hooked everything up correctly, and installed the software according to the directions, you should hear glorious sound emanating from you speakers. If you don't hear anything, you need to shift yourself into troubleshooting mode. First, check that Pro Tools is actually playing. Is the software "tape counter" running? Do you see meters moving on the Pro Tools mixer? If not, the Session probably isn't playing. Try clicking Play again.

If the counter is rolling, are the signal indicators lighting up on your audio interface hardware? Quit Pro Tools and make sure that the interface is connected

correctly.

If Pro Tools is playing, and the audio interface seems to be working like it's supposed to, check that the volume is turned up on the interface hardware. Make sure that the interface isn't muted…the 002, for example, powers up with its monitor outs muted.

Next check that your speakers are connected correctly, that the speakers are turned on, and that any volume controls on the speakers or their amplifier are turned up. If you still don't get anything from the speakers, and you're sure Pro Tools is playing, try hooking a set of headphones to the Pro Tools interface and listening on them. If you hear the sound on the headphones, then the problem lies in your speaker system, how it's connected to your interface, or it's not turned on or up.

THE TRANSPORT WINDOW

Wonderful, we've got Pro Tools making some noise! As long as we're here, let's take a quick look at some of the basic features of the Transport window—we'll learn about the rest of the advanced features later. If the Transport window isn't open, go **Windows →
Show Transport** or hit type ⌘+1 (Ctrl+1).

Figure 8-17

In the upper-left section we've got familiar looking controls—you've probably seen similar buttons many times before on tape players, VCRs, CD and DVD players, and the like.

Figure 8-18

The Return to Zero button on the far left will take you to the beginning of the session. Next up are Rewind, Stop, Play, and Fast-forward—just like on a tape deck. The only difference from the way you'd expect these buttons to act (for now) is that you can click repeatedly on Rewind or Fast-forward to step through the session instead of winding all the way to beginning or end. Next is the Go to End button; it may surprise you, but yes, it takes you to the end of the session. Rounding things out is the Record button. Just like on a tape recorder, clicking this button then clicking the Play button (or hitting the spacebar) will start Pro Tools recording (more on this in Chapter 13, Record!).

The section to the right of the transport controls contains the time counters.

Figure 8-19

The time counters show you where you're at in the Session. There are two: The Main counter on top, and the Sub counter below. Each can display one of three time scales: Samples (as in the Main counter shown here), minutes, seconds, and milliseconds (as in the Sub counter shown here), or bars and beats. If you have the optional DV Toolkit, the counter can also display timecode.

To change the time scale displayed by a counter, click the little white down-facing arrow to the right of the green counter digits. *See Figure 8-21.*

You can set the Transport window to show some or all of its controls. As the Transport window opens up in the demo song, it's displaying the "expanded" view—all the controls are visible. Try this: Go **Display → Transport Window → Shows → Expanded**. The bottom half of the Transport window will fold up like

this: *See Figure 8-22.*

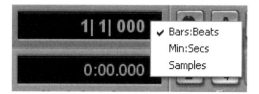

Figure 8-20

Figure 8-21

Next go **Display → Transport Window Shows → MIDI Controls**. The four buttons on the right—which control some MIDI functions that we'll discuss later—will disappear.

Figure 8-22

Next go **Display → Transport Window Shows → Counters**. The time counters will disappear, leaving you with just the transport controls—handy if your screen is becoming cluttered.

Figure 8-23

You can choose to check any combination of the three "Transport Window Shows" menu selections to configure the Transport window exactly as you want it. For now, go back and reselect all three (so that "Expanded," "MIDI Controls," and "Counters" are all checked) to fully expand the Transport window.

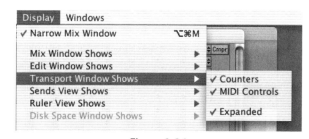

Figure 8-24

Figure 8-25

nine

THE MIX WINDOW

One of the beauties of Pro Tools LE is that there aren't a lot of software windows to deal with—there are only a few main windows we'll be seeing over and over. Two of those, the Edit and the Mix windows, are where most of the action takes place. Let's take a closer look at the Mix window; next chapter we'll delve into the mysteries of the Edit window.

If you haven't already copied the contents of the CD enclosed with this book onto your hard drive, please do so now. Open up the Session labeled "Chapter 9." The Session will look something like this:

Figure 9-1

One note: Don't save this Session as we work through this chapter. If you run into problems, or the pictures aren't pretty much matching what you see here, go **File → Revert to Saved…**, which will take the Session back to where it was when you opened it.

Click the Play button or hit the space bar to listen to the Session. When you've heard all you want (or can stand), click the Stop button or hit the space bar again.

Close the Transport window—the small one that looks like it has tape recorder controls and counters on it. You can do this by clicking the close button on the window itself, going **Windows→Hide Transport**, or typing ⌘+1 (Ctrl+1).

Figure 9-2

The Mix window should now be on top—it has the vertical "slider" controls across the lower middle.

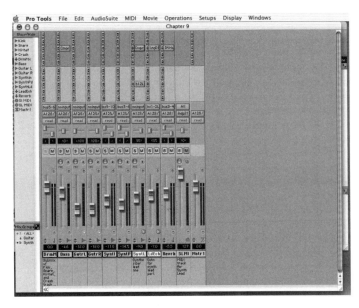

Figure 9-3

You can switch to the Edit window (the one with the horizontal audio tracks) by going **Windows → Show Edit**, or typing ⌘+= (Ctrl+=).

Figure 9-4

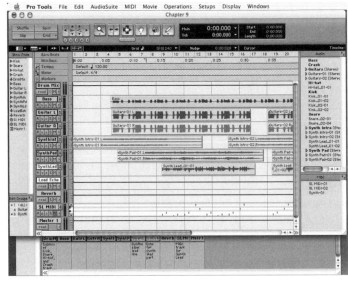

Figure 9-5

You can switch back to the Mix window by going **Windows → Show Mix**, or typing ⌘-= (Ctrl+=).

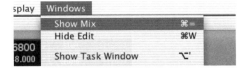

Figure 9-6

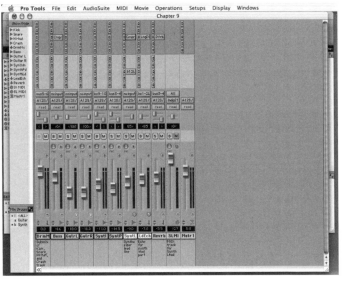

Figure 9-7

I recommend that you become very familiar with using the ⌘+= (Ctrl+=) key command. You'll be switching between the Edit and Mix windows a lot, and this is the fastest, easiest way to do it. (Besides, you'll look like a real Power User if you use the key commands instead of pulling down menus—won't your friends be impressed?)

MIX WINDOW

Let's begin our tour of the Mix window. This is the part of the Pro Tools software that duplicates the functionality of a hardware mixing console. Make sure that the Mix window is in front. If you prefer, you can close the Edit window completely by bringing it to the front then clicking its close button, going **Windows → Hide Edit**, or typing ⌘+W (Ctrl+W). If you've accidentally closed the Mix window, go **Windows → Show Mix**, or type ⌘+= (Ctrl+=).

And we're off, touring the Mix window. If you want to follow along on your computer, it will be easier if we make the channel strips a bit bigger. Do that by going **Display → Narrow Mix**, or typing ⌘+Opt+M (Ctrl+Alt+M).

Figure 9-8

The channel strips will become quite a bit wider; allowing you to see things more easily.

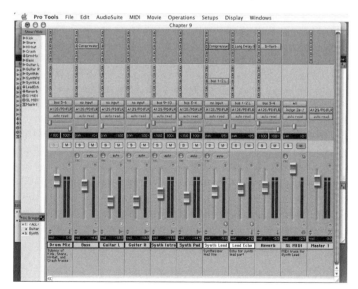

Figure 9-9

Let's begin by looking at the types of channel strips you'll find in the Mix window. A channel strip in the Pro Tools LE mixer represents the controls for one Audio or MIDI track, or the controls for an Auxiliary (Aux) input or a Master Fader.

First up we have the audio channel strip, which in Pro Tools LE comes in two flavors: Mono and stereo. The two types are similar, except for the mono strip handling one channel of audio...

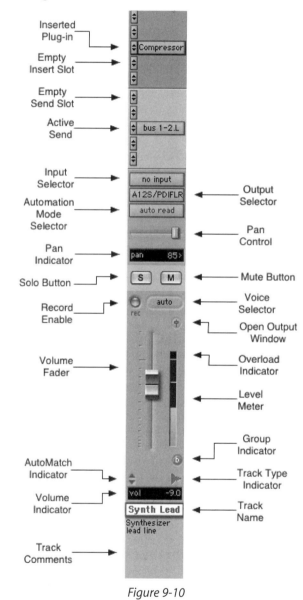

Figure 9-10

...while the stereo strip handles two channels (stereo signals). *See Figure 9-11.*

COMMENTS AND TRACK NAMES

At the bottom of the channel strip is an area for entering notes or comments on the track—a good place to make note of special gear or settings used when recording the track, for example. Click in this area of the Synth Lead channel strip once. It will highlight; you can now enter, delete, or edit comments. When you're finished hit Return (Mac) or Enter (Windows) to exit. *See Figure 9-12.*

Figure 9-11

Figure 9-12

Many Happy Returns

You can enter a line return in a track's comment box by hitting ↑ +Return (↑+Enter).

Above the track comments is the track name. Double-click the Synth Lead track name. This will open a dialog where you can type in and edit the track's name. This dialog also features another way to enter track comments. From this dialog, you can click Previous or Next to move on to other tracks. Click OK when you're finished. *See Figure 9-13.*

VOLUME INDICATOR

Above the track name is the volume indicator, which by default shows the setting of the volume fader in decibels. *See Figure 9-14.*

⌘**-click** (Ctrl-click) in the volume indicator to toggle this display to show headroom based on the peak level of playback for the track. *See Figure 9-15.*

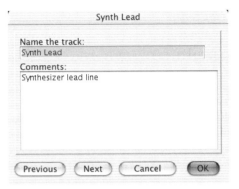

Figure 9-13

Figure 9-14

Figure 9-15

⌘**-click** (Ctrl-click) in the volume indicator to switch the display to track latency—although the latency display is meaningless with our LE systems. It's a holdover from TDM systems, which have latency (delays) due to plug-ins.

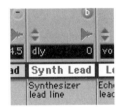

Figure 9-16

⌘**-click** (Ctrl-click) again to switch the display back to volume.

AUTOMATCH INDICATOR

Above the volume indicator on the left of the strip are the two arrow-shaped AutoMatch indicators. Pro Tools LE can remember and play back any fader moves you make; these indicators light to tell you the direction you need to move the fader so it matches the automation level. (More on this in Chapter 22, Automation.)

TRACK TYPE INDICATOR

The Track Type Indicator does two things: First, it tells you what kind of track you're looking at. There are four Track Types in Pro Tools LE, Audio (stereo and mono share the same track type) and Auxiliary tracks, Master Faders (stereo and mono share the same track type), and MIDI tracks.

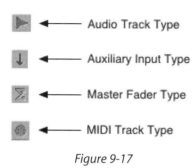

— Audio Track Type

— Auxiliary Input Type

— Master Fader Type

— MIDI Track Type

Figure 9-17

Second, when you **Ctrl+⌘-click** (Ctrl+Start-click) the track type icon, the track becomes inactive—basically, the track and all its processing is turned off. When inactive, the track will be grayed out. **Ctrl+⌘-click** (Ctrl+Start-click) again to re-activate the track.

GROUP ID INDICATOR

Groups in Pro Tools LE provide a way to link the controls for various tracks. For example, you might group all your drum tracks, so that when you mute one, all of them mute. There's a great deal more you can do with groups; we'll get into all that in Chapter 12, On the Right Track, and in Part 5: Editing. The group indicator shows if a track belongs to a group, and if so, which group.

In this Session, Guitar L and Guitar R are grouped together, as are Synth Lead and Lead Echo. Start the Session playing by hitting the space bar. When the guitar parts enter, use your mouse to grab and drag the volume fader for the Guitar L track (see below for more on volume faders) and move it up and down. You'll hear the volume of the guitar track change as you move the fader. Notice that the Guitar R volume fader moves along with it—it's grouped with Guitar L, so the two move together.

VOLUME FADER

The volume fader sets the volume for the track. There are two modes for the volume fader ("fader" for short). When Pro Tools LE is playing back, the fader sets the volume for the audio coming off the hard drive—but you might have guessed that. When Pro Tools LE is recording, the fader sets the monitor

volume for the track, but doesn't affect the volume of the audio as it is recorded to hard disk—this is an important concept that we'll revisit when we're recording tracks in Chapter 13, Record! This is useful when you're overdubbing tracks—you can create a nice mix for your performer to listen to without making the recording levels too high or low.

If you moved the Guitar L fader above (and Guitar R followed along with it), return it to its original setting of −18.0dB. To make fine adjustments, hold the ⌘ (Ctrl) key while dragging the volume fader.

Zero Balance

You can quickly set a volume fader to its default setting ("0dB") by Option-clicking (Alt-clicking) on it. Actually, this works with almost every parameter control in Pro Tools LE: Option-click (Alt-click) the control to return it to its default setting.

LEVEL METER AND OVERLOAD INDICATOR

This may be obvious, but the level meter shows the level of the audio signal being played back or recorded by Pro Tools—you've seen them moving when you played Sessions back. The meter changes color as you hit it with higher levels. Green is within safe-range levels, yellow means you're getting close to distortion (about 6dB below clipping), and the overload indicator lights red when the signal clips.

By default, the metering in Pro Tools is "pre-fader," meaning that it shows the level of the audio coming off the hard drive, regardless of where the volume fader is set. If you want the meters to show the level after the volume fader, go **Operations → Pre-Fader Metering**, so that it is un-checked.

Wide Load

Here's a cool trick: You can make the channel level meters wider by **Ctrl+Opt+⌘-clicking** (Ctrl+Start+Alt-clicking) on the meters (hold the modifier keys and click again to switch back to narrow meters). *See Figure 9-18.*

OPEN OUTPUT WINDOW

Clicking this little innocuous button opens up a sub-window with another, slightly different view of the fader, meter, and output section of the channel strip. Either a mono and stereo version will open, depending on whether the track is mono or stereo.

The Output Window can be quite useful; one example is when you're working in the Edit window and want access to a track's main controls without taking up all the space required by the full Mix window. Another is when you have a very large Mixer that requires scrolling to see all the channels. You might open up Output Windows for important channels that you need to access often. *See Figure 9-20.*

Figure 9-18

Figure 9-19

Targets

Here's a tip that's useful when dealing with Output Windows: At the upper right of the Output Window is a red and white "target." If this target is "lit," the next window you open will replace the current window.

Figure 9-20

If you deselect the target, the window will be "anchored"; the next window you open will appear in addition to the first one. This lets you have multiple windows available at the same time, without having to reopen them each time you need them. As we'll see later, this also works with Plug-in and Auxiliary Send windows.

Figure 9-21

Try it for yourself: Hit the Synth Lead track's Open Output Window button; its Output window opens up.

Now click the Synth Pad track's Open Output Window button. Its Output window replaces the Synth Lead Output window.

Turn off the Synth Pad Output window's target.

Click the Synth Intro track's Open Output Window button; its Output window will open, probably right on top of the Synth Pad Output window.

Drag the Synth Intro Output window to one side to reveal that the Synth Pad Output window is still open. As long as the Synth Pad Output window has its target turned off, you can open other Output windows at will and it will stay open. You can keep as many windows open as you want by turning off their targets.

Close all Output windows when you're finished checking this out.

RECORD ENABLE

Clicking the Record Enable button "arms" an audio or MIDI track for recording—if you click the Record and Play buttons on the Transport window, recording will begin. When you record-enable a track, its Record Enable button will light; the track's fader will also be highlighted in red. When a track is record-enabled, or armed, it will pass input signal so you can hear what you're sending into Pro Tools for recording—even if Pro Tools isn't playing or recording.

Figure 9-22

VOICE SELECTOR

Back in Chapter 3, Basic Pro Tools Concepts, we learned that while Pro Tools LE can have 128 audio tracks, only 32 of those can actually be "voiced" or play at a time. If you have more than 32 audio tracks, you have to tell Pro Tools which ones to voice. The Voice Selector on each audio track is where you do this. Click and hold the Selector, and you can choose between "Auto" and "Off."

Figure 9-23

Choose "auto," and the track will play as normal. If you turn the track off, it won't be heard when Pro Tools plays. This is different than making the track inactive, as described above. When a track is made inactive, all the resources it uses—track voice, CPU power used by plug-ins, etc., are returned to the "pool" for use by other tracks. When a track's voice is turned off, only the voice is available for another track to use. Any plug-ins, etc., on the unvoiced track will still consume CPU power.

Figure 9-24

Figure 9-25

SOLO AND MUTE BUTTONS

Pro Tools Solo and Mute buttons work in opposite fashion. When you hit the Solo button for a track, the button will light and all other tracks will be muted—the only track you'll hear is the one that's soloed.

Start the Session playing by hitting the space bar. Once all the parts enter, Click the Bass track's Solo button. All other tracks will drop out. If you want to hear another track, you can click its Solo button as well—try clicking the Guitar L track's Solo. The Bass track will continue playing, and both Guitar tracks will also go into solo. Why both? Remember that the Guitar tracks are grouped…soloing one will also solo the other.

To un-solo the tracks, click the Solo buttons again. Stop the Session by hitting the space bar.

Safe Soloing

There are certain tracks that you may not want to mute when you solo other tracks. Examples include Auxiliary inputs used for effects and submixes, and MIDI tracks. You can make a track "solo safe" by ⌘-**clicking** (Ctrl-clicking) its Solo button. The track's Solo button will be grayed out, and it will be heard even when another track is soloed. Return the track to solo as normal by ⌘-**clicking** (Ctrl-clicking) its Solo button again.

Try it out. Play the Session by hitting the space bar. When the Synth Lead track comes in, click its Solo button. You'll hear the Synth Lead, but you won't hear the echo that's supposed to accompany it. Un-solo the track and stop the Session.

Now ⌘-**click** (Ctrl-click) the Lead Echo track's Solo button; it will gray out. Play the Session again. When the Synth Lead track comes in, click its Solo button. You'll hear the Synth Lead, but this time you'll also hear the echo—the Lead Echo track has been made "solo safe."

Figure 9-26

Muting works the opposite way: If you click the Mute button for a track, its Mute button will light and that track will be silenced, while all the rest of the tracks continue to play. Try it: Play the Session. When all the tracks come in, click the Drum Mix track's Mute button. The drums will fall silent. Click the channel's Mute button to make it play again. When you're finished, stop the Session. Note that muting a track doesn't free up its voice or DSP resources—the track is still active, you just can't hear it.

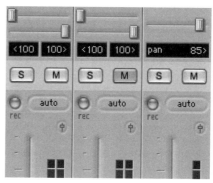

Figure 9-27

PAN CONTROL AND PAN INDICATOR

The Pan slider sets the left-right balance for a track assigned to a stereo output. The Pan Indicator displays the pan setting; "100>" is panned full right (only coming out of the right side of the stereo output), "<100" represents full left. A pan value of ">0<" means that equal-strength signal is going to both sides of the stereo output; the track will appear centered in the stereo field.

Try this: Play the Session. When the parts come in, **Ctrl-click** (Start-click) the Guitar R Solo button. This will suspend (turn off) the guitar group, and allow you to just solo the one track. Grab and drag the Guitar R pan slider. You'll hear the guitar track move from side-to-side across the stereo field. When you're finished, stop the Session and pan the track back far right. **Ctrl-click** (Start-click) the Guitar R Solo button again to leave solo and turn the guitar group back on.

Figure 9-28

With stereo tracks, each side of the stereo pair can be panned independently. *See Figure 9-29.*

If you're routing to a mono output, the pan control and indicator will disappear, as they're not needed. *See Figure 9-30.*

AUTOMATION MODE SELECTOR

Pro Tools can remember and play back moves you make on a track's volume fader, pan slider, and other parameters; this feature is called "automation," and it's an incredibly powerful tool for creating perfect mixes of your songs. The Automation Mode Selector contains settings that determine how the track will record and respond to automation data. We'll be

getting hot and heavy with automation in Chapter 22, Automation. *See Figure 9-31.*

Figure 9-29

Figure 9-30

Figure 9-31

INPUT AND OUTPUT SELECTORS

The Input Selector is where you assign the input that will feed an Audio or Auxiliary track in Pro Tools. Inputs can come from either your Pro Tools hardware interface or from a bus within the Pro Tools mixer. If the track is mono, you can assign a single mono input or bus; if the track is stereo, it will be assigned a consecutive pair of inputs or buses. *See Figure 9-32.*

The Output Selector assigns where the signal will go when it leaves an Audio or Auxiliary track, or Master Fader. The output may be a hardware out on your Pro Tools interface, or it may be an internal bus in the Mixer that's used to feed another track. A mono track may feed either a mono output or a stereo output pair. A stereo track can only feed a stereo output pair. *See Figure 9-33.*

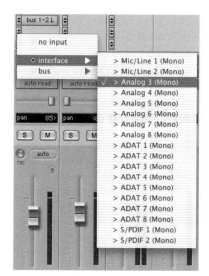

Figure 9-32

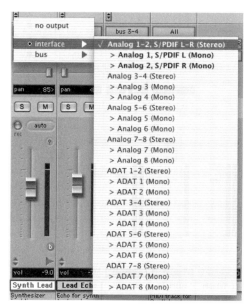

Figure 9-33

Don't worry if all this talk of inputs, outputs, tracks, and buses seems confusing. We're going to be learning more about Pro Tools inputs and outputs when we reach Chapter 11, Session File.

SENDS

Each Pro Tools LE audio track and Auxiliary Input can have up to five Sends. A Send splits off from the track's main signal and is sent somewhere else, leaving the main channel signal path untouched. A send might go to feed an effects processor, it might be sent to headphones for the musicians to listen to, etc.

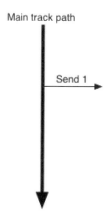

Figure 9-34

Sends are assigned by clicking and holding the little box with the up/down arrows on one of the five slots in the Send Assignment section of the channel strip. Both mono and stereo tracks can feed either a mono or stereo send.

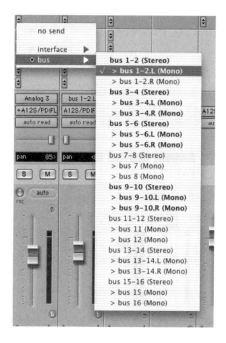

Figure 9-35

Does Figure 9-36 look familiar? It should—it's the same type of Output Window as we saw earlier with the channel strip outputs. When you select a Send, its Send Output Window will open automatically, allowing you to set the Send level, panning, and so on. Click the send labeled "Bus 1-2.L" on the Synth Lead track to see for yourself. *See Figure 9-36.*

So far, we've been looking at the Sends in what is called the Assignment View—you can see all five Send slots (labeled A, B, C, D, and E) and where each is assigned. There's another view that gives you more access to the controls for each send. On the Synth Intro track, click and hold the Send Assign for Send C

(the third send of the five). Assign it to the first bus.
See Figure 9-37.

Figure 9-36

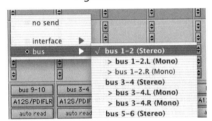

Figure 9-37

The Send Output Window will open. Close it. Go
Display → Sends View Shows → Send C.

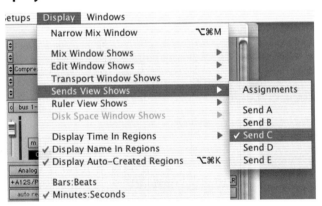

Figure 9-38

The Sends section of the channel strip will change
so that it shows all the parameters for the selected
Send (in this case, Send C). This view contains a level
fader for the Send, as well as a level meter with
overload indicator. Also included is a pan slider (if the
send is to a stereo bus or output), send mute button,
a pre/post fader button, and a Send Assignment
selector.

Figure 9-39

To change back to Send Assignments View, go
Display → Sends View Shows → Assignments. We'll
learn a lot more about sends in Chapter 20, In the
Flow.

INSERTS

An Insert differs from a Send; as we've seen a Send
splits off from the main track signal path and goes
somewhere else. An Insert interrupts the main track
signal path completely, sends the signal somewhere
else (such as through a plug-in) and returns it to
continue on through the channel strip.

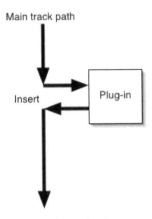

Figure 9-40

Each audio track, Auxiliary Input, and Master Fader
can have up to five inserts; these can either be routed
to internal software plug-ins, or they can feed out of
an output of your Pro Tools interface, then return
through an input on your interface (if your interface
supports this). This allows you to use external
hardware boxes to process the audio on a track. *See
Figure 9-41.*

We've only scratched the barest surface; I'll have a
lot more to say about inserts and plug-ins in Chapter
20, In the Flow and Chapter 21, Plugged In.

OTHER TRACK TYPES

The other three track types—Auxiliary Inputs, Master
Faders, and MIDI Tracks have much in common with
audio tracks.

Figure 9-41

Figure 9-42

AUXILIARY INPUTS

Auxiliary Inputs are almost identical to audio tracks, except that they don't have Record Enable buttons or Voice Selectors—they're inputs, not tracks, so there are no tracks to record or play, nor is there a need for a voice.

MASTER FADERS

Master Faders (see Figure 9-42) are simpler than audio tracks or Auxiliary Inputs. A Master Fader simply receives outputs from audio tracks and Auxiliary Inputs. There's no need for many of the controls found on an audio track. There's no Solo or Mute button, and no Record Enable or Voice Selector. Master Faders don't need pan controls, as they directly feed hardware outputs or buses; they also have no need for inputs—everything going into a Master Fader is being sent out on a specific output, so input assignment is unnecessary, as are sends. However, Master Faders do have five inserts so that final processing can be applied to the combined audio tracks and Auxiliary Inputs.

You can check out what a Master Fader does by playing the Session, then dragging the Master 1 fader up and down—the Master Fader controls the overall output level of the Session.

MIDI TRACKS

Considering that they're quite different functionally from audio tracks, MIDI tracks are surprisingly similar in features and appearance. Differences include that the MIDI Volume Fader sends out MIDI controller 7 (MIDI volume) data to synths and samplers that can receive it; the meter shows MIDI velocity instead of signal level.

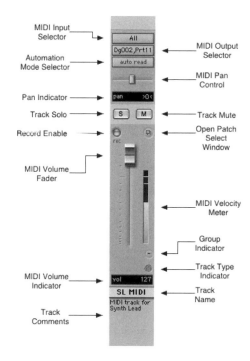

Figure 9-43

Instead of an Open Output Window button, MIDI tracks use a similarly placed button to open a Patch Select Window, for calling up presets on your synthesizer.

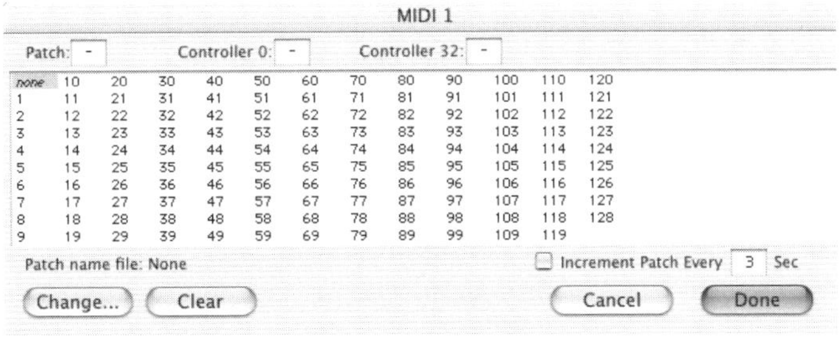

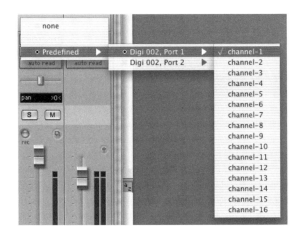

Figure 9-44

MIDI tracks have a pan control that sends out messages to synths and samplers that support MIDI panning. The MIDI Input Selector opens up to show whatever MIDI inputs are available on your system—it will depend on how you've set up your MIDI connections, if you have any software synthesizers installed, and so on. (I have a Digi 002, so I see one hardware port available when I click on the input selector.)

Each MIDI input will likely have 16 channels; you must also select one of these channels (or all channels) for each MIDI track. The four Pro Tools Inputs are virtual MIDI connections to Pro Tools; they allow Pro Tools to receive MIDI information from compatible third-party programs such as Ableton Live and Propellerhead Reason that are running on the same computer.

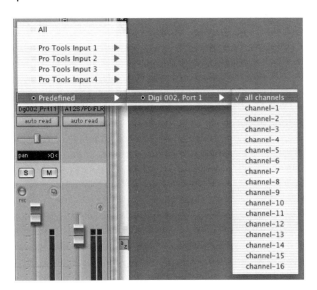

Figure 9-45

Like other Pro Tools tracks, MIDI tracks can be assigned to one (or more) outputs. And like MIDI inputs, each MIDI output will have 16 channels to choose among. The outputs you see will again depend on how you have your system configured. (My Digi 002 has two MIDI output ports, each supporting 16 MIDI channels.)

Figure 9-46

There will be much more on MIDI tracks in Chapter 24, MIDI Tracks, and in Part VII: MIDI to the Max.

MIX GROUPS LIST

There are two other sections (called "panes") to the Mix window. The first of these is the Mix Groups List, found on the lower left of the window. You can change the sizes of the panes by clicking and dragging on the boundaries between them.

Figure 9-47

When you create a Session, there will automatically be an "All" group (by default the All group is inactive; not highlighted). As you create new groups, they'll show up in this list. A group is active when it's highlighted in blue. Click on a group name to suspend it—click again to re-highlight it and make it active again. Try it: With the Guitars group highlighted move either the Guitar L or Guitar fader; the other guitar fader will move along. Now click on "Guitars" in the Mix Groups List to de-select it. Move a guitar fader again; the other won't follow along. Turn the Guitar group back on.

There are more options for groups; to see them, click and hold on the Mix Groups pop-up menu. *See Figure 9-48.*

The pop-up menu lets you create new groups, display either Edit or Mix groups (normally groups apply to both the Edit and Mix windows, so the list will be the same in both windows), suspend all groups (make them all inactive), and delete groups.

Figure 9-48

To the right of the Mix Groups pop-up, is a small box with "a-z" in it, called the Groups List Key Focus. (In the Mix window it's always on; in the Edit window it can be turned off.)

Figure 9-49

Key Focus allows you to turn groups on and off by simply typing the Group ID letter. In this Session, for example, if you type an "a" on the computer keyboard, the Guitars group will switch between enabled and disabled status.

We'll learn more about groups in Part V: Editing and Part VI: Mixing.

SHOW/HIDE TRACKS LIST

The upper-left section or pane of the Mix window contains the Show/Hide Tracks List.

Figure 9-50

This list shows all the tracks in the Session. Those that are highlighted in blue are visible in the Mix window. If a track isn't highlighted, it won't be visible in the Mix window, but (assuming it has a voice, is active, and isn't muted) will still play.

In the case of our Session, the top four tracks, Kick, Snare, Hi-hat, and Crash, are not highlighted so they don't show up. But we're actually hearing them—they're being submixed through the Drums Mix Auxiliary track. Click on these four tracks in the Show/Hide Tracks List to make them visible.

Figure 9-51

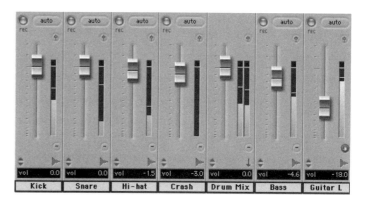

Figure 9-52

Like the Mix Groups List, the Show/Hide Tracks List has a pop-up menu that offers additional options.

Figure 9-53

This menu allows you to show or hide all the tracks in a Session, show or hide only those that are selected, and more. If you go **Show/Hide → Show Only**, you can choose to display tracks of only one particular type. *See Figure 9-54.*

Likewise, if you go **Show/Hide → Hide**, you can choose to hide tracks of a particular type. *See Figure 9-55.*

Figure 9-54

Figure 9-55

You can use the last item in this menu to sort the tracks in the Mix window by various criteria; this may help you to organize your tracks more effectively in large sessions.

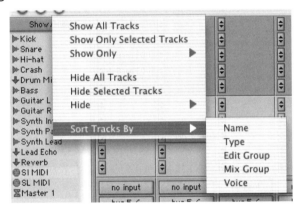

Figure 9-56

There's another way that you can arrange your tracks to your liking; simply click and drag the track in the Show/Hide Tracks List. For example, click on the Kick track and drag it down between the Crash and Drum Mix tracks. A dotted line will follow where you drag the track, showing you where it will end up.

Figure 9-57

The tracks will be re-ordered in the list with the Kick in its new location.

Figure 9-58

The way in which the tracks are ordered in the Mix window will change to match the List as well.

Figure 9-59

You can also change track order in the Mix window by clicking and dragging on a track's name. Click and drag the Kick track back to the far left to restore the original track order. The order in the Show/Hide Track List will change to reflect the new order.

Figure 9-60

That's it for this chapter. Close the Session by going **File → Close Session** or typing ⇧+⌘-**W** (⇧+Ctrl-W), and get ready to explore the Edit window!

ten

THE EDIT WINDOW

There are two ways to use Pro Tools… well…there are certainly many, many ways to use Pro Tools, but two come to mind right now. The first is to use Pro Tools as a basic replacement for a mixer and multitrack recorder—record your tracks, mix them down, and you're done. The second isn't quite as straight-ahead: Record your tracks. Edit them until you're satisfied with the arrangement you've created. Mix down, and you're finished.

The second method is where the Edit window, the next item on our little Pro Tools tour, mainly comes into play. In the Edit window, we can cut and paste, buff and polish, perfect, rough-up, slice and dice, mutilate, re-arrange, demolish, de-construct, re-construct…in other words, we can get in there and operate on our audio at both the micro and the macro levels. We'll be spending a bunch of time learning about editing techniques in Part V: Editing. In this chapter we'll be learning our way around the Edit window.

Let's get started! Find and open the file "Chapter 10" from the CD-ROM.

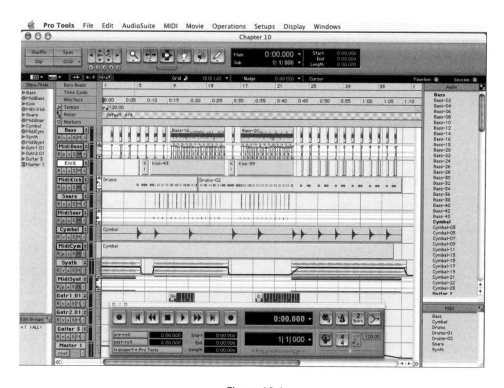

Figure 10-1

Click the Play button or hit the space bar to listen. When the song ends, click the Stop button or hit the space bar again. If necessary, move the Transport window so you can see the Edit window more clearly, and let's begin our tour.

Right smack-dab in the center of the Edit window is where the action takes place; the tracks you record—both MIDI and audio—show up here, as do Aux Inputs and Master Faders.

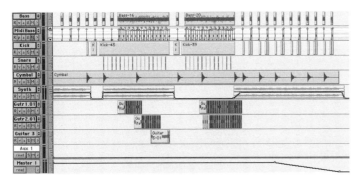

Figure 10-2

The tracks run horizontally across the screen, with some controls and info on the left, and the "data" display—waveforms, automation, MIDI notes, and various regions on the right.

In this example, we have a variety of track types and views. We've got large audio regions, such as the one on the Cymbal track that spans the entire song. We also have short audio regions, such as those on the Snare track. MIDI regions are present on the MIDIBass track. Aux 1 is an auxiliary input; remember that Aux tracks don't actually contain audio, they serve to route and combine other tracks. Master 1 is a Master Fader, providing final level control and processing for the entire collection of other tracks. We'll be getting into more detail about how the various tracks work in the Edit window later in this chapter.

WHERE ARE WE?

Hit the space bar or press the Play button. Notice the thin black line that scrolls across the screen as the song plays? *See Figure 10-3.*

That thin black line is called the Playback Cursor. It shows the current playback position in the song. We can position this cursor wherever we want—you don't always have to play from the beginning of the song.

Here's how: First make sure that the Selector tool is highlighted at the top of the screen—we're going to talk more about the Selector tool later, don't worry;

for now just make sure it's selected. If it's not selected, click on the button so it highlights. *See Figure 10-4.*

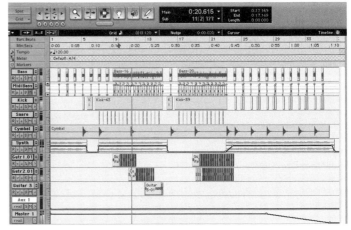

Figure 10-3

Figure 10-4

With the Selector tool selected, you can click anywhere in the track display to set where playback will begin. Try it: On the Cymbal track, click before the third cymbal hit waveform. Notice that a blinking cursor line (called the Edit Cursor) appears across that track showing where you clicked. Start the song playing. It will begin right where you clicked in the track. Stop playback. The Edit Cursor will still be blinking; if you start Pro Tools playing again, it will start from the same spot as before; where you clicked in the track.

To jump to somewhere else in the song, click in another spot along any of the tracks and start playback. When you're finished, hit the Return to Zero button on the Transport window to take Pro Tools back to the beginning of the song. You can also click the Fast-forward and Rewind buttons in the Transport window to locate to a particular point in the session.

To let you know exactly where the Cursor is at, the Edit window features Location Indicators.

Figure 10-5

Using the down arrows to the right of the counters, you can pull down a menu and choose what time format is displayed. You have your choice of bars and beats, minutes and seconds, or samples.

Figure 10-6

RULERS

Above the tracks in the Edit window is a set of rulers—as many as six. The gray rulers at the top—the timebase rulers—display the location in bars and beats, minutes and seconds, or samples. The lower three colored rulers—the Conductor rulers—show the tempo, time signature, and track markers, which are memorized locations in the song. You can click in a ruler to set the position of the Playback Cursor. You can change the order of the rulers by clicking on the name of a ruler and dragging it up or down.

Figure 10-7

You can choose which rulers are visible in one of two ways. You can go **Display → Ruler View Shows**, and select which rulers you want to see.

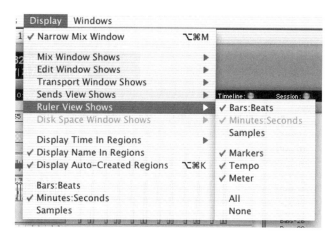

Figure 10-8

There's also a Ruler Display button located near the upper left of the Edit window.

Figure 10-9

If you click this button, a menu will drop down

that will allow you to choose which rulers are visible. Try it out. Click the Rulers button or go **Display →Ruler View Shows**, and select Samples. A third timebase ruler will show up in the Tracks part of the window.

Figure 10-10

THE TRACKS

Now let's take a closer look at the tracks themselves. Feast your eyes on the Cymbal track.

Figure 10-11

This is an example of a basic audio track. In this case, I've recorded the crash cymbal from an electronic drum kit. The main part of the track shows a waveform representing the audio performance.

Figure 10-12

In this view, you can clearly see each of the cymbal hits, which, individually, look like this:

Figure 10-13

On the left side of the track are basic track controls. These are similar to what we saw in the Mix window. Across the top is the track name. As in the Mix window, double-click it to open up a window where you can change the name and enter comments. And like the Mix window, you can click and drag on a track name to move tracks and change the track order. Note that if you change the order of the tracks in the Edit window, the order will also be changed in the Mix windows, and vice-versa.

Figure 10-14

Below the track name are buttons similar to those found in the channel strips in the Mix window: Record, voice select, automation, solo, mute, level meter, and so on. But let's make things a bit bigger so we can more clearly see what we're talking about. Click on the vertical strip to the right of the level meter, the one with the markings that look sort of like those on a tape measure or yardstick.

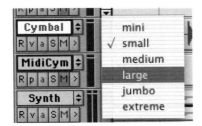

Figure 10-15

This menu allows you to set the vertical height of the track. Select "large." The track will become substantially taller, and the controls section will expand to give you a better view.

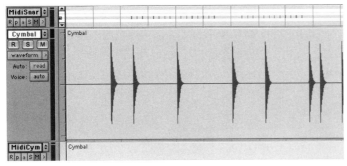

Figure 10-16

Looks much more like the controls in the Mix window, right? In fact, the Record Arm (R), Solo (S), Mute (M), Automation menu (Auto), and Voice Selector (Voice) function exactly the same way in the two windows. There are two other controls available. The first is the Track View Selector, which changes how track data is displayed. Right now, it's set to "waveform," so the track shows the audio waveform for the track. Click it to see the other options.

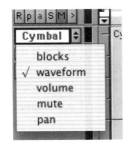

Figure 10-17

Choose "blocks."

This view shows where in the track audio is recorded, but doesn't show the waveform. It's useful if you're not doing waveform editing, and just need to reference the location of audio. If you have a slow computer, it will also free up some CPU power for faster operation.

Go back to the Track View Selector and choose "volume."

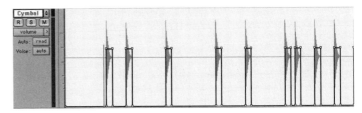

Figure 10-18

This view shows what's happening with volume automation in the track. Pro Tools can remember and play back volume fader moves for the track. In this View, you can see, enter, and edit that information. Here I've automated the volume fader so that it comes up and goes down with each cymbal hit. If you want to see the effect of this, go to the Mix window— remember the fastest way to do this is ⌘+= (Ctrl+=).

If the Transport window is closed, open it—⌘+1 (Ctrl+1). Click the Return to Zero button.

Note the position of the volume faders for each channel. Start the session playing.

As the session plays, you'll see the various channel faders moving up and down. This is automation in action. Even the Master Fader has been automated, note the long, slow fade out that ends the song. When you're finished, stop the session, and close the Mix window. We'll be learning all about automation in Chapter 22, Automation.

In the Edit window, go back to the Cymbal track's Track View Selector and choose "mute."

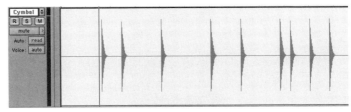

Figure 10-19

This view shows mute automation information—Pro Tools can remember when you mute and un-mute the track. There's no mute information on this track, so the mute line stays up at the top of the display.

Go back to the Track View Selector and choose "pan."

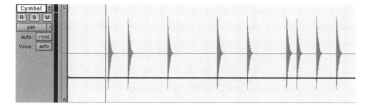

Figure 10-20

This view shows pan automation data. In this case, we're not moving the track around—it stays panned about halfway between center and right in the stereo field—so the automation line doesn't change position.

Depending on what you have happening in the track, you may see other Track View Selector options. For example, if you have automated any plug-in parameters, you'll find them added to the list of available Views.

Other track types have their own views. Aux Input tracks allow you to view volume, mute, or pan automation data.

Figure 10-21

Generally, Master Faders don't have any extra selections; they just display volume information. Check it out in the track Master 1. The exception is if you have plug-ins on the Master Fader inserts, and you've automated their parameters. In that case, those parameters can also be displayed on the Master Fader track.

Figure 10-22

MIDI tracks, on the other hand, offer lots of options. You can display all kinds of MIDI data—we'll be talking much more about this in Part VII: MIDI to the Max. *See Figure 10-23.*

Take a look at some of the other tracks in the session; there are examples of a variety of track views.

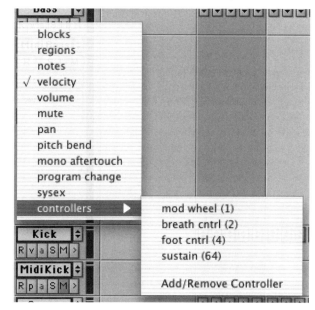

Figure 10-23

There's one final control to be discussed here: the Playlist Selector. This is found directly to the right of the track name; it's the button with the up/down arrows on it. A playlist is an arrangement of data on a track—audio regions, or MIDI regions and notes. An advantage of playlists is that you can have multiple takes and arrangements without using multiple tracks or voices. There is one limitation: Each track only supports one set of automation data, so the same volume, pan, and other information will be shared by all of a track's playlists.

You can use playlists to try out different performance takes, and different edit and arrangement ideas. On the Cymbal track, click the Playlist Selector, and pull down to select "Cymbal.01," a second playlist for the track.

Figure 10-24

The track will change to show the second playlist's arrangement of regions. *See Figure 10-25.*

See the difference? In this playlist, the empty space between cymbal hits has been edited out—you won't hear much difference if you play back the song with this playlist selected. To hear a bigger difference, change the playlist for the Guitar 1 and Guitar 2 tracks. The original playlists for these tracks were edited to create the "stuttering" chord effect. The second playlist for each track has the original sustaining guitar chords. Switch between the playlists for each track and play back the song to hear the difference.

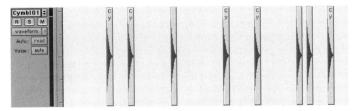

Figure 10-25

But Wait, There's More!

Even though you can quickly switch from the Edit window to the Mix window and back again to change settings, in some cases, this will interrupt the flow of what you're doing. Fortunately, the Pro Tools LE designers thought of that. We can display pretty much everything from the Mix window channels in our Edit window track controls. Here's how: Go **Display → Edit Window Shows** to see the options that are available.

Figure 10-26

Go **Display → Edit Window Shows**. Select Comments View.

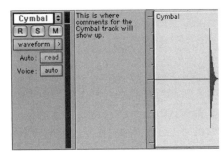

Figure 10-27

Any comments you have entered in the Mix window's comments area will show up here, and vice-versa. Go back to the **Display → Edit Window Shows** menu and select I/O View.

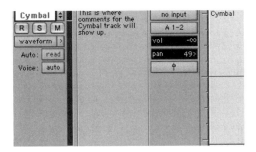

Figure 10-28

Here we see the Input and Output Selectors, volume and and pan indicators. Click the little fader at the bottom of the I/O View section. Yes, there it is again, our old friend the Output window. If you need to adjust volume, pan, or any other basic track controls from the Edit window, this is an easy way to find them. Also, remember that you can de-select the Output window's target to keep it open when you access other windows.

Figure 10-29

Go **Display → Edit Window Shows**. Select Inserts View.

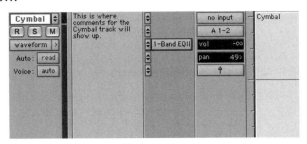

Figure 10-30

The Inserts View will open up, showing and giving you access to the plug-ins that are being applied to the track.

Go **Display → Edit Window Shows**. Select Sends View.

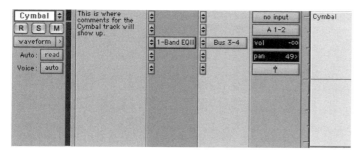

Figure 10-31

This view shows the sends for the track. Click on the Send Selector to add a send; click on the send to open its Send Output window. By using all these views, you can do everything in the Edit window that you can in the Mix window. If you don't need to see everything, you can open any combination of views. Go **Display → Edit Window Shows**. Choose None to return to the default track view. Choose All to open all views.

With All views selected, scroll down to the track named Aux 1. Make it Large using the Track Height selector. Aux tracks can display comments, and inserts and sends, just like audio tracks. There are Inputs and Outputs, volume and pan indicators, and a button for opening the Output window.

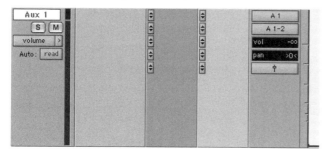

Figure 10-32

Next, look at the Master Fader track, named Master 1. Make it large. There's not a lot of extra features available; you can select the track's output, there's a volume indicator, and a button for opening the track's Output window. You can also enter comments and access inserts. *See Figure 10-33.*

The MidiBass track shows the extra features you can show for MIDI tracks. Make it large and check out the comments section, the Input and Output selectors, and volume and pan indicators. For everything else, you'll need to go to the Mix window. *See Figure 10-34.*

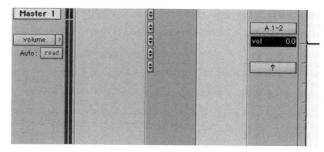

Figure 10-33

Figure 10-34

When you're finished looking at the Edit window track features, go **Display → Edit Window Shows**, and select None to return to the default track displays.

If you're getting tired of going all the way up to the Display menu to set what's showing in the Edit window, you can aim your mouse over to the upper left of the window, near the button we used to pull down the Rulers menu earlier.

Figure 10-35

There's a similar button that can be used to set what the Edit window shows. Click it to pull down the Edit Window Display menu.

Figure 10-36

Options Galore

Hold the Option key down while making a selection, and it will be applied to all tracks of the same type. For example, if you've been checking out the various Edit track views, you've probably got some tracks set for large height, and others smaller. Hold down the Option key and change one track to Small using the Track Height selector. All tracks will change to small height.

THE BIG LIST

There are two panes on the right side of the Edit window; the Audio Regions List and the MIDI Regions List. The two are similar, but one holds audio regions and the other holds MIDI regions—maybe you can guess which is which. The lists show every region that has been recorded or created by editing.

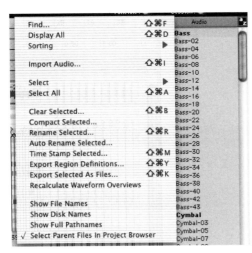

Figure 10-37

The Audio and MIDI Regions Lists each have pull-down menus. The pull-down menu for the Audio Regions List provides commands for finding, sorting, displaying, and performing operations on audio files.

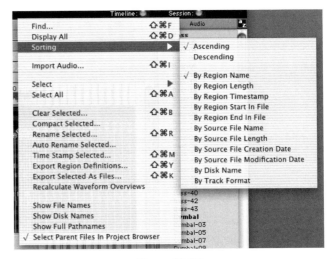

Figure 10-38

The Sorting submenu allows you to arrange the list of regions to your liking. Since the Audio Regions List can get quite long, these functions make it much easier to find what you're looking for.

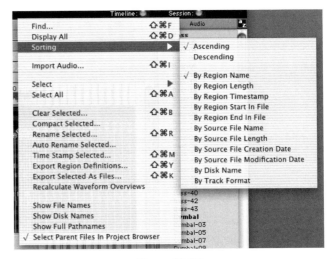

Figure 10-39

The Selection submenu let's you find regions that are no longer in use in the song; you can use the "Clear Selected..." command to remove them from the Session.

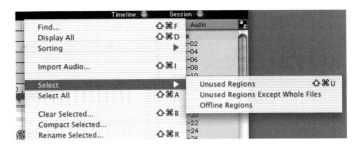

Figure 10-40

The MIDI Regions List has a similar pull-down menu that offers the same functions as applied to MIDI regions.

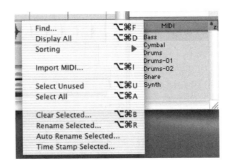

Figure 10-41

As with the Sorting submenu in the Audio Regions List, the MIDI Regions List has options for changing the order in which the MIDI regions are displayed.

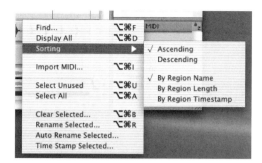

Figure 10-42

You can hide the Audio and MIDI Regions list section of the Edit window by clicking on the right-facing double-arrow button at the bottom of the window.

Figure 10-43

GO FOR WHAT YOU KNOW

Hidden among all those colorful doodads in the Edit window, there is some ground we've already covered. Like the Mix window, the Edit window is divided into several panes—in fact, the two panes on the left are identical to those on the Mix window.

Figure 10-44

On top is the familiar Show/Hide Tracks List area, and below that is the Edit Group List area. These not only look like their counterparts in the Mix window, but they work like them, and contain similar menu selections. Feel free to hide and show tracks at your leisure….

If you don't need to see the Show/Hide list and Edit Groups list, you can close those panes of the window, making the main track edit section larger. To

do this, click on the left-facing double-arrow button at the bottom of the screen.

Figure 10-45

You can also adjust the size of the various window sections by clicking a dragging on the borders between them.

PUT ON YOUR TOOLBELT

The Edit window offers a variety of tools for manipulating tracks. These are found across the top of the Edit window in three groups.

Figure 10-46

On the far left are the four Edit Mode buttons. These are used to control how regions are placed and moved in time in the tracks as they're edited. You can cycle through the Edit Modes by repeatedly typing the tilde (~) key.

With Shuffle mode (click its button or type **F1**), regions snap as far left on the track as they can—either to the right edge of the nearest region or the beginning of the track if there are no regions present.

When you're using Spot mode (click the button or type **F2**), regions snap to a particular time on a track. This is useful for sound effects, etc., where you want a sound to occur exactly at the right time.

Slip mode (click the button or type **F3**) lets you slide regions around however you like; you're free to place them anywhere.

In Grid mode (click the button or type **F4**), a time grid is set up on the track, and regions snap to the nearest grid point—you can set the grid resolution in musical terms (8th-note, 16th-note, etc.) or time units or samples. I used Grid mode to create the rhythmic 16th- and 32nd-note stuttering guitar edits on the Guitar 1 and Guitar 2 tracks.

We'll be talking a lot more about the Edit Modes in Chapter 15, The Mode You're In.

Figure 10-47

To the right of the Edit Mode buttons is the Zoom button area. These buttons let you magnify the tracks so that you can see more detail. The buttons with arrows are used to zoom in and out on the tracks. The numbered buttons below are used to memorize zoom settings.

Figure 10-48

If you click the right- or left-facing arrows, all tracks will zoom horizontally. Try this: Click the Return to Zero button on the Transport window to make sure Pro Tools is at the beginning of the session. Make the Bass track large height. Click the right-facing zoom arrow four times.

All tracks will expand out horizontally, zooming in on the waveforms or regions on the tracks. Next, to zoom all audio tracks vertically, click the second button from the left—the one with an audio waveform in the middle, between up and down arrows. Click the up-arrow portion of the button three times to zoom in.

Figure 10-49

Figure 10-50

You can zoom all MIDI tracks vertically using the button with the up and down arrows above and below the MIDI note symbol. *See Figure 10-51.*

Use the arrows that face the opposite direction to the ones we've used to zoom out; the left-facing

button zooms all tracks out horizontally; the down-facing arrows on the Audio and MIDI Zoom buttons zoom out horizontally.

Figure 10-51

Zoom!

Make your life infinitely easier with some handy tricks for zooming!

- Zoom button key equivalent commands:
  Horizontal Zoom In: ⌘+] (Control+])
  Horizontal Zoom Out: ⌘+[(Control+[)
  Audio Vertical Zoom In: ⌘+Option+] (Control+Alt+])
  Audio Vertical Zoom Out: ⌘+Option+[(Control+Alt+[)
  MIDI Vertical Zoom In: ⌘+↑+] (Control+↑+])
  MIDI Vertical Zoom Out: ⌘+↑+[(Control+↑+[)

- Click and drag up and down on a Vertical Zoom button to continuously zoom in and out vertically; click and drag side-to-side on a horizontal zoom button to continuously zoom in and out horizontally.

- To zoom completely out, so that all regions are visible, press Option+A (Alt+A).

ZOOM PRESETS

The five Zoom Preset buttons let Pro Tools remember five horizontal zoom levels. Zoom all the way out by pressing **Option+A** (Alt+A). Now click each of the five Zoom Preset buttons. You can do this using key commands as well: Hold the **Control** key (Start key) while typing the 1 through 5 alphanumic keys (the number keys above the letters, not the ones on the numeric keypad).

Figure 10-52

You can store your own horizontal zoom presets. Do it this way: Zoom in horizontally to the level you want. While holding the ⌘ key (Control key), click on one of the Zoom Preset buttons. Your Zoom Preset is stored and can be selected.

EDIT TOOLS

Figure 10-53

Next to the Zoom buttons are the Edit Tools. You're going to be using these babies a lot; we'll discuss them extensively in Part 5: Editing. For now, let's identify them. You can cycle through the Edit Tools by repeatedly typing the **Esc** key, or by typing ⌘**+1** through ⌘**+7** (Ctrl+1 through Ctrl+7).

Zoomer

Figure 10-54 and 10-55

Click the magnifying glass icon or press **F5** to select the Zoom tool. The Zoom tool can zoom in and out on a track. It has two modes: "Normal" (left) and "Single" (right). In Normal Zoom mode, after you use the Zoom tool, it stays selected. In Single Zoom mode, after you use the Zoom tool, it reverts to the tool you were using previously. You select between the modes by either clicking on the Zoom tool icon and pulling down its menu or by repeatedly pressing **F5**.

You can zoom in a number of ways. If you click and drag in a track, it will zoom in horizontally. Hold the **Option** (Alt) key while dragging the Zoom tool and the track will zoom out. **Option-click** (Alt-click) to revert to the previous zoom level; double-click the Zoom tool icon to zoom all the way out.

If you hold the ⌘ key (Control key) and click and drag, the track will zoom both horizontally and vertically.

You can zoom in the Rulers by pressing ⌘**+control** (Control+Alt) and clicking or clicking and dragging with the Zoom tool in a Ruler.

Trimmer

Figure 10-56 and 10-57

The Trimmer tool (left) lets you trim the beginning or end of regions and notes, or adjust the level of automation. Click the icon or press **F6** to choose the Trimmer. The Trimmer tool has two modes; you can choose the one you want by clicking the Trimmer icon and pulling down its menu. You can also cycle through the tools by repeatedly pressing **F6**.

The second Trimmer mode, the Time Trimmer (right), allows you to time-compress/-expand an audio region. In other words, you can change the length of a piece of audio without changing its pitch. You can use the Time Trimmer to match the tempo of a loop to another region, to match the length of a region to a song's tempo, and more.

Selector

Figure 10-58

We already used the Selector tool earlier in the chapter to locate the Playback Cursor in a track. (Click the icon or press **F7**.) The Selector is also used to select portions of a track for editing; try dragging in a track with the Selector tool to see how it works.

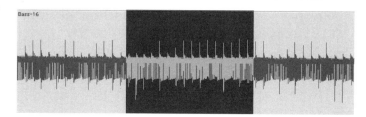

Figure 10-59

To the right of the Locate display is a display that shows where a selection made with the Selector tool (or by any other means) begins, ends, and how long it is.

Figure 10-60

Grabber

Figure 10-61 and 10-62

Press **F8** or click on the "hand" icon to choose the Grabber tool (left). As its name implies, the Grabber can be used to select regions or automation points and move them around. Press the **F8** key again, or click on the icon to pull down the Grabber menu to choose a second mode, the Separation Grabber tool (right). This mode can be used to split regions up into smaller sections.

Scrubber

Figure 10-63

The Scrubber tool is selected by clicking its icon or pressing **F9**. Scrubbing duplicates an effect possible on analog tape recorders, where you can manually move the tape reels and hear the recorded audio play back at slow speed. Try it: Select the Scrubber. Click and drag in one of the regions in the Synth track. The speed of the scrubbing will depend on how far you are zoomed in or out. You can scrub either forward or backward.

Pencil

Figure 10-64

The Pencil tool allows you to "draw" data into a track; this includes re-drawing waveforms, entering automation, entering MIDI notes, and more. Select the Pencil tool by clicking on its icon or by pressing **F10**. The Pencil tool has more than one mode of operation; if you click on it and pull down its menu you can select among the modes. Or you can press the **F10** key repeatedly to step through the various options.

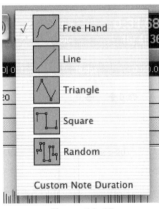

Figure 10-65

Smart Tool

Figure 10-66

The Smart tool is sort of a combination mode. Depending on where you place your mouse cursor in the track section of the Edit window, the tool changes among the Trimmer, Selector, and Grabber, among other things. You can select the Smart tool by clicking on the oval beneath the Trimmer, Selector, and Grabber, or by pressing **F6+F7** or **F7+ F8**. As you're editing, use the Smart tool most of the time rather than selecting individual tools; you'll find it makes editing go much faster.

BUT THAT'S NOT ALL...

There's much more to the Edit window, which we'll be getting to in later chapters. But before we go, check out a few more features:

KEY FOCUS

Like the Mix window, the Edit window has Key Focus capabilities. But where Key Focus is only available in the Groups List in the Mix window, there are a number of places in the Edit window where hitting a single key on the keyboard can make a selection. By clicking the "a…z" button in the Edit Groups List, Audio Regions List, or MIDI Regions List, you can use the keyboard to select a region or group. For example, select the "a…z" button at the upper-right of the Audio Regions List. Now type a "c." The first Cymbal audio region will be selected.

There's also a Key Focus button at the upper left of the Edit window.

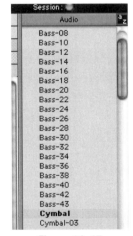

Figure 10-67

Figure 10-68

Selecting it allows you to perform various functions. For example, with the Key Focus selected (it will outline in blue), hit the "e" key. Whatever track you have selected will expand in height (how far it expands is set in the Pro Tools Preferences). Hit "e" again to toggle back to the previous track height.

You can toggle through the four possible Key Focus buttons (main window, Audio Regions List, MIDI Regions List, Edit Groups List) by typing ⌘+**Option**+**1** through ⌘+**Option**+**4** (Ctrl+Alt+1 through Ctrl+Alt+4).

TAB TO TRANSIENT

If you click the little "arrow aiming at a waveform" button to the left of the Key Focus button so it's highlighted in blue, you'll turn on "Tab to Transient."

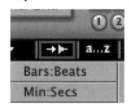

Figure 10-69

This feature allows you to step through a track based on the transients it contains. (Transients are sounds with sharp, fast attack, such as a drum, guitar, or piano—as opposed to the slow attack on, say, a violin.) Tab to Transient is great for quickly stepping across a track to where you want to be. It's excellent if you're trying to create drum loops; you can easily jump exactly from hit to hit to find the loop length you want.

With Tab to Transient selected, click near the beginning of the Cymbal track. If you press the Tab key, you'll step across the track, jumping from cymbal hit to cymbal hit. If you hold the Shift key while tabbing, you'll select the area between cymbal hits. **Option+tab** (Alt+tab) steps you through the transients backward (right to left across the track).

LINK EDIT AND TIMELINE SELECTION

Normally you'll want to leave the "Link Edit and Timeline Selection" button selected (highlighted in blue).

Figure 10-70

You can also make this selection by going **Operations → Link Edit and Timeline Selection** or typing ↑+**/**.

Figure 10-71

With the Link Edit and Timeline Selection active, when you make a selection in the tracks, you'll simultaneously be making the same selection in the Rulers, which determines where Pro Tools will play back. This is the default operation, since you normally want to play back what you have selected.

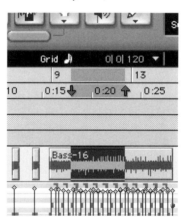

Figure 10-72

There are times, however, where you want the edit and playback selections to be in different places. Maybe you have a specific area you're working on and listening to, but you want to jump outside that area to audition another area. You can do this by unlinking Edit and Timeline Selection, and making another selection in a track. *See Figure 10-73.*

Now if you hit the space bar or click Play, the area selected in the ruler will play back. But you're actually editing the area that's selected in the track (in the Bass track in Figure 10-73). If you go **Operations → Play Edit Selection** or type **control+[** (Start+[) the area that's selected for editing in the track will play.

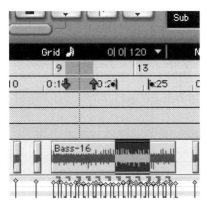

Figure 10-73

eleven

SESSION FILE

Now that we've got our studios set up and have learned our way around Pro Tools, it's time to dig in and start using Pro Tools to create some sounds!

To begin, we'll create a new Session file, and get Pro Tools ready for recording. We had a brief introduction to Session files back in Chapter 3, Basic Pro Tools Concepts. The Session file is the "master" Pro Tools document. It contains all the information for a project: The tracks, routing and processing information, edit information, locations of all the audio and other component files for the project—basically anything associated with a particular project is contained in the Session file.

CREATING A NEW SESSION

In order to start a project, you have to create a new Session file. There are two ways you can do this: Go **File → New Session...** or you can type ⌘+**N** (Ctrl+N).

Figure 11-1

Once you've given Pro Tools the order to create a new session, you'll need to give the file a name, and set up a few overall parameters. Type the name you want to use into the "Save As:" space. (I'm using the

very clever name "First Session" for my first session....) At this time you should also set the location where you'd like the Session to be stored on your hard drive using the "Where:" pull-down menu or by navigating in the browser part of the window. I've stored this Session in the folder "Pro Tools Files" on the hard drive named "160GB."

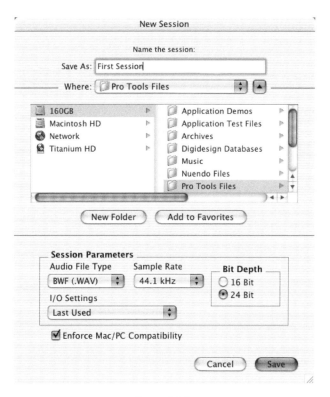

Figure 11-2

Before saving the file and moving on, there are a few Session parameters to set or verify in this window. You can choose among three audio file types: Broadcast Wave Files files (a variation on the Microsoft WAV file format), AIFF (Audio Interchange File Format; developed by Apple), or Sound Designer II (developed by Digidesign). Once upon a time, the file format you used could cause compatibility problems with other platforms and systems or other types of software you wanted to use, but these days most systems and applications support most file formats. I tend to use BWF files to ensure broadest compatibility with either Mac or Windows users.

Figure 11-3

You'll also need to set a sample rate for your session. The selection of sample rates that appears in this menu depends on what hardware interface you're using with Pro Tools. I'm using a Digi 002, so I can decide among 44.1, 48, 88.2, and 96kHz rates; you may see different options if you're using a different hardware interface.

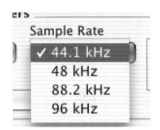

Figure 11-4

Which Rate?

There are a few things to consider when choosing a sample rate for your session: Obviously your hardware is a big consideration—it will determine what rates are available to you. In general, higher rates sound subtly better, but that's not the complete story. Higher rates also use more hard disk space, and require a more stout computer if you want to play or record a lot of tracks.

Another consideration is where your music will end up—what format will you be distributing? CDs use a 44.1kHz rate. It is possible to reduce other sample rates to the CD rate, but this process, called "sample rate conversion" sometimes has a negative effect on the audio quality. DVDs support higher rates, but not many of us are set up to burn audio to DVD yet—expect that to become more commonplace soon.

For the Web, you're probably going to be data-

compressing the heck out of your audio files to make them small enough to easily download. A higher sample rate's quality benefits may be lost in the process.

So which way to go? Here's my take: I work at the highest rate I can for the best quality. This way, I'm ready if future delivery media supports better quality. I'd rather ratchet down to lower rates now—and put up with the higher hard drive and system demands—with the prospect that listeners will be able to enjoy the full quality of my tunes in the future.

Next, set the bit depth or sample resolution. Remember that higher bit depth makes a big difference in audio quality, even if the final distribution will be on 16-bit CD or over the Web.

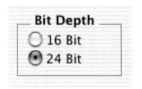

Figure 11-5

Pro Tools can remember the overall input and output routings you've used for a Session, and allow you to recall those settings for use in future Sessions. The first time you create a session, you'll have a choice of two I/O (input/output) settings: "Last Used" and "Stereo Mix." Since this is our first new session, they're identical, so it doesn't really matter which one you choose. Once you start creating your own I/O Settings (in fact, we'll get into just that topic later in this chapter) choosing the right one will be more important.

Figure 11-6

If you're a Mac user and you're going to be collaborating or sharing files with a Windows user—or vice versa—select the Enforce Mac/PC Compatibility check box. Even if you don't expect to use your Sessions on the other platform, I recommend checking this box. It doesn't hurt anything, and you never know which platform your Session might end up being used on in the future. *See Figure 11-7.*

Click Save, and the new Session will open up. Both the Mix and the Edit windows will be completely empty—no MIDI or audio tracks, no Aux Inputs, and no Master Faders.

Figure 11-7

At the same time as the Session opens up on your screen, a folder containing the Session and its associated components will be created on your hard drive at the location you specified.

I know you're anxious to get some sounds recorded into Pro Tools, so I'm going to be a nice guy and give you a choice. I don't recommend it, but if you just can't wait to get recording, you have my permission to jump ahead to the next chapter and dive right in. Pro Tools is set up with defaults that will get you going without problems. Wait, wait, hold your horses, there's one condition: You have to come back and read the next section on setting up Pro Tools' inputs and outputs after you've satisfied your recording jones.

THE PATH TO GREATNESS

Pro Tools uses "paths" to define its input and output routing. There are four types of paths: inputs, outputs, inserts, and buses. Let's take a closer look. Go **Setups → I/O Setup...**

Figure 11-8

The I/O Setup window will open. Across the top of this window are four tabs, which match the four types of Pro Tools paths. To begin, make sure the "Output" tab is selected. *See Figure 11-9.*

WORKING WITH PATHS

The center of the I/O Setup window is a matrix that allows you to set up paths from Pro Tools tracks, sends and returns, and inserts to your hardware interface's physical inputs and outputs. Across the top of the matrix are the ins and outs; I've got a Digi 002, so with the Output tab selected, my matrix shows 18 outputs: eight analog, and eight ADAT optical and two S/PDIF digital. In the boxes below, you

select which paths go to which outputs. When you assign an output in a Pro Tools track, you select the path you want, and signal is routed to the corresponding output or outputs. *See Figure 11-10.*

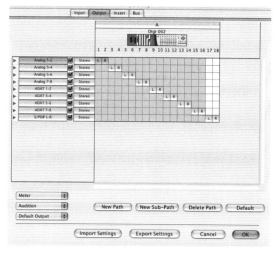

Figure 11-9

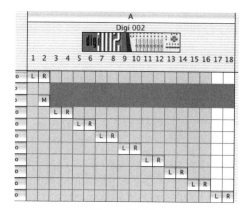

Figure 11-10

You select a path by clicking its name. The name will highlight. Select the top path, labeled "Analog 1-2."

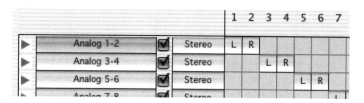

Figure 11-11

Click the Delete Path button or hit the Delete key; the path you have selected will be deleted. This is how you remove paths you won't be using in a session (should you want to do so). *See Figure 11-12.*

If you click the New Path button or type **⌘+N** (Ctrl+N); a new path will be added to the list. *See Figure 11-13.*

Click and drag in the path's name to bring it to the top of the list. *See Figure 11-14.*

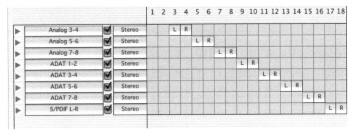

Figure 11-12

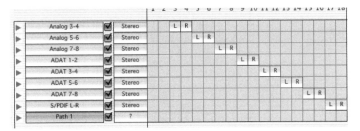

Figure 11-13

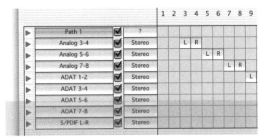

Figure 11-14

Next, double-click the path name. You can now name the path however you like. These are the names you'll see when you assign an input or output for a track, so it makes sense to use names that mean something in the context of your studio. The names shown here are the generic defaults, and allow you to choose specific analog or digital paths. Once you have Pro Tools integrated into your studio, you may want to follow the lead of many engineers and producers who prefer to name the paths based on what gear is hooked to each input and output. For now, let's name the path "Analog 1-2." Hit the **Return** (Enter) key when you're finished naming the track.

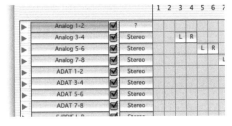

Figure 11-15

The checkbox to the right of the path name makes the path active or inactive. With the box checked, the path will show up and be available for tracks to use. If the box is unchecked, the path will show up in track

input and output selectors, but it will be inactive—not available for use. Inactive paths are shown in italics wherever they appear. To the right of the checkbox is a pull-down menu marked with a "?" that lets you set the format for the track: mono or stereo. Choose stereo for our newly created path.

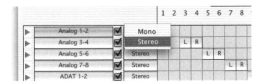

Figure 11-16

The last step is to assign which hardware outputs our new path will be feeding. Move the mouse cursor over the matrix part of the window. The pointer arrow will change to a pencil. Click in the box under output 1; since this is a stereo path, both outputs 1 and 2 will be assigned to the path.

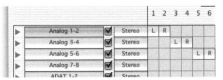

Figure 11-17

SUB-PATHS

A sub-path is a secondary path within the main path. Each of the stereo paths in the I/O Setup window has two sub-paths within it (except the one we just created above); one for the left channel, the other for the right channel. You can look at the sub-paths by clicking the arrow to the left of the path name. When you've finished checking out the sub-paths, click all the arrows you've "opened" to close them and hide the sub-paths.

Figure 11-18

Now let's add some sub-paths to our new Analog 1-2 path. Start by clicking its name to select the path. Now click the "New Sub-Path" button twice to add two new paths. The two new sub-paths will be mono, since their parent path is stereo. There's no checkbox; as long as the main path is active, its sub-paths will be active. *See Figure 11-19.*

Change the sub-path names by double-clicking each sub-path name and typing in the new name you desire. Name them "Analog 1" and "Analog 2." *See Figure 11-20.*

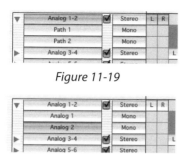

Figure 11-19

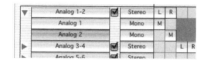

Figure 11-20

Now assign the sub-paths to physical outputs in the same way that you did the main path: Move the cursor over the matrix until it turns into a pencil, then click in the boxes. Note that you can only select from the outputs that are assigned to the main path.

Figure 11-21

That's all there is to deleting, creating, naming, and assigning paths and sub-paths. We'll learn more about how paths are used in the next chapter.

OTHER I/O SETTINGS

There are a few other settings in the I/O Setups window. The Meter pull-down menu allows you to assign which path will be feeding the meters on a Digidesign ProControl. Since it's doubtful anyone would use a ProControl with a Pro Tools LE system, you can pretty much ignore this menu.

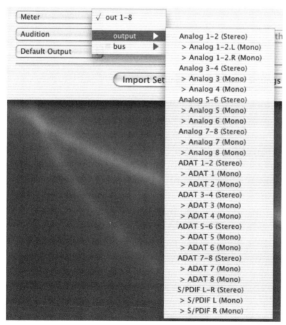

Figure 11-22

The Audition pull-down menu sets the path that will be used when you're previewing regions in the region list and before importing them into a Pro Tools Session. We'll find out more about auditioning and importing audio in Chapter 14, The Import Business. Generally you'll want this menu assigned to the path where your studio speakers are connected; usually the path feeding outputs 1 and 2 (Analog 1-2 in our example).

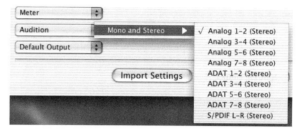

Figure 11-23

The Default Output pull-down menu selects which path will be used as the default output for any new tracks that are created. In other words, if you create a new Audio Track, Aux Input, or Master Fader, it will show up automatically assigned to the path you select here. Generally you'll want this assigned to the path where your studio speakers are connected; usually the path feeding outputs 1 and 2 (Analog 1-2) in this case.

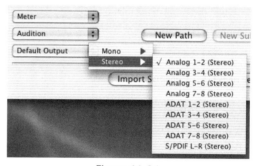

Figure 11-24

The Import and Export buttons at the bottom of the I/O Setup window allow you to save I/O Setups and load them into another Session. Saved I/O Setups will also show up in the I/O Settings pulldown (remember it from the beginning of this chapter?) when you create a new Session. Click the Export button to save your settings, and click Import to load saved settings into a Session.

Figure 11-25

INPUTS, INSERTS, AND BUSES

There are three other tabs across the top of the I/O Setup window. Click the Input tab to bring the input paths to the front. Input paths work exactly the same as output paths, with the obvious exception that they are dealing with routing paths to physical hardware inputs rather than outputs.

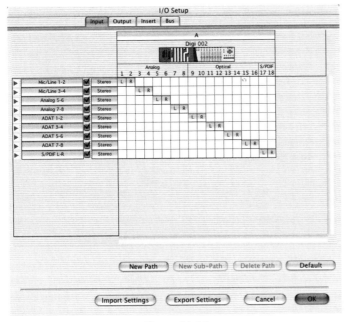

Figure 11-26

If you click the Insert tab, the insert paths will be brought to the front. Inserts are used to route signal out of your Pro Tools interface, usually to a processor, such as a reverb or another effects device, then bring the processed signal back into Pro Tools. So when you're setting up an insert path, you're assigning both an input and an output at the same time. You can assign an insert to inputs and outputs that are already assigned to input or output paths, but only one of the assignments can be active at once. For example, an insert path that's assigned to input and output 3 will be inactive if output 3 is already in use by an output path. We'll learn more about inserts in Chapter 20, In The Flow.

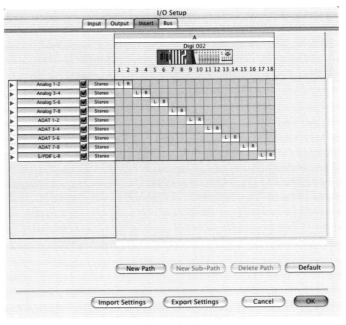

Figure 11-27

Buses are the only paths that don't get assigned to physical hardware inputs or outputs. Buses are used to route signal internally in the Pro Tools mixer—think of them as software audio pipelines. You can name buses if you like, but generally you'll want to wait until you have them in use before you name them. For example, once you're using a bus to feed a reverb plug-in, you might name the bus "Reverb Feed," or something equally descriptive.

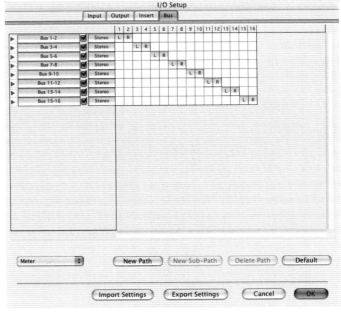

Figure 11-28

Recording

twelve

ON THE RIGHT TRACK

The time has come—the moment you've been waiting for! In Chapters 12 and 13 we're going to work up to hitting the Record button and getting the first strains of your glorious music laid down in Pro Tools.

First up, we need to prepare an empty Audio Track and set up a click (metronome). If you closed the empty session we created in the last chapter, open it up and bring the Mix window to the front.

CREATE A NEW AUDIO TRACK

In order to record sound, we've got to have an audio track available. To create a new track, you can go **File → New Track...** or you can type ⇧+⌘+N (⇧+Ctrl+N).

Figure 12-1

The new track dialog will open. You'll need to set a few parameters here. First, type the number of new tracks you want into the field on the left. One track should do us for now.

Figure 12-2

Next choose whether your new track will be mono or stereo using the pull-down menu in the center.

Figure 12-3

Now choose what type of track to create using the pull-down on the right. Choose "Audio Track."

Figure 12-4

Click the Create button or hit **Return** (Enter). Your new track will appear in all its glory at the left of the Mix window. Hit ⌘+S (Ctrl+S) to save the Session with your new track in it.

INPUT AND OUTPUT

Now that we have brought a new track into existence, we'll need to assign which input path will be feeding it. I'll be recording into the first hardware input on my Digi 002, so I'll choose the first path, Mic/Line 1. Choose the path you'll be using to record on your interface. The paths you see as options in this menu will depend on which hardware you're using.

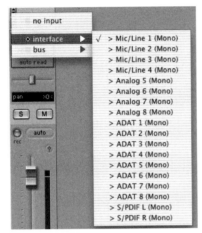

Figure 12-5

In the same way, we now need to assign the output path our track will be feeding. The track will automatically be set to the default path assigned in the I/O Setup window (as discussed in the last chapter). But you if you want, can change to whatever path you'd like to use.

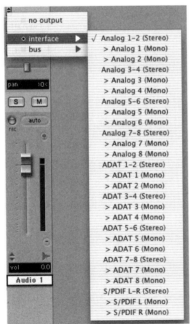

Figure 12-6

Multiple Outputs

There are many situations where you'll want a track to feed more than one output, whether more than one hardware output or more than one internal bus. Assign a track to multiple outs by **Ctrl-clicking** (Start-clicking) its Output Selector button.

Figure 12-7

A track that's been assigned to more than one output will have a "+" in its Output Selector button.

Figure 12-8

Before you record, I recommend that you name the Audio Track. Yes, I'm a control freak, but this is more than me wanting control over everything you do. When Pro Tools records into a track, the resulting audio file is named based on the track name. It will make the files associated with a Session easier to manage later if you name the track first, so the associated file name makes sense. Hit ⌘+S (Ctrl+S) to save the Session.

Figure 12-9

MASTER FADER

The next step is optional—you can record without doing it—but I recommend always creating a Master Fader for your Sessions. The Master Fader will give you a final master level control and meter before signal leaves Pro Tools for your speakers. A Master Fader is created in the same way as an Audio Track: Enter "1" for the number of tracks, choose "Stereo" from the track format pull-down (unless for some reason you want a mono song), and choose "Master Fader" from the track type pull-down menu. Click

window is selected, then Pro Tools will follow the tempo set in the Conductor track in the Edit window. If you deselect the Conductor button, you can set the tempo in several other ways: You can move the tempo slider below the click buttons. You can double-click in the numeric field and type in the exact tempo you want. You can also click the "tap" button, then click your mouse a few times at the tempo you want the song to use.

Figure 12-22

Or you can go **MIDI → Change Tempo...**, which will open the Tempo/Meter Change window.. This window is intended to be used to set up tempo changes in the Conductor track, but you can also use it to specify the tempo for the entire track; simply enter the tempo you want into the BPM (Beats Per Minute) field and hit Apply.

Figure 12-23

At the bottom of the Tempo Change window, you can click on the rhythmic value that should receive the click. Another, more convenient way to do this is to click on the button with the "note =" icon on the Transport window. You can select from whole or dotted rhythmic values by clicking on the dots below the notes.

Figure 12-24

The final click parameter to be set is the meter. You can open the Meter Change window by double-clicking on the button with the meter on it on the Transport window or by going **MIDI → Change Meter...** Enter the meter you want, then click Apply.

Figure 12-25

Hit ⌘+S (Ctrl+S) to save the Session. That's it, turn the page, let's get recording!

thirteen

RECORD!

The time has come: Let's *record*! If you closed the Session we were working on in the last chapter, open it up. Make sure the Mix window is at the front.

HOOK IT UP

Connect whatever source you're going to record to the input you have selected for your Audio Track. In my case, I've got a microphone connected to input 1 of my 002; I'm going to put the microphone in front of an acoustic guitar I'll be strumming. You can use a mic on an instrument or vocalist, an electric guitar or bass plugged directly in, a keyboard, a drum machine, a CD player—whatever you want to use as a source of audio. If you can't think of anything else to do, plug in a microphone and count along with the click.

Positive Feedback

If you're using a microphone, be careful that you don't get feedback from your speakers. Feedback happens when sound comes out of the speakers, into a mic, back out of the speakers, into the mic, and on and on…the result is squealing, screaming feedback.

You've heard it a million times before, but it's not something you want to hear in your studio, especially if you happen to be wearing headphones at the time—ouch! The easiest way to avoid feedback when using microphones is to turn off your speakers completely and use headphones instead. As a bonus, cutting out any potential speaker "bleed" will also result in a cleaner recording.

AND WE'RE OFF....

In order to record on an Audio Track, we have to "arm" it—put it in "record-ready" mode. You do this by clicking the little button labeled "Rec" above the volume fader. When you do this, the button will highlight in red.

Figure 13-1

As you record-arm a channel, its fader also highlights. When the track is armed for recording, the fader sets the monitoring levels signal coming into the channel, not playback level coming from hard disk. In other words, by moving the fader, you can adjust the volume of the channel you're listening to without affecting the level that's being recorded to hard drive. This allows you to optimize recording levels while still being able to create a balanced sound while recording. *See Figure 13-2*.

Play your source and watch the meter on the track you're recording on. You want the meter to go as high as possible without overloading—without turning on the red overload indicator. As long as the signal is pushing the level into the upper parts of the meter, you'll be fine. There's no need to try to get the meter exactly to the top. Note that you can't adjust the level of the audio being recorded using Pro Tools software; you have to use your hardware interface to make input level adjustments at this point.

Figure 13-2

Once you're happy with the levels going into Pro Tools, hit the Return to Zero button on the Transport window, to make sure the track is at the beginning of the Session.

Here we go, the moment of truth! There are several ways to start recording: Click the Record and Play buttons on the Transport window, hit ⌘+**spacebar** (Ctrl+spacebar), or hit the **F12** key. The Pro Tools click will count down, and the track will begin recording. Play or sing your heart out!

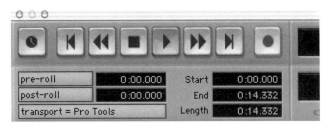

Figure 13-3

When you've finished recording, hit the **spacebar** to stop. Pro Tools will automatically rewind to the beginning of the track, but if you want to be sure, click the Return to Zero button on the Transport. Click the Rec button to dis-arm the track. Hit the spacebar or click Play to listen to your masterful recording. Congratulations, you've done it! Go ahead, play it back a few more times, just to savor the feeling…you know you want to.

If the perfectionist in you would like to try another

take, simply go back, re-arm the track, and record again. The new take will record over the first one. The cool thing is that when you do this, the old take isn't lost—Pro Tools is non-destructive, so it remembers old takes for you. We'll learn how to go back and retrieve old takes later.

If you absolutely hate what you've recorded and don't want to take a chance that anyone will ever hear it—if it's so bad it may be blackmail material— you can throw it away and start over by hitting ⌘+**Z** (Ctrl+Z), which will undo the recording. You can also press ⌘+**.** (Esc or Ctrl+.) to stop recording and throw away the take.

When you're satisfied with what you've recorded (don't stress over it too much, we're just learning our way around right now), go back to the Mix window, take the track out of record-arm by clicking the Rec button again, and save your Session.

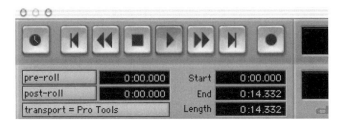

Figure 13-4

If you would like to see the waveform for the track you've recorded, switch to the Edit window. The waveform for your track will be displayed in all its glory. You'll also see the name of the region you've recorded listed in the Regions List on the right of the Edit window.

Figure 13-5

Take Two

Wonderful, so you've recorded your first track! Again, may I congratulate you on your artistic achievment. But one track does not a song make—most of the time, at least. In most cases, you'll record other tracks to complete your song. This process of recording tracks in separate passes is called "overdubbing," and it's a standard recording technique in every studio.

Here's how to do it:

• If you've switched to the Edit window, bring

the Mix window to the front.
- Add a new Audio Track to the Session.
- Set the track's input to the one you want to use to record—it can be set to the same input as the first Audio track you recorded, no problem.
- Make sure the new track's output is set to same one as your Master Fader.
- Record-enable (arm) the track for recording, and check its level on the channel's meter.
- That's it, hit Record/Play and lay down your next track!

You'll hear the click count off, then your first track will begin playing. Start playing or singing your second track. When you're finished, hit the spacebar to stop, then hit it again to play back your 2-track masterpiece. Save your Session for future generations to enjoy. Repeat for as many tracks as your song needs.

Reducing Latency

There's a delay—called latency—introduced as an audio signal enters your interface, passes through Pro Tools, and comes back out of Pro Tools through your interface, and on to your headphones or monitors. If your interface hardware supports it, go **Operations → Low Latency Monitoring**. This sets up your Pro Tools hardware so that it will have the least possible delay.

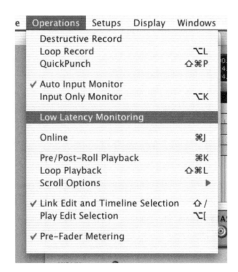

Figure 13-6

There's a trade-off to using Low Latency Monitoring, though: Plug-ins are made inactive, so you can't use the Click plug-in in (or any others). There are two solutions: Record your first track without turning on Low Latency Monitoring. Once you have the first track laid down, turn off the click and switch on Low Latency Monitoring, since you'll have the first track to play along with.

A better solution is to "bounce" the click to a track, so

it becomes audio. Then you can turn off the click plug-in, and just listen to the bounced track. We'll learn how to do track bouncing in Chapter 20, In the Flow.

If you're using an Mbox, you can forget all the above; you've got the Mix knob on the Mbox's front panel, which lets you directly monitor (listen to) incoming audio.

LOOP RECORDING

Pro Tools has a few tricks up its sleeve when it comes to recording. One of these is loop recording. Loop recording allows you to make as many passes through a track or part of a track as you want—perfect when you want to keep trying, say, a guitar solo or vocal chorus until you get it right.

Open up the CD-ROM Session "Chapter 13." Make sure that the Edit window is on top. If you play the Session, you'll hear an amazingly creative drum track. No need to hold back, I can tell you're impressed with my drum composition talents. We're going to loop record a track on top of these stellar drums.

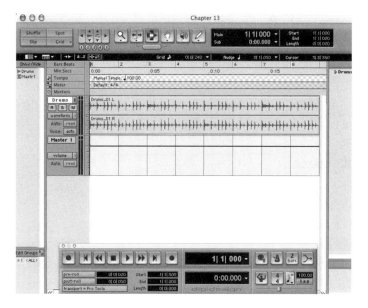

Figure 13-7

You can turn on Loop Recording in a few different ways. One is to go **Operations → Loop Record**. A second is to repeatedly **Ctrl+click** (right-click) the Record button. The best way (in my opinion) is simply to type **Option+L** (Start+L), which will jump you straight to Loop Record mode.

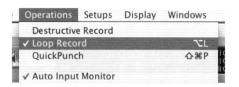

Figure 13-8

Pro Tools is in Loop Record mode when you see the Record button's icon change to include an arrow.

Figure 13-9

Let's try this loop recording thing out. First, we'll add a track to record onto. Here's a tip: A newly created track will show up after the last selected track. Select the Drums track, then create a new monophonic audio track.

Figure 13-10

The new track will show up after (below) the Drums track.

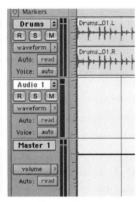

Figure 13-11

Name the new track; since we're trying out Loop Recording, let's name it "Loop test."

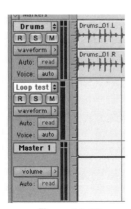

Figure 13-12

Flip over to the Mix window (or change the view in the Edit window) so you can set the "Loop test" track input and output. The input should be whatever path you want to record from; the output should be the same as the Drums track and Master Fader.

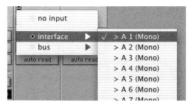

Figure 13-13

Back in the Edit window, arm the "Loop test" track and check input levels. We're ready to record; now we have to set up our loop.

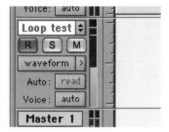

Figure 13-14

Click on the Selector tool at the top of the Edit window.

Figure 13-15

Using the Selector tool, drag across the Bar:Beat ruler (the top ruler in this Session) or in the track you want to record on. Select from measure 3 to measure 7 (the selection should be four bars long).

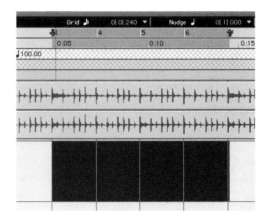

Figure 13-16

Unless you're a lot better than I am at dragging with the mouse, it will be tough to exactly select four bars—and if we're not exact, our loop will be rhythmically lopsided. Verify your selection by looking at the Start, End, and Length readouts at the top of the Edit window, to the right of the time counter (the same readouts appear in the Transport window).

Figure 13-17

We can use these displays to make our loop start and be exactly the length we want. Click in the Start numbers, and make them read 3|1|000; hit **Return** (Enter). Now click in the End numbers, and make them read 7|1|000; hit **Return** (Enter). The Length field should read 4|0|000, or exactly four bars long.

Figure 13-18

As things are set up now, if you click Play or Record/Play, Pro Tools will begin playing and recording at 3|1|000—unless you're really fast, you'll have trouble playing your part on time. To give yourself a bit of a lead, you could set up a click with a countoff (although we really don't need a click, since we're recording along with a drum track). Rather, let's use another Pro Tools feature, "pre-roll." Pre-roll allows you to set a specified time that the track will play before entering record. Here's how to set it up: Go to the Transport window. Click on the "pre-roll" box to highlight it and to turn on pre-roll. Next click in the pre-roll numbers and set them to two bars (2|0|000). Now when you click Record and Play, Pro Tools will pre-roll for two bars, then enter record and begin loop recording.

Figure 13-19

We're set! Begin loop recording just as you would regular recording, by clicking Record/Play, hitting ⌘+**spacebar** (Ctrl+spacebar), or typing the **F12** key.

Pro Tools will begin playing from the beginning (because of our 2-bar pre-roll), then enter record as soon as it hits our selected loop region. When Pro Tools reaches the end of our selected loop region, it will jump back to the beginning of the loop region and continue recording. There's no pre-roll on subsequent passes through the loop—only on the first pass. Go ahead and make four passes through the loop, then hit the spacebar to stop. Let's save our work: Go **File → Save Session As...**, type in a new name—"Chapter 13 Loop Test" works for me—and click Save. It's good practice to do this periodically as you're working, as it saves a new Session with all the current tracks, audio, and edits, but without overwriting older versions of the Session. This way you can easily jump back to an earlier version of your Session should you need to make major changes.

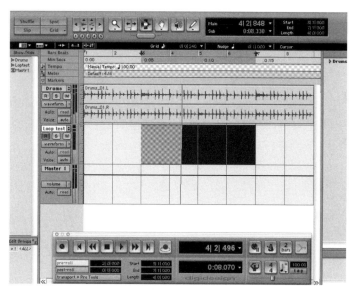

Figure 13-20

Each time Pro Tools makes a pass through the loop region, it will generate a new audio region called a "take." Turn your gaze toward the Audio Regions list on the right of the Edit window. In addition to the Drums region that was there when you opened the session, you'll see five more regions. The one in bold, "Loops test_01" is the "master" take; it contains all the other loop takes. Below it are listed the four actual loop takes.

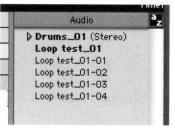

Figure 13-21

Back in the "Loop test" Audio Track, the last take you recorded will be the one that shows up and is played by Pro Tools.

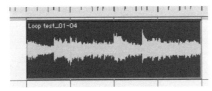

Figure 13-22

You can switch among the takes you recorded by ⌘-**clicking** (Ctrl-clicking) in the loop region. A drop down menu will let you choose among the regions that match your loop. Play the Session and switch among the takes you recorded.

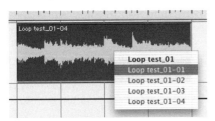

Figure 13-23

Loop Playback

In addition to loop recording, Pro Tools can loop playback. This is useful for rehearsing or working on a particular section of a track, among other things. To enter Loop Playback mode, you can go **Operations → Loop Playback, Ctrl+click** (right-click) the Record button. Or type ⇧+z+L (⇧+Start+L).

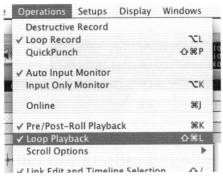

Figure 13-24

Now when you play Pro Tools, it will loop playback over the region you have selected. If you've done some loop recording, you can even switch takes on the fly, while Pro Tools plays, to audition them.

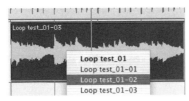

Figure 13-25

PUNCH-IN/PUNCH-OUT

There you are, steaming along, recording the take of a lifetime—the performance that will bring the world to its feet in a rousing ovation! Then…oops…you make a mistake. You could record the entire take over again, hoping to recapture the magic. Or you could use Pro Tools punch-in/punch-out capability to fix the mistake.

Punching works similarly to the loop recording we just did. You make a selection on the track so that the selected region contains the error you want to fix. Set up a pre-roll to give you a "run" at performing the fix. When Pro Tools reaches the selection, it will drop into record, when it reaches the end of the selection, it will drop out of record.

Let's try it. Open the Session called "Chapter 13.1." Make sure the Edit window is on top, then give the Session a listen. We're going to be punching on the Synth Bass track. Don't worry if you don't have a synth (or a bass)—any sound source will work for our purposes. Or even no sound source (which is what I'm going to do for this example—I'll just record silence so you can clearly see where the punch is at). The point is just to get a look at how punching works so you can use the technique on your own tracks.

Figure 13-26

Before we begin punching, we need to check one thing. You won't have to make this setting for each track, just verify it before you punch the first track in a Session. Pro Tools has two input monitoring modes, which decide how you hear the audio when you're recording a track. (Any tracks you're not recording on will play back as normal, regardless of the Input Monitor setting.) With Input Only Monitor, you'll hear what is coming into Pro Tools, not what is recorded on the track. With Auto Input Monitor, you'll hear anything that was recorded on the track until the track actually goes into record; at that point you'll hear the audio that's coming into Pro Tools and being recorded. I generally leave input monitoring set to Auto Input Monitor when I'm punching, so I can hear what leads up to the punch. To make this setting go **Operations → Auto Input Monitor**. If you prefer to use key commands, **Option+K** (Start+K) will toggle back and forth between Auto Input Monitor and Input Only Monitor.

Figure 13-27

You can punch in extremely small regions—just one note, if you want. For this example, let's make it easy, and punch in an entire measure. First up, make sure the Selector tool is active at the top of the Edit window.

Let's do a 1-measure punch, at bar 4 in the Synth Bass track. Drag in the top ruler or in the Synth Bass track to make the selection. You can also make a selection "on the fly": Play the track; when you reach the spot where you want to punch-in, hit the down-arrow key. Where you want to punch-out (stop recording), hit the up-arrow key.

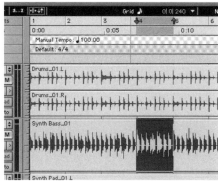

Figure 13-28

To make our selection fall perfectly on the beginning and end of bar 4, fine-tune the selection Start and End points at the top of the Edit window (or in the Transport window).

Figure 13-29

Pre-roll will let us hear a bit of the track before the punch takes place, post-roll does the same thing after the punch ends. To turn on pre-roll and post-roll, go **Operations → Pre/Post-Roll Playback** or type ⌘+K (Ctrl+K) or simply click on the pre-roll/post-roll buttons on the Transport window.

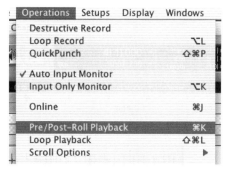

Figure 13-30

Next, set up how long you want pre-roll and post-roll to last. Click in the pre-roll numbers, set it for one measure (1|0|000), and hit **Return** (Enter). Do the same for post-roll—set it to 1|0|000, then hit **Return** (Enter).

Figure 13-31

You can also set the pre-roll and post-roll times by dragging the little green flags in the rulers of the Edit window. You can adjust the punch-in selection by dragging the blue arrows.

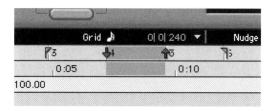

Figure 13-32

Arm the track for recording, and verify that the incoming signal matches the level in the original track. If the two levels don't match, you'll get an audible level jump at the punch-in and punch-out spots.

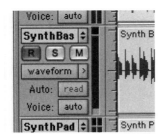

Figure 13-33

To begin, click the Record and Play buttons, hit ⌘+**spacebar** (Ctrl+spacebar), or type **F12**. Pro Tools will start playing at the pre-roll location, then when it hits the selection, it will automatically drop into record ("punch in"), allowing you to play or sing corrections for the track. When Pro Tools reaches the end of the selection, it will automatically drop out of record ("punch out"), and continue playing until it reaches the end of the post-roll.

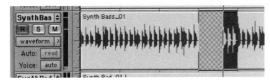

Figure 13-34

Here's how the track will look after we've punched on it. The punch region is empty—it has a flat line instead of a waveform—since for this example I didn't send any audio into Pro Tools while punching. Normally, there would be a waveform for your new audio in the punch-in region.

Figure 13-35

If you compare the regions in the Audio Regions list with the regions on the Synth Bass track, you'll see what happened during the punch-in/punch-out process. The original beginning-to-end Synth Bass track region was "Synth Bass_01." Punching in created a new region on the track, "Synth Bass_02." The process of punching in on the track also created two new regions—sub-regions of "Synth Bass_01." One of these, "Synth Bass_01-01" shows up on the track before "Synth Bass_02." The other, "Synth

Bass_01-02," follows the new punch region.

Figure 13-36

QUICK, PUNCH!

If you need to fix more than one mistake in a track, regular punching may not do the job, as you have to stop and reset your in and out points, as well as pre-roll and post-roll for each spot you want to punch. For these situations, QuickPunch is the perfect solution. Basically, with QuickPunch, you're manually dropping in and out of record as the track is playing. With QuickPunch, you can switch in and out of record up to 100 times per take.

Here's what's happening in QuickPunch: In QuickPunch mode, Pro Tools is recording as soon as you hit Play—even before you click Record. So whenever you switch into Record, Pro Tools just drops the new audio in, replacing the old.

Open up the "Chapter 13.1" Session again. Make sure the Edit window is on top.

Figure 13-37

As with everything in Pro Tools, you can get in and out of QuickPunch mode in several ways. You can go **Operations → QuickPunch**, you can **Ctrl-click** (right-click) on the Record button repeatedly until a white "P" shows up in the red circle, or you can type ⇧+⌘+**P** (⇧+Start+P).

Figure 13-38

Once you're in QuickPunch Record mode, all you have to do is arm your track, and make sure levels are consistent with the original audio on the track. As with regular punching, if you QuickPunch with levels that are different than the original track, your punched-in fixes will be noticeable to listeners.

Figure 13-39

We're set. Start Pro Tools playing. Wherever you want to punch in, click the Record button, hit ⌘+**spacebar** (Ctrl+spacebar), or type **F12**. When you've finished with the punch, click the Record button, hit ⌘+**spacebar** (Ctrl+spacebar), or type **F12** to drop out of record—but *don't* stop playback. Let Pro Tools keep playing.

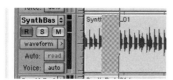

Figure 13-40

When you reach the next place you want to punch in on, go back into record. You know the drill: click the Record button, hit ⌘+**spacebar** (Ctrl+spacebar), or type **F12**. When you're finished with the punch, come back out of record. Again, don't stop Pro Tools playback.

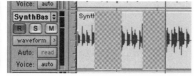

Figure 13-41

Continue this way until you've made all the punches you want to make on the track. In our example here, I've QuickPunched a number of times without running any audio into Pro Tools. So all the regions I punched in are empty (flat lines—no waveforms).

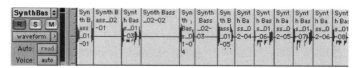

Figure 13-42

Remember how I said that in QuickPunch mode, Pro Tools is recording in the background as soon as you hit Play? You can verify this by looking at the Audio Regions List on the right of the Edit window. The original beginning-to-end audio region on the Synth Bass track is "Synth Bass_01." Each time we QuickPunched, we created new regions in the original region—these are the regions labeled "Synth Bass_01-01," "Synth Bass_01-02," "Synth Bass_01-03," and so on.

The new beginning-to-end region created in the background by Pro Tools in QuickPunch mode is "Synth Bass_02." The small regions that actually show up in the spots where we QuickPunched in the Synth Bass track are labeled "Synth Bass_02-01," "Synth Bass_02-02," "Synth Bass_02-03," and so on.

Figure 13-43

MURDER, DEATH, DESTRUCTION

Pro Tools has one more recording trick up its sleeve: Destructive recording. As we learned earlier, Pro Tools is generally non-destructive—it's a kinder, gentler sort of DAW. If you record over a previously recorded track, for example, you aren't erasing the old audio, you're simply recording new audio on top of the old. You can go back and restore the old audio if you want to.

Destructive recording, however, *does* erase whatever audio might already be on a track. It's not a mode you'll generally see Pro Tools users working in, as the odds of accidentally recording over something you want to keep are high. But if you want to live on the edge, go ahead and destructive record—but don't say I didn't warn you! You can enter this mode by going **Operations → Destructive Record**, or by repeatedly **Ctrl-clicking** (right-clicking) on the Record button until a white "D" appears in the red circle.

Figure 13-44

fourteen

THE IMPORT BUSINESS

Recording may be the main way in which most users get audio into Pro Tools, but it's not the only way! You can also import audio files from hard drives and from CD—you can even import stereo audio tracks off of commercial music CDs. There are, of course, several ways to import audio files into Pro Tools—you'd hate to be limited to just one.

IMPORTING FROM THE AUDIO REGIONS LIST

Get started by creating a new session. Name it "Chapter 14 Import." Make sure the sample rate is set to 44.1kHz.

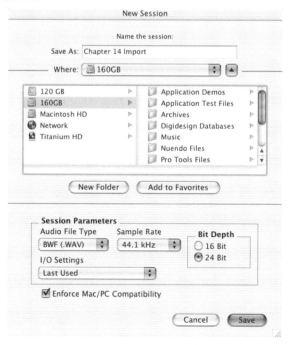

Figure 14-1

Add tracks to your empty session. We'll need three stereo and two mono audio tracks. We'll also want a stereo Master Fader. Label the three stereo tracks "Drums," "Guitar 1," and "Guitar 3&4." Label the mono tracks "Bass" and "Guitar 2." You can arrange the tracks in any order you prefer. For rock/pop sessions, I generally work with the rhythm section on the left and other instruments on the right.

Figure 14-2

Switch over to the Edit window. Go **Audio → Import Audio...** *See Figure 14-3.*

When the Import Audio window opens, navigate to the folder holding the folder "Chapter 14" from the CD-ROM. Inside this folder are the audio files we'll be importing. *See Figure 14-4.*

Figure 14-3

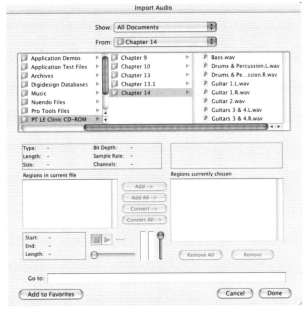

Figure 14-4

Single-click on Bass.wav. The Import Audio window will give you information on the type of file (WAV), bit depth (24), length (24 seconds), sample rate (44.1kHz), size (around 3MB), and number of channels (mono). There's also a message that Bass.wav can be added directly into our session. This is because the format (WAV, AIF, etc.) and sample rate of the file (44.1kHz) match the format and sample rate of the session. If the sample rate and format didn't match, you could still import the file, but Pro Tools would automatically convert the file to match the session.

"Bass" shows up in the "Regions in current file" field. You have two options, to Add or Copy the file. (If you have more than one file selected, you can add or copy all off them at once.)

If you Add the file, it will be imported to the Session from its original location. If you Copy the file, a copy of the file will be created in the Session's folder before it is imported. Copying is a good idea if you're trying to keep all components of a Session in one place. Click Copy to move "Bass" into the "Regions currently chosen" field.

There's another cool feature in this window. Below the "Copy All" button are controls for playing the selected file. The file will play back through the Audition path set in the I/O Settings window. This allows you to listen to the files in a folder, to make sure that you're importing the right one.

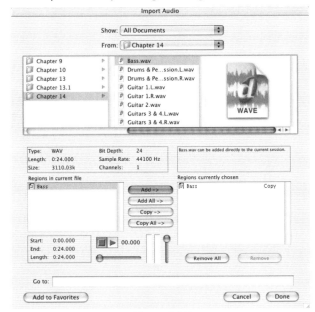

Figure 14-5

Select the rest of the files in the Chapter 14 folder by shift-clicking on them. Click "Copy All" to move them to the "Regions currently chosen" field. All the files are now ready to be imported. Click Done to import them.

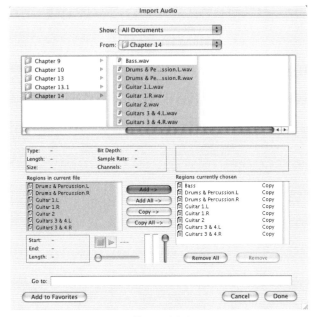

Figure 14-6

Since we've Copied the files, rather than simply Adding them, we need to choose a destination folder for them to be copied into. Pro Tools will default to selecting the Audio Files folder for the Session you're importing to. Click Choose to finish copying and importing.

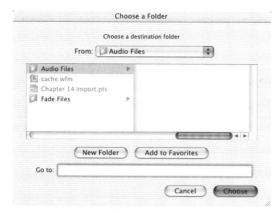

Figure 14-7

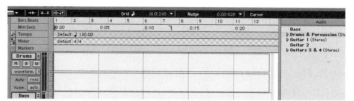

Figure 14-10

You can verify that the files have been added by checking the Audio Regions List. Does it seem strange that we imported a total of eight files, but only five appear in the Audio Regions List? This is because several of the files we imported were the separate left and right sides to stereo regions. Pro Tools automatically combines these into stereo regions in the Audio Regions List.

When you release the mouse, the file shows up in the track.

Figure 14-11

Figure 14-8

Go ahead and drag the remaining regions to their respective tracks.

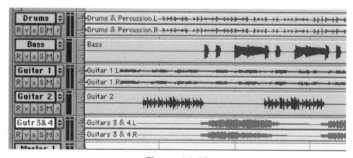

Figure 14-12

You can also verify that the imported regions have been copied by checking the Audio Files folder in the folder for your Session.

Figure 14-9

Back in the Edit window, click and drag the region "Drums & Percussion" to the drum track. An outline of the region shape will follow as you drag. Make sure you drag the file all the way to the left of the track.

If you want to listen to the tracks you've imported, switch over to the Mixer window, and set the channel levels in mixer: Drums at 0, Bass at –6, Guitar 1 at –1.5, Guitar 2 at –10, and Guitar 3&4 at –12. The Master Fader can stay at 0, unless you need to turn it down to control the volume going to your speakers or headphones.

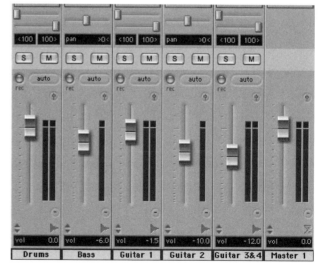

Figure 14-13

IMPORT TO TRACK

If you want to streamline the task of importing audio, Pro Tools will allow you to import an audio file directly into a track, in one step—it will even automatically create the new track for you. To make this happen, go **File → Import to Track...**

Figure 14-14

The Import Audio dialog will open. Choose the file and Add or Copy it as we did when importing from the Audio Regions List. Click Done when you're finished.

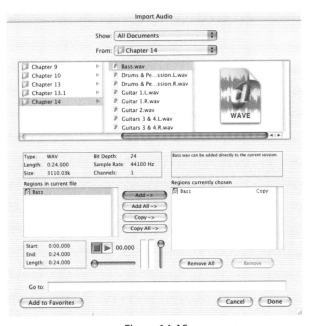

Figure 14-15

If necessary, choose the folder where you want the audio file to be placed. *See Figure 14-16.*

The audio will be imported to the Audio Regions list, and simultaneously a new Audio track will be created with the audio file already in place, ready to play. *See Figure 14-17.*

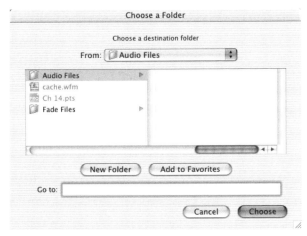

Figure 14-16

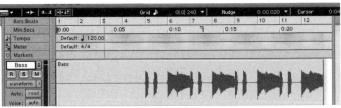

Figure 14-17

IMPORTING USING THE WORKSPACE BROWSER

Version 6 of Pro Tools included a powerful new tool for data management: DigiBase. DigiBase works like a database for viewing, searching for, auditioning, and importing Pro Tools data. In Pro Tools LE, DigiBase consists of two "browser" windows. The first, the Project Browser, deals with the data associated with a particular Session. The second, the Workspace Browser, manages all the storage devices mounted on your computer—all the hard drives and CD-ROMs you might be using at a given time. For importing audio, we'll want to use the Workspace Browser.

To begin, create a new empty Session. Name and save it as you normally would. Go **Windows → Show Workspace** or type **Option+;** (Alt+;). *See Figure 14-18.*

The Workspace Browser will open. It will have entries for any storage devices you might be using. In my case, I have two hard drives in my computer, "Macintosh HD" and "160GB." *See Figure 14-19.*

Click the little arrows next to the hard disk icons to "open" the drives and see their contents. In my case, I store all my audio files on the 160GB drive. Navigate to the location on your system where you stored the files for Chapter 14. *See Figure 14-20.*

When you find the audio files, you'll see that the Workspace browser imparts a lot of information about the files—the kind of file, size, etc. In the right pane of the window, you can click the speaker icon to audition the files. If you scroll over to the right, you'll find even more information, such as when the file was created and last modified, the file format, number of channels, sample rate, and much more. By clicking on the button with the magnifying glass on it, you can search for particular files using different criteria.

Figure 14-18

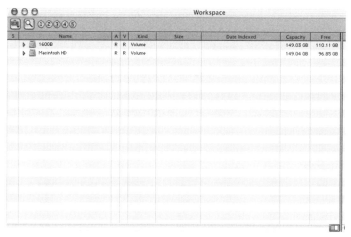

Figure 14-19

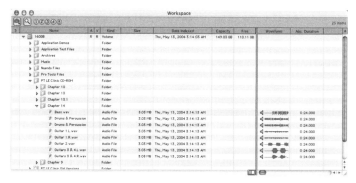

Figure 14-20

What we're mainly interested in right now is importing audio into our Session. The Workspace browser lets us do this with a few cool twists.

First up, we can simply drag a file from the browser to the Audio Regions List in the Edit window. *See Figure 14-21.*

It can then be placed in an audio track. Or, to save a step, you can simply drag the file from the Workspace browser straight into the track—skip putting it in the Audio Regions List first. *See Figure 14-22.*

Figure 14-21

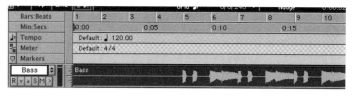

Figure 14-22

To make the file you're dragging automatically snap to the beginning of the track, hold the **Control** (Start) key while dragging the file to the track.

Figure 14-23

In fact, you don't even have to create a track before dragging the file. Ctrl-drag a file from the browser into the Edit window. A new track will be created, and the region will automatically snap to its beginning.

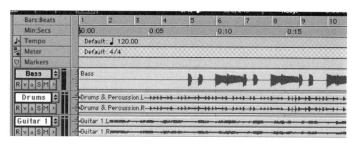

Figure 14-24

For stereo files, ⇧-**click** the left and right sides of the file in the browser window, then **Ctrl-drag** to the Edit window. A new stereo track will be created, and the two sides of the stereo file will snap perfectly into place. *See Figure 14-25.*

One final trick: If you hold the **Option** (Alt) key while dragging or Control-dragging, a copy of the file you're dragging will be created in the Session's audio file folder.

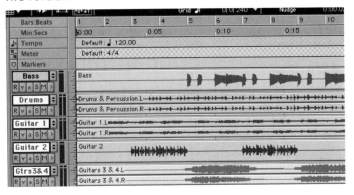

Figure 14-25

IMPORTING FROM CD (MAC ONLY)

So far we've covered importing files from hard disk into Pro Tools. There will be many occasions when you'll want to import tracks from an audio CD into a Session—one example is when loading loop files from a CD into a track. There isn't an "Import Audio from CD" command in Pro Tools. Rather, the task is handled via QuickTime.

Insert an audio compact disc into your computer's CD drive—any stereo audio CD will work. Create, name, and save a new Session. Add a single stereo Audio track. Go **Movie → Import Audio from Other Movie...**

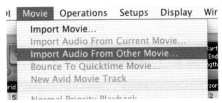

Figure 14-26

When the Open Movie dialog opens, navigate to your CD.

Figure 14-27

Select the CD track you want to import into Pro Tools, then click Open.

Figure 14-28

The Track Import window will open. Click OK.

Figure 14-29

Choose the folder where you want the CD track to be stored. Pro Tools will default to putting it in the Audio Files folder for the current Session. Click Choose when you're ready.

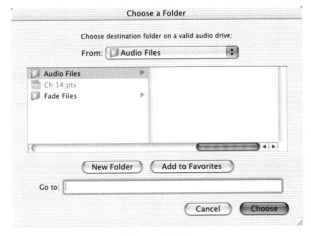

Figure 14-30

A "processing" dialog will show the progress as the audio track is loaded off CD, converted to an audio file, and stored on your computer's hard drive.

Figure 14-31

When your computer is finished importing the CD track, it will show up as a stereo region in Audio Regions List in the Edit window.

Figure 14-32

Drag the region to the stereo track you created earlier.

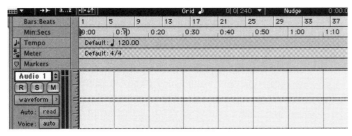

Figure 14-33

Play Pro Tools; the imported CD track will play back. It can now be processed, edited, and worked with just like any other audio file in a Session.

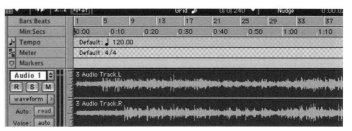

Figure 14-34

PART FIVE 5

Editing

fifteen

THE MODE YOU'RE IN

Now that we've learned how to get our precious sounds into Pro Tools, let's start learning how to mold and shape them to get exactly the results we want. Pro Tools offers a tremendous amount of audio editing power, both for fixing errors and for re-casting audio into something completely new and different—editing can be both a repair tool and a creative technique.

FOUR MODES

On the "macro" level, Pro Tools has four operating "modes" that determine how regions are handled in tracks. We were briefly introduced to the Edit Modes in Chapter 10, The Edit Window. Let's renew our acquaintance, and see if we can't deepen the friendship.

Open the CD-ROM Session named "Chapter 15." *See Figure 15-1.*

If you'll recall, there are four buttons in the upper-left of the Edit window used to select among the Edit Modes. Remember that in addition to directly selecting the buttons, you can cycle through the Edit Modes by repeatedly typing the **tilde** (~) key. Let's begin exploring the Edit Modes. *See Figure 15-2.*

SHUFFLE MODE

In Shuffle Mode, an audio region placed on a track will snap as far left as it can. To enter Shuffle Mode, click the "Shuffle" button or type **F1**. Shuffle Mode is useful when you're working with sections of a song or with loops, as the left edge of each region will snap

to the right edge of the previous region. Try it: Drag the Drums_01 region from the Audio Regions List to anywhere on the Drums track, and release it. It will snap to the left edge of the track, at location 1|1|000. *See Figure 15-3.*

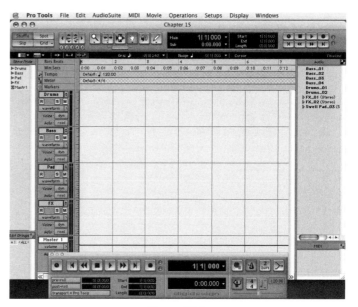

Figure 15-1

Figure 15-2

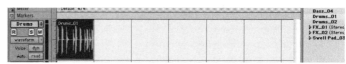

Figure 15-3

Now return to the Audio Regions List and drag Drums_01 over to the Drums track again. Release the mouse, and the new region will snap to the right edge of the first region you dragged over. Click Return to Zero to rewind, then play the Session to hear your work so far.

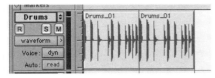

Figure 15-4

In Shuffle Mode, if you drag a new region on top of an existing region, the existing region will shuffle over to the right. Try it: Drag Drums_02 (which contains a cymbal crash at its beginning) on top of the left-most region in the Drums track.

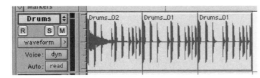

Figure 15-5

Now drag another Drums_02 region to the division between the two Drums_01 regions on the Drums track. They will spread apart to make room for the new region to drop in. Rewind and play the Session to hear the results.

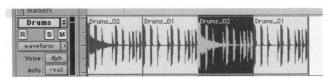

Figure 15-6

Our drum part is finished. Save your work, and let's check out Grid Mode.

GRID MODE

In Grid Mode, the track is subdivided into a rhythmic or time-based grid. New regions dropped on or moved across the track will snap to the nearest grid division. Click the Grid button or type **F4**. Notice the dividing lines that appear in the tracks when you switch to Grid Mode.

If you click and hold on the Grid button, you can select between two types of grids: Absolute and Relative. For most editing work, you'll want to be in Absolute, where a region's beginning or an edit selection snaps to the grid. Relative grid is useful if a

region works better slightly off the grid, but you need to move it across the track and maintain its position relative to the grid. This will often be the case when you're recording live musicians—players often play slightly ahead of or behind the beat. In Relative mode, you can preserve the "feel" while still being able to edit using the grid. For now, stay with Absolute grid.

Above the Edit window rulers is a pulldown menu where you can set the grid division.

Figure 15-7

For most music-oriented work, using the bars: beats division for the grid works well. From this menu you can also change to other division types, such as minutes:seconds, samples, or regions/markers. To continue working on our song, select "1/4 note" from the menu.

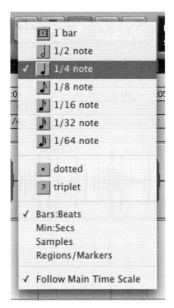

Figure 15-8

We'll be constructing a bass line. Drag the Bass_01 region from the Audio Regions List to the beginning of the Bass track. It will snap into place.

Figure 15-9

Next, drag Bass_02 to the first beat of measure 2,

Bass_03 to first beat of measure 3, and Bass_04 to the first beat of measure 4. Notice how the regions snap along the grid division as you drag them across the track. In this Edit Mode it's virtually impossible to place something out of rhythm—the grid makes sure that each region is perfectly in time as it's placed or moved in the track. Rewind and play the Session to hear the results. Save your work.

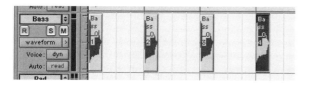

Figure 15-10

SLIP MODE

Slip Mode, which you enter by either clicking the Slip button or typing **F3**, could be considered the opposite of Grid Mode. In Slip Mode, a region can be freely moved anyplace on a track—wherever you let go of the mouse is where the region will end up. And once a region is in a track, you can freely slide it back and forth in time. You can even slide one region over the top of another; whichever one is on top is the one that will be heard.

Drag the Swell Pad_03 region onto the Pad track. This particular region has a slow start and finish, so it doesn't need to be placed exactly in rhythm. Listen to the Session play and find a spot that sounds good to you by sliding the region around until you like the results. Save your work.

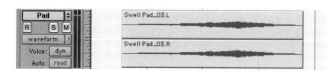

Figure 15-11

SPOT MODE

Click the Spot button or type **F2** to enter Spot Mode. Spot Mode allows you to exactly specify where a region will be placed in a track. It's great if you're trying to place a sound effect for a video project, for example. For music work, it will likely be your least used mode, but knowing your way around is still useful.

Drag the FX_01 region to the FX track. When you release the mouse, the Spot Dialog window will open allowing you to enter the region's start time. In the Start field, enter 1|3|360. Note that you can change the time scale to minutes:seconds or samples.

Instead of the region Start point, you can choose to set the End point, or the Sync point—a point within the region that you can assign. Click OK when you've entered the Start time.

Figure 15-12

The region's beginning will snap to the exact time you entered.

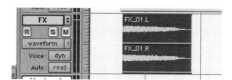

Figure 15-13

Now drag FX_02 to the FX track and set its Start point to 3|2|100. Rewind the Session and give it a listen.

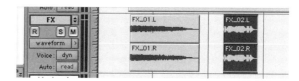

Figure 15-14

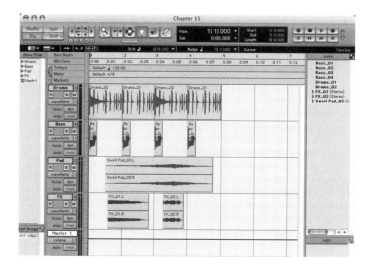

Figure 15-15

Congratulations! You just used the Pro Tools Edit Modes to create a musical arrangement.

sixteen

SLICE AND DICE

Last chapter we learned our way around Pro Tools' Edit Modes...but we've only scratched the surface of Pro Tools' editing power. Pro Tools has the capability of editing audio on the most microscopic level—we can tear the audio apart and stick it back together again, if we want. But even if you're not going to work much on the microscopic level, it's a good bet that you'll use some of the editing features and techniques found in this chapter, whether for fixing a near-perfect take or for creating new arrangements and performances.

Know When to Say When

The editing power of Pro Tools can be a double-edged sword: You can do damage with it just as you can do good. So I'll offer one bit of brotherly advice: Please don't feel that you *must* edit your tracks. One of the keys to successfully using Pro Tools to create compelling music is knowing when to edit and when to leave well enough alone. Perfection can be boring—not every performance benefits from being rhythmically corrected and polished to the point of sterility. Used tastefully, Pro Tools editing is a fabulous tool. But if you take things too far, you'll drain all the life from the tracks. A word to the wise...practice restraint.

Let's take a look at some of the things we can do using basic Pro Tools editing tools. Open the CD-ROM Session "Chapter 16." Play it; you'll hear that this Session contains one track of vocals—counting from one to five. However, the recording quality was, shall we say, less than stellar. There's a bunch of noise, loud breaths, and clicks in between the words. Plus, the

guy who did the counting didn't exactly have rhythm in his blood!

Time to work some magic, and turn this sorry recording into a high-fidelity wonder. There are several ways in which we can proceed to clean up this track. One approach is to isolate what we want to keep, then get rid of everything else. Another is to cut out the garbage, leaving behind the words we want to keep. Let's try both. To begin, create two more mono audio tracks. Leave them named "Audio 1" and "Audio 2."

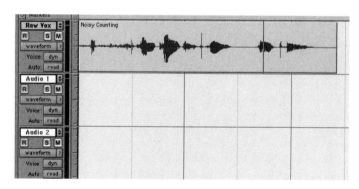

Figure 16-1

Click the Grabber tool (the one with the hand) or type **F8. Option+drag** (Start+drag) the region in the top track to the track below. This will create a copy of the region. Do the same thing, **Option+dragging** (Start+dragging) the top region to the third track. You've now got three identical tracks. For this type of work, you'll want to be in Slip Mode.

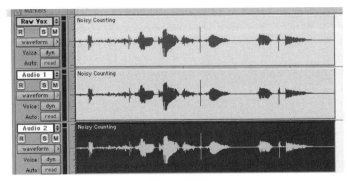

Figure 16-2

KEEP THE GOOD STUFF

We'll begin work on the second track, "Audio 1." Solo it. We want to select each word, and turn it into its own region. Change to the Selector tool (the one with the waveform) by clicking its button or by typing **F7.** Play the track, noting where the word "one" occurs. Using the mouse, select the word. You want to get in close, selecting just "one" without cutting any of the word off, but without leaving any empty space or noise. Zoom in horizontally and vertically on the track if it will help you get right on the word—make the track taller if it will help you see. Hit Play to hear what you've selected. Don't worry if you have to re-select a few times to get the complete word without any extra noise. And don't stress too much—remember that editing in Pro Tools is non-destructive. Nothing is permanent, we can adjust the regions later.

Figure 16-3

If All Else Fails, Trust Your Ears

It can be tricky making selections on a track, as the waveform is just a guide. It may not show every detail. This is especially true with vocals, where certain sounds—"f" at the beginning of a word, for example—may not show up well in the waveform.

In some cases, if you edit too close, vocals can start to sound unnatural. Be careful of cutting out all the breaths and little mouth "noises" the speaker or singer makes; leaving some or all of these in will help your track sound more natural.

In the end, it comes down to using your ears. Listen, and approve every edit aurally before you move on.

Now we'll make our word "one" into its own

region. Go **Edit → Separate Region...** or type ⌘+E (Ctrl+E). Using Key Focus, typing "B" will do this for you. If you find you've made a mistake, simply go **Edit → Undo** or type ⌘+Z (Ctrl+Z) to go back.

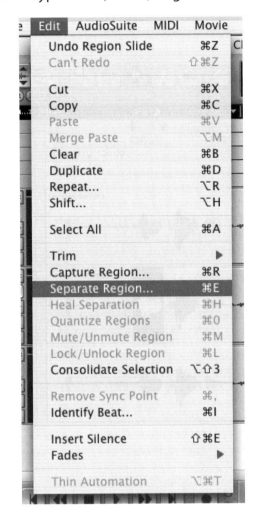

Figure 16-4

You'll be asked to name the new region; go with something clever, like "One." The word will be cut loose from the rest of the track, becoming its own audio region flanked by two other regions.

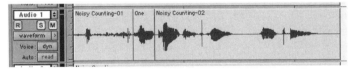

Figure 16-5

Continue in this fashion, selecting each word, and separating it into its own cleverly named region. Remember that as you make each selection, you can click Play to hear what you're doing. *See Figure 16-6.*

Now we want to select the regions containing the garbage—all the junk before, after, and between our words. Change back to the Grabber tool. Using the Grabber, click on the first junk region, the one that runs from the beginning of the track up to the word "One." *See Figure 16-7.*

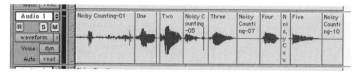

Figure 16-6

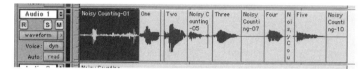

Figure 16-7

There are several ways to get rid of the selected region: Go **Edit → Cut** or type ⌘+X (Ctrl+X). Go Edit → Clear or type ⌘+B (Ctrl+B). Or (my favorite) simply hit the Delete key. Remember, if you find you've made a mistake, you can go Edit → Undo or type ⌘+Z (Ctrl+Z) to reverse the error.

Figure 16-8

Go through the rest of the track, using the Grabber to select the unwanted regions between the words, then deleting them. If a region seems too small to select, zoom in to make things easier.

When you're through, you'll have a track with five regions, one for each word. Rewind, then Play to hear your work. Much better than the original!

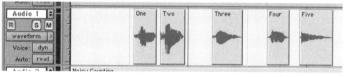

Figure 16-9

If, on listening back, you find that you've cut a word too close or left a bit of noise before or after a word, no worries! Change to the Trimmer tool by clicking its button or typing F6. Move the Trimmer cursor so that it is located over the left edge of "one." When you're in the right spot, the cursor will look like a "C." Click and drag to the left; you'll see an outline of the region extend out. You can go all the way to the beginning of the track if you want, or you can drag to the right, which will cut off the first part of the word. If you release the mouse, the region will expand or contract as far as you've dragged. The Trimmer is very

useful for tweaking the start and end of regions—practice with it on the words in this track, noting the results as you drag the left and right edges of each region around.

Figure 16-10

TAKE OUT THE TRASH

Let's try a different approach to cleaning up this recording. Un-solo Audio 1, and solo Audio 2. Change back to the Selector tool. Use the mouse to select all the garbage in the track leading up to the word "one." If you want, zoom in on the track and change track height so you can clearly see what you're doing. Play the track to hear what you've selected—all the noise before "one."

Figure 16-11

Cut, clear, or delete the selected area.

Figure 16-12

Go through the rest of the track, selecting the garbage between words and deleting it. In the end, the results will look the same as what we did above.

Figure 16-13

There are certainly other ways in Pro Tools to accomplish this kind of thing. Experiment with using various combinations of the Trimmer and Selector to select and eradicate noise and garbage.

SLIP SLIDING AWAY

Since we're in Slip Mode, you can freely slide the various word-regions around on the track. Grab the "three" region and pull it all the way to the left.

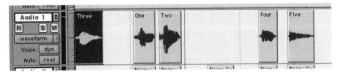

Figure 16-14

Slide the rest of the words over so that the rhythm is consistent. While you'll be able to get close visually; use your ears to make the rhythm sound even.

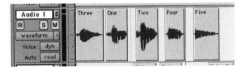

Figure 16-15

CUT, COPY, PASTE

If you've worked with a word processor—or pretty much any other computer program—you've probably cut, copied, and pasted data before. Pro Tools can work in much the same way. We've already "cut" when we were cleaning up the tracks above. Now let's try some copying and pasting. Using the Grabber, select the word "one" in the track Audio 1. Go Edit → Copy or type ⌘+C (Ctrl+C) to copy the region. (You don't necessarily have to select and copy an entire region. You could use the Selector tool to select part of a region and just copy that.)

Figure 16-16

Switch to the Selector tool. Click in the same track, somewhere after the last word. Go Edit → Paste or type ⌘+V (Ctrl+V) to paste the region into the track at that point.

Figure 16-17

You don't have to paste into a blank space or even on the same track. Select and copy "Four." Paste it into the beginning of Audio 2.

Figure 16-18

PLAYLIST

If you want to try a different arrangement for a track, you could create a new track and work on it. Another solution is to use a new playlist on an existing track. Remember that a playlist is an arrangement of regions. Let's try it out.

Solo track Audio 2. Click the button to the right of the track name to pull down the playlist menu. Choose "new."

Figure 16-19

Name the playlist (or use the default name that appears), then click OK. The new blank playlist will open on the track—the track name will change to the one you gave the new arrangement. We can drag whatever regions we want onto the track, and edit them as we see fit.

Figure 16-20

Switch to Grid Mode. Set the grid to 8th notes. All the regions we created for the other tracks appear in the Audio Tracks List. Drag the regions named "one" through "five" onto the blank track—for fun, do it so they appear in reverse order: "five," "four," "three," "two," and "one." Use the grid to space them evenly. Play to hear your work.

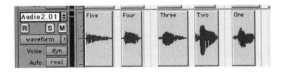

Figure 16-21

You can switch among a track's playlists by going to the playlist menu and choosing the one you want to use. It's an easy way to try out new arrangements and editing ideas without using an extra track or losing your existing work on a track.

DELETING TRACKS

While we've done amazing work on this Session, let's

clean it up, taking it back to its original state. First up, we'll delete the tracks we're no longer using. (Important note: You can't undo deleting a track. Be sure!)

Never Delete
Since deleting a track is permanent, you might want to avoid doing it altogether. One way to do this, while still getting rid of Session clutter, is to make the track inactive, then hide it. The track is gone from the Edit and Mix windows, and since it's inactive it doesn't consume any system resources.

Click on the track name to select the track; Start with Audio 2.

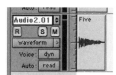

Figure 16-22

Go **File → Delete Selected Tracks...**

Figure 16-23

Pro Tools may tell you that the track contains audio regions—click Delete to proceed. Pro Tools may also tell you that there are playlists being used by the track—click Yes to delete them. The track will be deleted. Now delete the Audio 1 track.

DELETING UNUSED REGIONS
Now that we've cleaned up the tracks, we'll clean up the unnecessary regions in the Audio Regions List. Go **Audio⚫Select → Unused Regions,** or type ⇧+⌘+U (⇧+Ctrl+U).

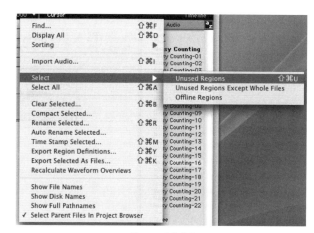

Figure 16-24

The regions that aren't being used in any tracks will be highlighted.

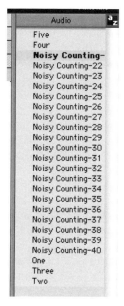

Figure 16-25

Go **Audio → Clear Selected,** or type ⇧+⌘+B (⇧+Ctrl+B).

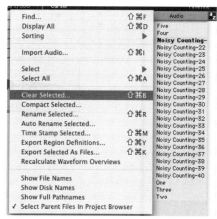

Figure 16-26

You have two choices: Remove the regions, which gets them out of the Session's Audio Region List, but leaves them on the hard drive. This is a good option, since the regions aren't erased completely. If you need to, you can import them back into the Session.

Or, you can choose to Delete the regions. If you do so, the audio files will be completely nuked from the hard drive. No way to get them back—be sure before using Delete! In most cases, choose Remove, just to be safe.

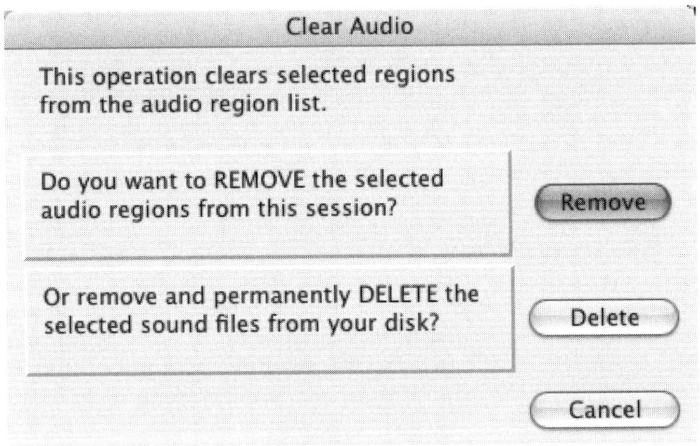

We're now down to just our original track, and the regions that are in use on it.

You're going to be using these editing tools and techniques a lot—I recommend practicing as much as possible. Feel free to try whatever crazy edits you want. Remember, the undo command is your friend.

Figure 16-27

seventeen

FADE TO BLACK

Fade ins, fade outs, and crossfades are very important when using Pro Tools to edit audio. Yes, a "fade" can be the sort of long, slow fade out you hear on the end of song on a CD. And yes, you can do that kind of fade using Pro Tools (and we will, later in this chapter).

But the fades we're mainly talking about in this chapter take place more on the "micro" level. We'll mostly be using extremely short fades to clean up the edges of edited audio files—often you'll get a click when you perform an edit in the middle of a region where there's audio playing. A fade in or fade out smoothes over the edit, and removes the click. Another type of fade, a crossfade, is used to smooth the joint between two audio regions that you've edited together.

Open up the CD-ROM Session "Chapter 17." You can play it if you like, but it's really not ready for primetime. We need to do some editing to get it prepared for aural consumption.

REPAIR WORK

To begin, we need to fix a problem on the "Guitar Arps" track. If you solo the track, and listen to the last chord, you'll hear that it's distorted. I could have punched in to fix it, but instead a second track was added with the last chord on it. Solo "Guitar End Fix" and listen to the last chord. The plan is to trim this track down to just the final chord, then transfer that chord to the track above it to replace the distorted bit.

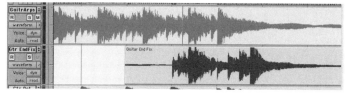

Figure 17-1

Zoom in on the tracks until you can see clearly—change track height as well. Listen to the track to identify where the final chord starts. (It should be right at measure 33.)

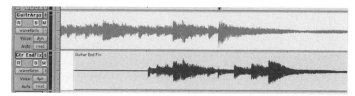

Figure 17-2

Using the Trimmer tool, pull the left edge of the Guitar End Fix track in to where the final chord starts.

Figure 17-3

As you're working, make the track taller and zoom in as far as you need to clearly see the notes. When you've got Guitar End Fix trimmed to where it enters right on the last chord, use the Grabber tool to **ctrl+drag** (right-click drag) the region to the track above. **Control+dragging** (right-click dragging) constrains the drag so you can only move it in one direction—up or down. This prevents you from accidentally shifting the region earlier or later in time while moving it between tracks.

The region you move will land on top of the existing region, replacing the end of it. Rewind a little bit and listen to the transition. Unless you're really lucky, there will be a small click at the transition between the old region and the one you dragged onto the track.

Figure 17-4

Zoom in on the transition between the regions. You'll be able to see the reason for the click: A mismatch between the end of the first region and the beginning of the second.

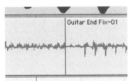

Figure 17-5

Using the Selector tool, make a small selection over the transition between the regions.

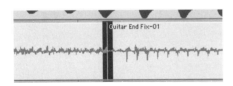

Figure 17-6

Go **Edit → Fades → Create Fades...** or type ⌘+F (Ctrl+F). The Fades dialog box will open. Since we've selected overlapping regions, the dialog will default to a crossfade, which fades out one region while fading in another. You can click and drag in the window to adjust the shape of the fade. Clicking on the buttons on the left will let you display the waveforms behind the fade display for reference. The speaker icon on top lets you audition the crossfade. The Shape controls on the bottom let you modify the fade curves.

For our purposes here, the default fade that shows up when you open the window will work just fine. *See Figure 17-7.*

Click OK to add the crossfade to the track. Rewind a bit to listen to the crossfaded track. The click should be gone, and the old region should transition smoothly to the final chord on the track. Have problems? You can Undo any of the changes we've made and try again. *See Figure 17-8.*

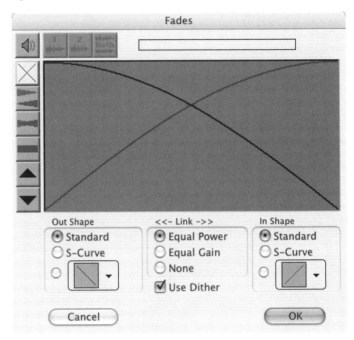

Figure 17-7

Figure 17-8

When you're finished, the Guitar End Fix track will be empty. Make sure it is un-soloed, then go ahead and hide it. Un-solo any other tracks that might be soloed.

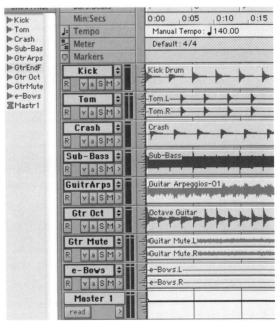

Figure 17-9

CONSTRUCTION WORK

As it stands, this song is pretty boring—a bit repetitious. We'll use some editing to make things somewhat more interesting by bringing in one part at a time.

Mute the Sub-Bass, Guitar Arps, Gtr Mute, and e-Bows tracks. This will leave the three drum tracks and Gtr Oct playing. Give the Session a listen to verify.

Figure 17-10

We want this song to start out with just drums, so we'll trim the Gtr Oct track to begin later. Solo the track. Zoom in, and use the Trimmer tool to drag the left edge of Gtr Oct over to the beginning of measure 5. We want to trim to just before the first chord enters in that measure. Listen to verify that you're hitting in the right spot.

Figure 17-11

Using the Selector tool, select a tiny bit of the region before the chord enters. Don't select any of the actual chord, just the space before the chord starts.

Figure 17-12

Go **Edit → Fades → Create Fades...** or type ⌘+F (Ctrl+F). This time, we're at the beginning of a region, so Pro Tools will default to a fade in. Again, you have options for adjusting the fade, but the defaults should work fine.

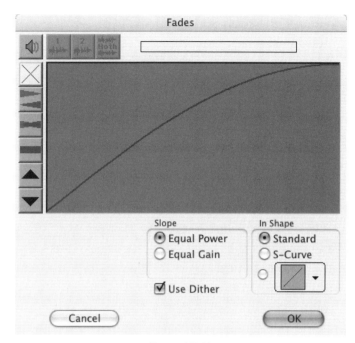

Figure 17-13

Click OK to add the fade in to the track; this will prevent any clicks when the region starts playing. Listen to verify, then un-solo the track. Listen to the Session if you like. You should hear the drums enter and play for four measures, then the strummed guitar chords should enter.

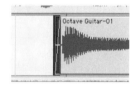

Figure 17-14

Next, un-mute and solo and trim the Sub-Bass track in the same way. We want the Sub-Bass to enter at measure 13.

Figure 17-15

You'll definitely want to add a fade to the beginning of the Sub-Bass region, otherwise there will be a substantial click when it starts playing. Be careful to add a very short fade, otherwise you'll hear the fade in on the first note of the part. *See Figure 17-16.*

Un-solo the Sub-Bass track and listen to your work so far. The drums start, guitar chords enter four bars later, then the Sub-Bass comes in eight bars later.

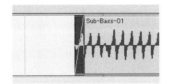

Figure 17-16

One at a time, un-mute, solo, and trim the rest of the tracks. We want Guitar Arps to enter at bar 17, Guitar Mute at bar 21, and e-Bows to come in around bar 25. On e-Bows, note that the part already fades in slowly, be careful not to trim so far that you cut off the entrance of the part. Listen carefully to make sure that you are trimming up to the beginning of the audio, without cutting anything off.

Take your time, and make sure that you're getting clean entrances for each part; use fade-ins to prevent clicks when the parts enter. When you're finished, the Session will look something like this.

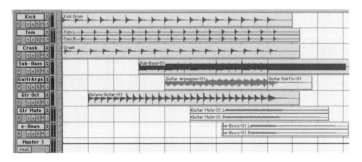

Figure 17-17

END GAME

Now we need to clean up the ends of our tracks, and complete the arrangement. Solo each track as you work on it, so you can clearly hear what you're doing. Zoom in and make the tracks taller as necessary for accuracy.

To begin, take a look at and listen to the end of the Tom track. There's one extra hit on the track that we'll want to get rid of.

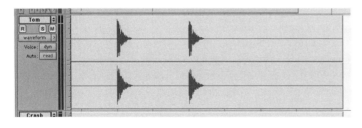

Figure 17-18

Using the Trimmer tool, trim back the right edge of the track to remove the extra hit. Since the hits are so far apart, there's only silence playing between

them. Because of this, we won't really need to add a fade out—there won't be any clicks to worry about. If you want to be certain, feel free to drop a short fade on the end of the track. (When you're working on your own tracks, be sure that what *looks* like silence really *is* silence—sometimes low-level noise or low frequencies may not show up visually, but will cause a click when editing. Use your ears to check!)

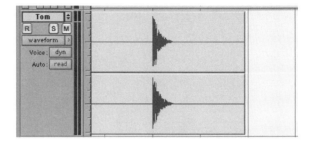

Figure 17-19

In the same way, trim the extra hit off the end of the Crash track. As with the Tom track, the hits are far enough apart that we won't have a click or need to fade.

Figure 17-20

Next go to the e-Bows track. We want the track to stop playing right when the last guitar chord hits. Using the Trimmer tool, drag the right edge of the track back to the beginning of measure 33.

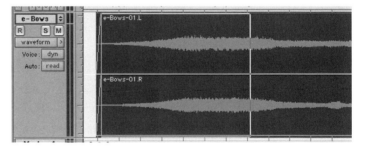

Figure 17-21

The e-Bow track is playing full steam at that point, so we'll definitely need a fade to prevent a click. Zoom in and make a very small selection at the end of the region. This time, you're at the end of a region, so when you open the Fades dialog, Pro Tools will automatically default to a fade out. The default settings should be fine. *See Figure 17-22.*

Click OK and a fade out will be added to both sides of the stereo track. Now trim the end of the Sub-Bass track back to the same spot (the beginning of measure 33), and add a fade. *See Figure 17-23.*

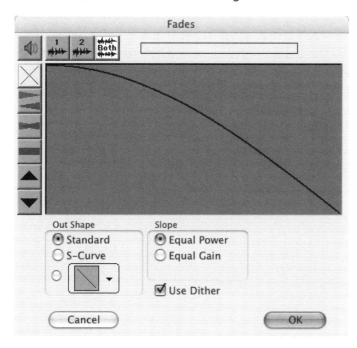

Figure 17-22

Figure 17-23

The three guitar tracks ring for different lengths of time after the last chord. Let's make them all end at the same time. Using the Selector tool, drag across all three tracks, simultaneously selecting them. You'll want to select so that all three tracks end about where Gtr Oct ends.

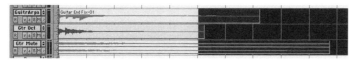

Figure 17-24

Delete, clear, or cut to remove the extra length from the tracks.

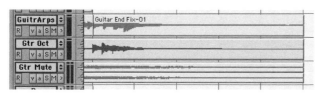

Figure 17-25

The Guitar Arps track will be cut off in the middle of ringing, so add a fade to it. This time, we'll create the fade in a different fashion: Switch to the Smart tool by clicking the oblong button beneath the Trimmer, Selector, and Grabber tools. If you now move the cursor over a track, it will change tools, depending on where it's located relative to the track.

Place the cursor in the upper part of the right end of the Guitar Arps track; it will turn into a square bisected by gray and white triangles. Click and drag toward the left; a fade will extend behind the cursor. When you've gone far enough—make it a long fade, so that the track gracefully fades out to the end of the track—release the mouse and the fade out will be placed on the track. You can use the Smart tool to do fade ins, fade outs, or crossfades.

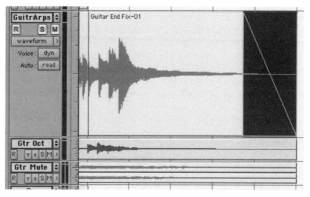

Figure 17-26

Likewise, add a long fade to the Guitar Mute track using the Smart tool, so it slowly fades down to the end of the track.

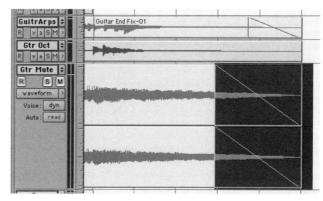

Figure 17-27

When you're finished, the final edited Session should look something like this. Give it a listen; hopefully you'll agree that it's much better than when we started. *See Figure 17-28.*

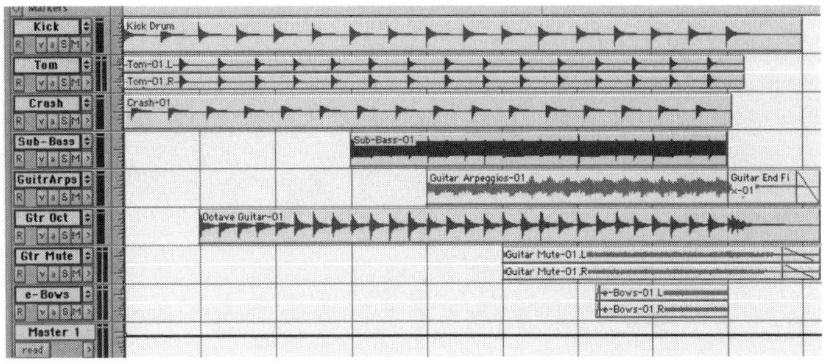

Figure 17-28

PRACTICE MAKES PERFECT

Don't worry if you had some trouble with working through this chapter. Editing is a skill that takes some practice. Over time, you'll learn to accurately make selections, what notes look like as waveforms, and when you'll need to add fades—and how long to make those fades.

Remember as you're practicing that you can always use the Undo command to jump back a step or two and try again.

eighteen

PROCESSING

There are two types of DSP (Digital Signal Processing) available in Pro Tools LE: The first, real-time RTAS plug-ins, will be discussed in Chapter 21, Plugged In. The second, AudioSuite plug-ins, don't operate in real time; they're applied to regions or audio files. Depending on the plug-in, many AudioSuite processes can be destructive; that is, they can actually change your existing audio files or create entirely new audio files. In some cases, depending on how you have things set up, you may not be able to undo AudioSuite processing.

That having been said (and seemingly having painted a negative picture), AudioSuite plug-ins offer powerful processing options. They can ease the load on your computer by taking processing offline, and they can provide options not available with real-time processes. However, as a trade-off, they create new files and therefore require more storage space. Pro Tools LE includes a nice bundle of AudioSuite plug-ins; pull down the AudioSuite menu and take a look.

The Audio Suite

Pro Tools LE comes bundled with the following AudioSuite plug-ins:

EQ
1-band EQ II—1-band equalizer (tone control)
4-band EQ II—4-band equalizer (tone control)

Dynamics
Compressor—controls signal dynamics
Limiter—sets a ceiling on maximum level of a signal
Expander-Gate—turns off signal between notes to reduce noise
Gate—turns off signal between notes to reduce noise
DeEsser—reduces level of "S"-type high-frequency sounds in vocals

Pitch Shift
Pitch Shift—changes the pitch of a region without changing its length

Reverb
D-Verb—adds reverb to a region or selection

Delay
Delay—adds echo to a signal
Multi-Tap Delay—four independent echo processors in one plug-in
Ping-Pong Delay—stereo echo, bounces between L/R channels

Modulation
Chorus—adds chorusing effect to region
Flanger—adds flanging effect to region

Other
Invert—flips polarity of signal
Duplicate—creates a single region from multiple selected regions
Normalize—sets overall level of a region higher or lower

Gain—raises or lowers volume of audio

Reverse—creates a version of region that plays backward

DC Offset Removal—removes DC offset artifacts from region

Signal Generator—creates audio tones

Time Compression Expansion—changes length of a region without changing its pitch

AudioSuite plug-ins can be applied to entire regions, to a selected part of a region, or to a selection that comprises multiple regions and/or parts of regions on one or more tracks. Conceptually, using AudioSuite plug-ins is simple: Make a selection on a track. Choose the AudioSuite plug-in you want to use. Optionally, Preview to hear what the processing will sound like. Process. Easy!

Let's take a look at a few AudioSuite plug-in examples. Open up the CD-ROM Session "Chapter 18."

It's a simple 1-bar drum part—make sure that the first track ("Reverse") isn't muted, then play it to hear what we're working with. For convenience sake, I've created four tracks, and put similar drumbeats on each one. We'll be using different AudioSuite plug-ins to process each track in a different fashion.

Using the Grabber tool, click on the region on the track "Reverse" to select the entire region.

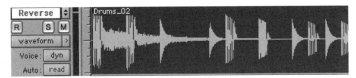

Figure 18-1

Go **AudioSuite → Other → Reverse** (in Pro Tools LE versions prior to 6.4, go **AudioSuite → Reverse**).

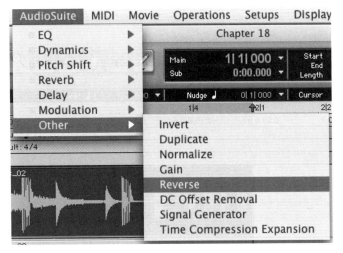

Figure 18-2

The Reverse plug-in window will open.

Figure 18-3

The five buttons at the top of this window are the same in every AudioSuite plug-in window. At upper-left is the plug-in selector. Pull this menu down to change to any AudioSuite plug-in.

The Playlist button offers you two options: Playlist and Region List. With "Playlist" selected, the regions selected in the track will be processed, but not their counterparts in the Audio Regions List. If "Regions List" is selected, the region in the Audio Regions List that corresponds to the one selected in the track will be processed, but not the one in the track. There's one exception; if "Use In Playlist" is selected (see below) along with "Regions List," both the region in the track and in the Audio Regions List will be processed. In most cases, you'll want to leave this set to "Playlist."

Figure 18-4

When the Use In Playlist button is turned off, a new version of the selected region will be created in the Audio Regions list, but not placed in the track.

If the button is on, and the Playlist menu is set to "Playlist," only regions selected in a track will be replaced with processed versions. Other copies of the region in the Session will not be replaced. So in our example here, only the region we've selected in the Reverse track would be processed and replaced; the other copies of this region in the Reverb and TCE tracks would not be affected.

If the button is on, and the Playlist selector is set to "Regions List," all the copies of a region in the Session will be processed and replaced. So in our example, every instance of "Drums_02" would be processed and replaced, even if those in the Reverb and TCE tracks weren't selected, they'd be replaced.

In most cases, you'll want this button turned on (highlighted)—just be careful when using this setting with the "Regions List" setting of the Playlist selector.

Figure 18-5

The File Mode selector has three options; these determine whether the plug-in is operating destructively or non-destructively. "Overwrite" replaces the original audio file on the hard drive; we're talking destructive here, folks! You can't undo after overwriting....

"Create Individual Files" processes each selected region, and creates a new file on the hard drive, and region in the track, for each one. It is non-destructive.

"Create Continuous File" combines all the selected regions and creates a single new file on the hard drive, and region on the track, that contains all of them. This is very useful if you're working on a track that contains parts of many regions that have been assembled to create a new performance. (This option isn't available with all plug-ins; if you don't see it, you can use the Duplicate plug-in or Consolidate Selection in the Edit menu to accomplish the same thing.)

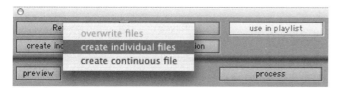

Figure 18-6

The Process Mode selector sets whether the plug-in will be applied to each region in a selection individually or to the entire selection as a whole.

Figure 18-7

The other common buttons in the AudioSuite plug-in windows are Preview (not found in all AudioSuite plug-ins) and Process. Preview lets you hear what the processed regions will sound like before you actually create new regions and replace the old ones. Process puts the plug-in to work and creates the new modified regions—it's the button you push when you're sure you're ready to go.

REVERSE

Some processes can only be accomplished in Pro Tools using certain AudioSuite plug-ins. Reversing a region, or part of a region, is one of these, as are most of the plug-ins found in the "Other" category in the AudioSuite Plug-ins list.

Let's try AudioSuite processing out. If you've changed anything since opening the "Chapter 18" Session, go back and select the region on the Reverse track. Open the Reverse plug-in from the AudioSuite plug-in menu. Set the selector buttons as follows:

Plug-in selector = Reverse, to choose the Reverse plug-in.

Playlist selector = Playlist, so processing will only be applied to the selected region in the track, not to the corresponding region in the Audio Regions List.

Use In Playlist = selected (highlighted), so the new processed file will be added to the Audio Regions List, and placed in the track.

File Mode selector = either "Create Individual Files" or "Create Continuous File"; we only have one region, so the result is the same with either setting.

Process Mode selector = either "Region By Region" or "Entire Selection" will work the same, as we only have one region selected.

Figure 18-8

Play the track to hear the original file one more time. Stop playback. Now click the Preview button. After a second—the plug-in has to do some calculating first—you'll hear the drum beat play back in reverse. But you've only previewed; the file hasn't really been processed yet. Click Preview again to stop the reverse playback. If you now play the Session, you'll hear the original region is still on the track.

When you're ready, click the Process button. After the plug-in finishes processing, you'll see that a new region appears in the Audio Regions List, and that region has been placed on the track in place of the original Drums_02 region. If you play the Session, you're ears will verify that the new, reversed region is on the track now.

Figure 18-9

Because we've created new regions, we can undo the processing; go Edit→Undo Reverse or type ⌘+**Z** (Ctrl+Z) to put the Session back where it was when we started. To reverse the region again, just reprocess with the plug-in or go **Edit → Redo Reverse** or type ↑+⌘+**Z** (↑+Ctrl+Z). You can bounce back and forth, processing and undoing, as much as you want.

Note that you don't have to process an entire region; you could use the Selector tool to just select one hit in the drumbeat. If you want to try it, undo if you've reversed the region. Now use the Selector to select just the first snare hit.

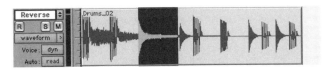

Figure 18-10

Process with the Reverse plug-in.

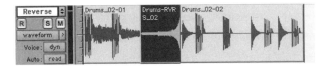

Figure 18-11

Rewind to the beginning of the Session, and play. The drums will play as normal, except the first snare hit, which will be reversed.

NORMALIZE

The Normalize plug-in sets the overall level of the selected region(s). It does this by finding the loudest peak in the region, and raising or lowering its volume to a user-set level. Mute the Reverse track, and unmute the Normalize track. Using the Grabber tool, select the region on the track. If you want, play the Session. Note how quiet the drums are, and how the waveform looks in the track. *See Figure 18-12.*

Go **AudioSuite → Other → Normalize.** The Normalize plug-in window will open. You'll see a sixth button in the top section of the Normalize plug-in

window: The Channel/Track Process Mode selector. With Peak On Each Chan/Track selected, each track will be normalized to its maximum level individually. With Peak On All Chans/Tracks selected, the plug-in will look for the highest peak in all the regions selected on all the tracks, and normalize all the regions based on that peak. *See Figure 18-13.*

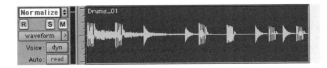

Figure 18-12

Figure 18-13

There are three controls for Normalizing; all do the same thing—set the level the region's loudest peak will be at. A setting of 0.0dB, 100.0%, or moving the slider all the way to the right means that the loudest peak in the region will be changed so that it is as loud as it can possibly go without distorting. (Maximum level is also known as "full code," since all the bits in the digital signal will be turned on.) Everything else in the region will be moved up by the same amount as the loudest peak. A setting of -6.0dB, 50%, or the middle of the slider range sets the loudest peak so that it is at 50% of maximum volume—the loudest peak will be set to -6dB.

Up or Down?

It's important to realize that Normalizing changes the level in absolute, not relative terms. That is, if the loudest peak is at maximum before normalizing, and you normalize to 50%, the loudest peak will be set to 50% of maximum volume. But if the loudest peak is very quiet, and you normalize by 50%, the region won't be turned down to 50% of its current level. Rather, the loudest peak will be set to 50% of maximum level before distortion—it will actually be turned *up.*

As an example, the following drum region's loudest peak is as loud as it can go—0dB, or "full code," in digital-speak.

Figure 18-14

This is what happens when you normalize it to 50%—it gets turned down so that the loudest peak is at 50% of full code, with the rest of the region turned down by a commensurate amount.

Figure 18-15

Here's the same drum region recorded at very low level.

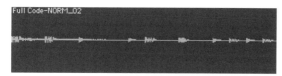

Figure 18-16

Notice what happens when you normalize the quiet region to 50%—it gets turned up so that the loudest peak is at 50% of full code, with everything else in the region turned up by a similar amount.

Figure 18-17

With the Drums_01 region selected on the Normalize track, open the Normalize plug-in. Set the plug-in parameters to 0.0dB, 100%, or full right on the slider. Click process. The plug-in will process for a second or two, then a new region will be added to the Audio Regions List, and the new region will be placed in the track, replacing the Drums_01 region.

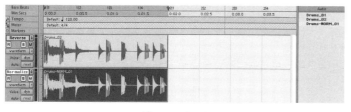

Figure 18-18

Note how much taller the waveform is, indicating that the level has been increased. Play the Session; hear how much louder the region is after being normalized?

It may seem like a good thing to normalize all your audio to the loudest possible level. But be cautious; normalizing raises the quiet parts of a region as well as the loud peaks, so any background noise will be turned up, too. And you may run into problems as you're mixing down your song if every region is maxed out in level. Working with 24-bit resolution, maximizing levels through normalizing isn't as commonplace as it was when everything was 16 bits. As with all processing, Normalizing is a great tool, but it should only be applied when absolutely needed.

REVERB

Reverb and delay (echo) processing are more commonly applied using RTAS plug-ins than AudioSuite. You may run into places where you want to use AudioSuite processing for these effects (although I'm having trouble thinking of one). There's one main difference when using reverb and delay AudioSuite plug-ins versus others: You have to allow extra length in your selection on the track for the reverb and delay to continue after the original region ends.

Mute the Normalize track, then unmute the Reverb track. Use the Grabber to select the region on the Reverb track. Open the D-Verb AudioSuite plug-in—lots of parameters in this one!

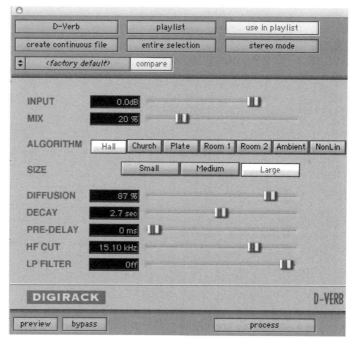

Figure 18-19

For now, set Input to 0.0dB. Set Mix to 30%. Set Decay to 2.5 seconds. Preview if you want, then click Process. When the plug-in is finished processing, a new region will be in the Audio Regions List, and placed in the Reverb track. Play the Session. You'll hear that the drums sound like they're playing in a large hall. But wait, there's something wrong...you'd expect the hall to continue ringing when the drums stop playing. Instead, the reverb cuts off at the end of the last drum hit.

This is why we need to extend our selection before applying the reverb processing—there was no space at the end of our region to store the new reverb data. Undo the processing you've done. Play the Session to verify the drums are back to their "dry" state, with no reverb.

Let's try again. Using the Selector tool, select the entire drum region, this time continuing the selection for a bit after the region ends.

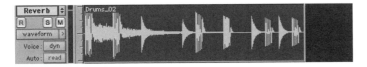

Figure 18-20

Now re-process using the D-Verb plug-in with the same settings as above. Note the change in the waveform; you can see that the reverb tail now continues ringing on into the end of the selection. Play the Session to hear the results.

Figure 18-21

TIME COMPRESSION EXPANSION

Time compression and expansion changes the length of a region without changing its pitch. The result is that the region plays back faster or slower than normal—vital when you're working with loops, for example, and need to match them to the tempo of your song.

Mute the Reverb track, unmute the TCE track. Play the Session if you like, to fix the sound and tempo of the original region in your ears. Now use the Grabber tool to select the region on the track. Open the Time Compression Expansion AudioSuite plug-in.

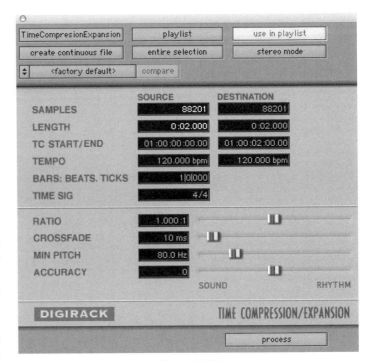

Figure 18-22

You can change any of the parameters in the "Destination" column to change the length (and therefore speed) of the processed region. Try setting the Tempo destination to 140 bpm. There's no preview on the Time Compression Expansion, so click Process, then play the Session to hear the results. You'll also notice how much shorter the Region is, since it's playing faster.

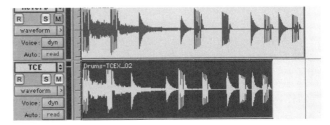

Figure 18-23

Undo, and try processing with a tempo of 100 bpm. Play to hear how much slower the result is, and check out how much longer the region is than before.

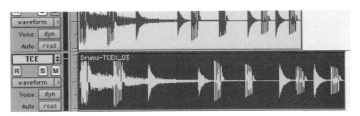

Figure 18-24

TCE Trimmer

If you want an even faster way to apply time compression or expansion to a region, look no farther than the Trimmer tool. If you click and hold the Trimmer button, you can choose the "TCE" Trimmer. Now when you click and drag the beginning or end of a region, instead of trimming the length, you'll actually be applying the Time Compression/Expansion plug-in.

nineteen

GOING DEEPER

In earlier chapters we explored some of the basics of Pro Tools editing. Now let's take a look at some more advanced and specialized editing tools and techniques. Open the "Chapter 19" CD-ROM Session.

EDIT GROUPS

Tracks in the Edit window can be grouped together so that as you perform editing operations on one, the same operation will be done on the others in the group. In the Session, select the Pad L and Pad R tracks (click on the Pad L track name, then ↑-click on the Pad R track name).

Figure 19-1

Go **File → Group Selected Tracks...,** go **Edit Groups → New Group...,** or type ⌘+G (Ctrl+G).

The New Group window will open. In this window you can name the group, set it so that it is in effect for just the Edit window, just the Mix window, or in both the Mix and Edit windows. You can also give the group an ID letter. Name the group "Pad," then click OK.

Figure 19-2

The new group will appear in the Edit Groups List at the lower left of the Edit window.

Figure 19-3

The Pad L and Pad R tracks are now grouped; what you do to one track, you'll do to the other.

Choose the Selector tool and make a selection in the Pad L track; the same selection will appear in the Pad R track. If you use the Trimmer tool to trim one track, the other will be trimmed as well. If you use the Grabber to move one track, the other will follow along—you get the idea, the grouped tracks act as one.

There are several things you can do using the Edit Groups list: Click the dot to the left of the group ID letter to select the tracks in the group. Click the group name (so it's not highlighted) to turn the group off so you can work on the tracks individually. Remember that you can also select the Edit Groups Key Focus button (a...z) and type the group's ID letter on your computer keyboard to enable or disable a group.

Click and hold the group name to open a menu allowing you to show or hide the tracks in the group.

Figure 19-4

Use the Edit Groups menu to create or delete a group or to suspend (turn off) all groups.

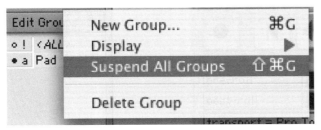

Figure 19-5

Grouping Groups?

You can have different combinations of tracks grouped in just the Mix window or just the Edit window, as well as groups that appear in both. This is so that you can have tracks grouped in the Mix window that you don't want to edit together in the Edit window. You may also want nested groups (groups within a group) in the Mix window, but you'll rarely want this in the Edit window. In other cases, tracks will always operate as a group—for example, the left and right sides of a stereo pair—both in the Edit and the Mix windows.

NUDGING

You can move a region in time by a specific amount using nudging. Nudging can be used to adjust the position of a region, automation data, and MIDI notes

and regions. Nudging works regardless of the Edit Mode, and can be used on regions selected on multiple tracks, as well as on regions on grouped tracks.

In order to nudge, you need to set a nudge value, or how far the region will be shifted in time. To set this value, use the Nudge menu, which is located above the rulers, in the center of the Edit window. (The nudge values in the menu will display with the same time scale as the main time counter unless you deselect "Follow Main Timebase" in the Nudge Menu.) Select "¼ note" as the nudge value.

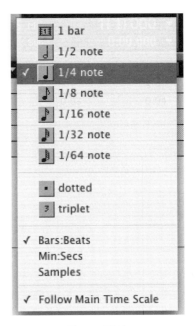

Figure 19-6

Using the Grabber tool, select the last region on the Bass track. You must select a complete region in order to use nudging. Type the "+" key to nudge forward in time, the "-" key to nudge backward.

You can type **Ctrl+/** (Start+/) to nudge forward using the next larger nudge value. (So if the nudge value is 1/4-note, this will nudge by 1/2-note.) Or use **Ctrl+M** (Start+M) to nudge backward at the next larger nudge value. If you have the Key Focus for the Edit window enabled (the "a...z" button above the left end of the rulers) just typing "/" or "M" will nudge by the next larger value.

You can also use nudging to trim the start and end points of a region or a selection. With the Grabber, select the Drums region. Type the Option and + or Option and - keys (Alt and + or -) to trim the start point. Type ⌘ and + or - (Ctrl and + or -) to trim the end point. Undo when you are finished to restore the Drums region to its original state.

Nudging can be very useful for fine adjustments in timing. In our example we used a 1/4-note setting, but you can nudge in increments as small as one sample (¹/₄₄, 100ᵗʰ of a second at 44.1kHz sample rate!) if you want exact control over region placement.

PENCIL TOOL

If you want serious editing, the Pencil tool can be used to actually redraw a waveform at the sample level. Normally you'll use the Pencil for tasks like removing a pop or click from a region.

Unmute the "Tone-Click" track, then solo it. Play the Session. You'll hear a tone with a bad click partway in. Make the track "large" or "jumbo" in height. Using the Zoomer tool, select the area containing the click—it looks like a spike in the otherwise smooth waveform.

Figure 19-7

Continue selecting the click with the Zoomer until the waveform turns into a thin line—you are now looking at the waveform at the sample level.

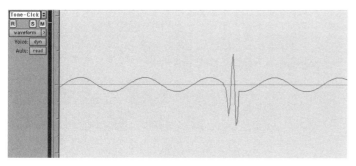

Figure 19-8

Now select the Pencil tool. While you can select the Pencil if you're not zoomed in to the sample level, it is inactive until you get to the point where the waveform becomes a line.

Use the Pencil to draw over the click in the waveform, making it look like the rest of the waveform in the region. When you're finished, rewind and listen to the track. The click should be gone.

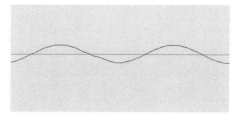

Figure 19-9

A caveat: Using the Pencil tool to do waveform editing is destructive—you're actually changing the audio file on the hard drive. Although you can generally undo a Pencil edit, be careful! This is a good place to put the Duplicate AudioSuite plug-in to work: Make a copy of a region for backup before you take the pencil to it.

STRIP SILENCE

Pro Tools' Strip Silence function looks at the selected region and removes areas of silence, dividing the region into smaller sections. Strip Silence considers anything quieter than a user-set threshold to be "silence," so it can also be useful for removing background noise such as hiss or hum.

If you soloed the Tone-Click track to try out the Pencil tool, unsolo and mute that track. Solo the Drums track. Using the Grabber tool, select the Drums region. Go **Windows → Show Strip Silence** or press ⌘+U (Ctrl+U). The Strip Silence window will open.

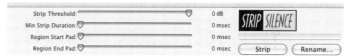

Figure 19-10

There are four controls in this window. There are four controls in this window; "Strip Threshold" sets the level below which "silence" will be removed. "Min Strip Duration" sets the smallest length of time that will be considered silence—it prevents too many tiny regions from being created by Strip Silence. "Region Start Pad" and "Region End Pad" set "pre" and "post" times at the beginning and end of the new regions. They prevent Strip Silence from cutting things too close and losing part of the attack or decay in the audio you want to keep.

To begin using Strip Silence, slowly adjust the Strip Threshold slider until white boxes begin to appear around the drum hits. In this case, we've got simple, defined material to deal with, so Strip Silence will have no problem deciding what is silence and what isn't—a threshold of -37dB should be fine.

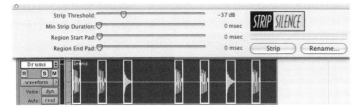

Figure 19-11

You can now adjust the other controls to see what they do. The Min Strip Duration won't be of much use in this example, as the silences are all well separated. Region Start Pad could be adjusted, but we're dealing with drum hits, which have a sharp attack, so we probably won't need much—18msec is plenty. You can experiment with Region End Pad, but again, not much will be needed; no more than 18msec.

Once you have Strip Silence set the way you want it, you can click the Rename button to specify how the newly created regions will be named, but in most cases the default will be fine. Click Strip when you're finished, then close the Strip Silence window.

Figure 19-12

The Drums region will be split into individual hits, with the silence between them removed. The new drum hit regions will appear in the Audio Regions List. Strip Silence is non-destructive, so go ahead and undo to return the Drums region to normal. Unsolo the Drums track.

ADDITIONAL EDIT MENU COMMANDS

We've already used Pro Tools' Cut, Copy, Paste, Clear, and Fade commands. But the Edit menu is well stocked with other useful editing commands and functions as well.

Duplicate

To make a copy of a selection (on one or more tracks) and paste it immediately after the selection, use the Duplicate command. Using the Grabber, select the Drums region. Go **Edit → Duplicate** or type **⌘+D** (Ctrl+D). The Drums region will be copied and placed immediately after the original on the track.

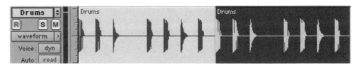

Figure 19-13

Repeat...

The Repeat command works the same way as the Duplicate command, except that you can enter the number of copies you want. Select the last region in the Bass track ("Bass_04"). Go **Edit → Repeat...** or type **Option+R** (Start+R). The Repeat window will open asking for the number of repeats you want.

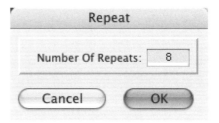

Figure 19-14

Enter "8," then click OK. Eight copies of the selected region will be created on the track, placed end-to-end.

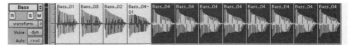

Figure 19-15

You can also select more than one region to be repeated. Undo the last operation. Now use the Grabber to select the last two regions on the Bass track ("Bass_02" and "Bass_04"). Use the Repeat command to make four copies.

Figure 19-16

Shift...

To move a region by a specific amount in time, use the Shift command. With the Grabber, select the second Drums region you created on the Drums track using the Duplicate command. Go **Edit → Shift...** or type **Option+H** (Start+H). The Shift window will open.

Figure 19-17

You can choose to shift the region either earlier or later in the track, and set how far. Set the window to shift later, by two beats—0|2|000. Click OK when you're finished.

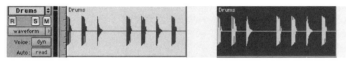

Figure 19-18

The region will be shifted over by two beats.

Capture Region...

The Capture Region command is used to create a new region in the Audio Regions List based on the current selection. The newly captured region is not added to the track's playlist, it only appears in the Audio Regions List.

Use the Selector tool to select a portion of the Drums region.

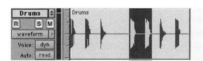

Figure 19-19

Go **Edit → Capture Region...** or type ⌘+R (Ctrl+R). When the Name window opens, enter a name for the new region.

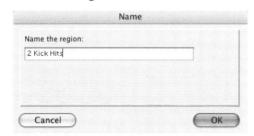

Figure 19-20

Click OK. The Drums track will remain unchanged, but a new region, with the name you just entered, will appear in the Audio Regions List. You can drag this

region onto a track or use it in any other way you choose.

Figure 19-21

Separate Region

The Separate Region command is similar to the Capture Region command, except that the selection you make is split off and made into its own region. If you haven't made a selection, the region will be split wherever the Edit cursor is located.

Make a selection on the Drums region (or use the same one you did when capturing the region above.

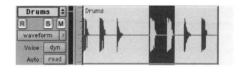

Figure 19-22

Go **Edit → Separate Region...** or type ⌘+E (Ctrl+E). Once again, you'll asked to name the new region. Name it, then click OK. The selection will be turned into a region and added to the Audio Regions List. Two Drums regions will also be automatically created to the left and right of the new region.

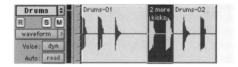

Figure 19-23

You can also use the Separate Region command to split a region at the cursor location. Using the Selector tool, click in the second Drums region at beats 3.

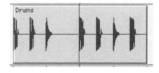

Figure 19-24

Go **Edit → Separate Region...** or type ⌘+E (Ctrl+E). The region will be split into two smaller regions.

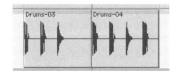

Figure 19-25

Separation Grabber

If you're going to be moving a separated region, you can do it with the Separation Grabber tool. Use the Selector tool to select part of a region. Click and hold on the Grabber tool to switch it to the Separation Grabber—change it to the hand with a scissors icon.

Use the Separation Grabber to grab and drag the selection; it will come free and can be moved wherever you want it. If you don't want to leave a hole in the original region, hold the **Option** (Alt) key while grabbing and dragging with the Separation Grabber. A copy of the selection will be moved.

Heal Separation

You can rejoin separated regions using the Heal Separation command, as long as you haven't modified either region or changed their start or end points. You can only heal regions that were once part of the same region. You can't heal the separation between regions that came from different places.

Use the Selector tool to select across the separation we created above when splitting the Drums region in two.

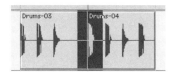

Figure 19-26

Go **Edit → Heal Separation** or type ⌘+H (Ctrl+H). The regions will be joined back into one region.

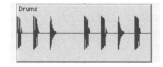

Figure 19-27

Quantize Regions

The Quantize Regions function is used to correct the timing of audio and MIDI regions. The start point of the region (or sync point, see below) is moved to the nearest grid location. The grid value is set up in the same way as it was in Grid Mode, using the pulldown Grid menu above the rulers.

Set the Grid to 1/4-note. In Slip Mode, slide a region

out of time; try it with the last region on the Bass track.

Figure 19-28

Go **Edit → Quantize Regions** or type ⌘+0 (Ctrl+0; that's a zero, not an "O"). The region will move to the nearest grid point (either before or after, whichever is nearest).

Figure 19-29

Mute/Unmute Region

One easy way to audition a quick change to an arrangement is to mute a region—turn it off so it doesn't play, but without turning off the rest of the track.

Select the region you want to mute. Try the first region on the Bass track.

Figure 19-30

Go **Edit → Change to Mute/Unmute Region** or type ⌘+M (Ctrl+M). The region will become dim to indicate its muted status.

Figure 19-31

Lock/Unlock Region

If you know you've got a region exactly where you want it, and you don't want to take a chance on accidentally moving it or otherwise screwing it up, you can lock it—prevent it from being moved or edited. Select the Pad L region using the Grabber, then go **Edit → Lock/Unlock Region** or type ⌘**+L** (Ctrl+L). A small "lock" icon will appear on the region indicating that it is locked and can't be moved or edited. (If you had the "Pad" group enabled, you simultaneously locked the Pad R region.) To unlock the region, go **Edit → Lock/Unlock Region** or type ⌘**+L** (Ctrl+L) again.

Figure 19-32

Consolidate Selection

If you do much editing on a track, you could end up with a bunch of little regions scattered about. To make things easier to deal with, you can combine all those regions into one big region using the Consolidate Selection command.

Use the Selector or ↑-click with the Grabber to select all the regions on the Bass track. (If you muted the first region on the track, unmute it first.)

Figure 19-33

Go **Edit → Consolidate Selection** or type **Option+↑+3** (Start+↑+3). The selected regions will be combined into one new, large region comprising the entire selection. A new audio file is created on the hard drive, a new region appears in the Audio Regions List, and the new region is placed on the track.

Figure 19-34

The regions you're consolidating don't need to be right next to each other. If they're spaced apart, the spacing between them will remain when the new consolidated region is created.

Identify Sync Point

By default the start point of a region is used when placing a region in Grid or Spot Mode, or when quantizing regions. But Pro Tools also allows you to define your own "sync point" in a region. This is useful for placing sound effects, or if there's a space in a region before the downbeat occurs.

Let's say that the fourth drum hit in the Drums region is actually the downbeat; the spot we want to use when placing or quantizing the region. To set this as the sync point, click right before the drum hit using the Selector tool.

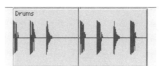

Figure 19-35

Go **Edit → Identify Sync Point** or type ⌘**+,** (Ctrl+,). A small downward arrow or triangle appears at the sync point.

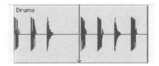

Figure 19-36

If you now quantize the region or move it in Grid Mode, it will snap based on the sync point defined by the arrow. If you want to get rid of the sync point, select the region with the Grabber, then go **Edit → Remove Sync Point** or type ⌘**+,** (Ctrl+,).

Identify Beat

Pro Tools' Identify Beat function allows you to create a "tempo map" for a Session based on a selection. This is especially useful if you're creating a song around audio that wasn't recorded to a click. Let's try it out.

Delete all the regions from the Drums track. Switch to Shuffle Mode. Drag the "Drums" region from the Audio Regions List to the Drums track. Now drag the "Drums 100 bpm" from the Audio Regions List onto the Drums track.

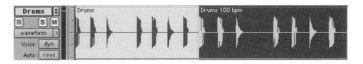

Figure 19-37

Using the Grabber, select the "Drums" region on the Drums track. Go **Edit → Identify Beat...** or type

⌘+I (Ctrl+I). The Bar|Beat Markers window will open.

Figure 19-38

The information in the window should be correct; the region starts at 1|1|000 and ends at 2|1|000, and is in Y time. Click OK. Tempo and meter information corresponding to the region will appear in the rulers.

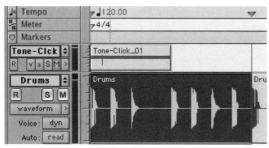

Figure 19-39

Now use the Grabber to select the "Drums 100 bpm" region on the Drums track. Go **Edit → Identify Beat...** or type ⌘+I (Ctrl+I). The Bar|Beat Markers window will open again.

This time we need to make some changes. The region does start at 2|1|000, but it's one measure long, so it ends at 3|1|000—change the End Location to reflect this, then click OK. Notice the change in the rulers: a new tempo, 100.00 has appeared at the beginning of our second region, and the Bars:Beats ruler has changed to show the beat locations based on the new tempo. The time signature is the same because both regions we analyzed are in Y time.

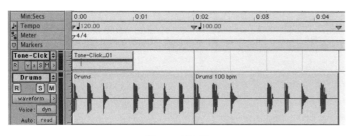

Figure 19-40

Solo the drum track and play Pro Tools. It will start out at 120 beats per minute tempo. When it reaches the second measure it will automatically switch to 100 beats per minute. If we were using the Pro Tools click as our metronome, it would change speed to match the tempo map we've created. Unsolo the drums when you are done listening.

Insert Silence

The cleverly named "Insert Silence" command inserts silence into a region or track. Exactly how the command works depends on the Edit mode you're in. If you are in Slip, Spot, or Grid modes, Insert Silence will clear any audio that is selected, replacing it with silence. If you're in Shuffle Mode, audio after the selection will be shuffled later on the track to make room for the inserted silence.

Solo the Bass track. Switch to Slip Mode. Use the Selector tool to select the fifth bass note.

Figure 19-41

Go **Edit → Insert Silence** or type ⇧+⌘+E (⇧+Ctrl+E). The selected bass note will be replaced with silence.

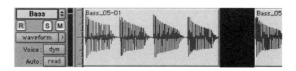

Figure 19-42

Undo to return the Bass region to the way it was before. Reselect the fifth bass note if necessary. Switch to Shuffle Mode. Go **Edit → Insert Silence** or type ⇧+⌘+E (⇧+Ctrl+E). The selection will again be filled by silence. But instead of replacing the fifth note, the fifth note (and everything after it) will be pushed over to make room for the insertion.

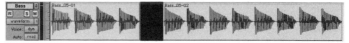

Figure 19-43

PART SIX

Mixing

twenty

IN THE FLOW

W e've recorded our tracks and edited them—they're exactly how we want them. Now we need to mix them to create our final masterpiece. In Chapter 9, The Mix Window, we looked at the different parts of the Mix window, and the various kinds of tracks. Let's move on to the next level, and learn how to use those tools to mix our music.

SIGNAL FLOW IN THE PRO TOOLS MIXER

We've already dealt with the basics of Pro Tools signal flow: how signals enter audio tracks, how they're routed out to Master Faders and the physical outputs on our hardware interface. But there's a lot more that we can do; the Mixer has a variety of routing capabilities we can use to our advantage. *See Figure 20-1.*

The input to each channel can accept a variety of sources: Audio from your hardware interface, audio playing from hard drive, or audio from a bus, which is like a virtual "wire" inside the Pro Tools mixer (more on buses below).

Once the audio is in a Mixer channel, up to five inserts can be used to process it. An insert can go to and come back from a software plug-in (plug-ins will be covered next chapter), or go out of a hardware output and return on a hardware input—this lets you use external hardware processors in the signal path.

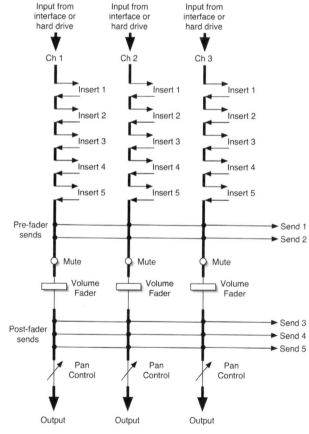

Figure 20-1

The signal continues on to the Mute button. On the way, you can tap off and send some of the signal elsewhere using any Sends that are set for "Pre-fader" (sends that are placed before the Volume Fader in the signal path). Sends can feed either hardware outputs on your interface or buses.

After the Mute button comes the Volume Fader. Following the Volume Fader are any sends that are set to be Post-fader. Then comes the Pan control.

The channel's output can feed a number of sources: a hardware output on your interface, a bus, or a Master Fader (which in turn can feed either a hardware output or a bus).

The signal flow is the same for mono and stereo tracks; it's also identical for an Aux Input, except that an Aux Input can't accept audio from hard drive as a source.

USING THE MIXER

Open up the CD-ROM Session "Chapter 20." Play the Session. Don't hear anything? There's a good reason for that: While I've created the tracks and the audio files, the mixer isn't set up for a mix yet. We've got some work to do.

This Session is a short excerpt from the guitar solo section of a rock song. There's a drum kit—with each drum recorded to its own track—electric bass, two rhythm guitars, a lead guitar, and another guitar playing harmony to the lead guitar.

Each recording engineer has his or her own approach to mixing a song. You'll develop yours as you work on songs. For now, let's begin by listening to the drums. Turn up all the drum tracks—conveniently located to the left of the Master Fader—to 0dB then play the Session. There's a brief silence before the toms enter.

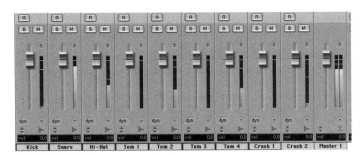

Figure 20-2

Right now all the drums are panned to the center. The mix will be more spacious if we pan them in stereo. Try the following pan positions for each channel:

  Kick: >0<
  Snare: >0<
  Hi-hat: <30

Tom 1: <45
Tom 2: <15
Tom 3: >15
Tom 4: >45
Crash 1 <60
Crash 2 >60

Figure 20-3

Listen to the drums again with the panning; adjust the volume of the individual tracks until you're happy with the balance. For exact fine adjustments, you can hold down the ⌘ (Ctrl) key while moving the fader—you'll be able to make 0.1dB changes. In my mix, I pulled the hi-hat and the four tom tracks down by 2.0dB. I also pulled down Crash 1 by 1.0 dB and Crash 2 by 2.0dB.

Most engineers try to balance the kick drum and the bass. Solo the Kick and Bass tracks. Raise the Bass up until you feel it's nicely balanced with the kick—try putting it at -3.5dB. When you're happy with the balance, un-solo the two tracks so you can hear the bass playing along with all the drums. Make volume adjustments as you listen, if you feel the need.

About this time you've probably noticed that the meters on the Master Fader have clipped—the overload indicators are showing red.

Figure 20-4

Click on the red squares to clear them. To prevent further overloads, let's pull down the Master Fader a bit; try -2.0dB.

Turn your attention to Guitar 1 and Guitar 2—the rhythm guitars. With the Session playing, raise the guitars. Since there are two rhythm guitars, the mix will be more open if you pan them opposite each other. Try panning Guitar 1 all the way to the left, and Guitar 2 all the way to the right. If you're having trouble balancing the guitars, set Guitar 1 to -7.0dB and Guitar 2 to -10.0dB.

Figure 20-5

Time for the Lead track; since it's the main focus, leave it panned right up the center. Bring it up to where it sounds right to you; I ended up putting it at about -10.0dB. Now bring up the Harmony track; we want it to sit "under" the lead track, not compete with or overpower it. You can leave the harmony panned to the center, but if you pull it a tiny bit off to one side, the mix will open up a bit more. Try panning it to >5—holding ⌘ (Ctrl) while moving the panner will let you make fine adjustments. I put the Harmony track at -15.0dB in my mix.

Now that you've got the mix roughed in, go back and tweak any levels or pan settings that you think will make things sound better. Go **File** → **Save Session As...** to save your work under a new name, use "Chapter 20.1." We'll be refining this mix over the next few chapters, so we'll want to be able to get back to it later.

Congratulations, you've just done a mix in Pro Tools!

BUSES AND SUBMIXING

We learned earlier that buses are like virtual wires in Pro Tools. We can use buses for a variety of routing purposes within the mixer. One of those applications is submixing—creating a smaller mix within the Session's main mix. Why would you want to do this? Normally the reason is to simplify mixdown, but submixes are also useful when you want to apply the same processing to a group of tracks (such as EQ on all the drums); you might do this to conserve DSP

power, or to get a more homogeneous sound by processing everything together.

As an example, take a look at the mix we created above. Let's say we want to turn all the drums up by 1.0dB. We could move each track individually (what a pain). We could group all the drum tracks (see below for more on grouping). Another method is to submix the drums using buses, then turn down the fader on the submix track.

Begin by creating a stereo Aux Input. Name it "Drums." Turn it up to 0dB.

Figure 20-6

Assign each individual drum track's output to Bus 1-2.

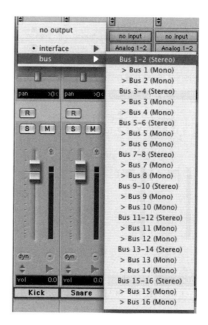

Figure 20-7

Assign the Drums Aux Input's input to Bus 1-2. *See Figure 20-8.*

Play the Session. It should sound exactly as it did before. But the nine individual drum tracks are now being routed—submixed—through the Drums Aux Input. If you change the position of the Drums fader, the overall level of the drums as a whole will go up or down. Set the Drums Aux Input at +0.5dB.

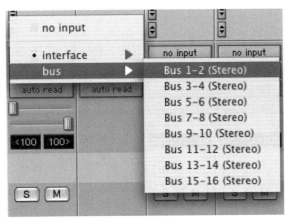

Figure 20-8

If you wanted to clean up the mixer and make it easier to work with, you could hide the individual drum tracks and just use the Drums Aux Input to control their level.

If you want to save your work, use the Save Session As... command to do so under a new name, "Chapter 20.2."

BUSES AND BOUNCING

Bouncing is the process of recording or re-recording an existing track or tracks to a new track. There are a variety of reasons why you might bounce a track: You could bounce the track with effects processing. You could bounce multiple edited tracks down to one track to combine the best parts of each—a process called "comping" that's often used to create a lead vocal or a lead solo track.

Or bouncing could be a matter of convenience. For example, we could bounce our stereo submix of the drums instead of doing a "live" submix through an Aux Input, as we did above. This will let us work with the drums as a stereo file in the Edit window and when processing in the Mix window.

Let's try it: Delete the Drums Aux Input track that you created earlier: Select the Aux Input, then go **File → Delete Selected Tracks...**

Now create a new stereo Audio Track. Name it "Drums" in honor of the Aux Input you just deleted. Set its input to Bus 1-2. The individual drum tracks are still set with Bus 1-2 as their output, so those tracks will serve as the source input for the stereo track. In order to hear the drums you'll need to record-enable the Drums stereo track. You'll also need to check that Input Only Monitor is selected under the Operations menu.

Figure 20-9

When you're ready, hit Record and Play. The individual drums will all be recorded to the stereo track. When you're finished, the stereo Drums track will contain all the drums; you can deactivate and hide the individual drums. (You could delete them, but deactivating and hiding them means they're still around if you need them later.) If you want to save your work, use the **Save Session As...** command to do so under a new name.

Bouncing The Click

Here's a cool use for bouncing: Remember how, when we used Low Latency Monitoring, all plug-ins were disabled, including the Click? Now we have a solution! Bounce the Click to an Audio Track. Here's how: Create a mono Aux Input. Select the Click plug-in. Turn up the Aux, and make sure you can hear the click.

Figure 20-10

Create a mono Audio Track. Set its input to Bus 1. Set the output for the Click Aux Input to Bus 1 as well. Record-enable the Audio Track. Name it "Click."

All that's left is to hit Record and Play. The click will be recorded to the audio track. When you're done you can delete the Aux Input with the Click on it, and use the audio track as your metronome. One caveat: Once the click is recorded as audio, it's needless to say harder to change tempos; make sure you have the right tempo before you bounce!

MIX GROUPS

In Chapter 19, Going Deeper, we learned about Edit groups. You can also have Mix Groups. When you group channels in the mixer together, moving the fader on one channel will move the faders on any grouped channels simultaneously.

In our Session, click on the Guitar 1 and Guitar 2 track names.

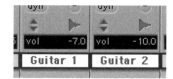

Figure 20-11

Go **File → Group Selected Tracks...** or press ⌘+**G** (Ctrl+G). The New Group dialog window will open. Name the group "Guitars," click OK. The new group will appear in the Mix Groups List.

Figure 20-12

Now move the fader for the Guitar 1 track. The Guitar 2 track will follow right along. If you mute or solo either guitar track, the other will mute and solo too. Remember that you can disable a group by deselecting its name in the Groups List.

Save your work, using the **Save Session As...** command to do so under the name "Chapter 20.3."

MEMORY LOCATIONS

Pro Tools has a powerful tool available that can make working on mixes—and editing, for that matter—go much faster: Memory Locations and Markers. Each Session can have up to 200 Memory Locations. These can be used to store Markers that allow you to easily jump to important points in the song—verse, chorus, solos, ending, and so on. Memory Locations can also

store zoom settings, pre- and post-roll times, track show/hide status, track heights, and group enables—which Mix and Edit groups are active.

There are several ways to create a Memory Location or Marker. Open the Session we saved with the first mix: "Chapter 20.1." Go to the Edit window. Click with the Selector tool at the beginning of the first region in the Tom 1 track. Click in the "Marker Well" — the little button to the left of the Markers Ruler.

Figure 20-13

The New Memory Location window will open. In this case, we only set a location, not zoom or other parameters that Markers can remember. Name the location "Start" and click OK. With these settings, the Marker will remember only the location.

Figure 20-14

Want another way to do it? You could also have held down the **Control** (Start) key and clicked in the Markers Ruler where you wanted the Memory Location.

Let's create a Selection Memory Location. Using the Selector tool, drag in a ruler or a track so that measure 3 of the song is selected. Zoom in horizontally so that the selection fills the window. *See Figure 20-15.*

Press **Enter** on the numeric keypad. The New Memory Location window will open. Click "Selection" in the Time Properties part of the window. Name the Memory Location "Measure 3." Select the check box by Zoom Settings. Click OK. With these settings, the Marker will remember the selection and the zoom level.

Figure 20-15

One more: Zoom out so that the Session fills the window—double-click the magnifying glass or press **Option+A** (Alt+A). Make the Bass track medium height. Press **Enter** on the Numeric keypad to open the the New Memory Location window. Under Time Properties, select "None." Select Zoom Settings, and Track Heights. Name the track "Tall Bass." Click OK. With these settings, no location is stored, but the zoom level and height of each track is remembered.

RECALLING MEMORY LOCATIONS

There are three ways to recall Memory Locations. You can click on the Memory Location name in the Show Memory Locations window (see below). You can click on a Marker in the Markers Ruler. Or, you can use the numeric keypad. Depending on how you have the numeric keypad preferences set, this may be done by pressing period (.) then the Memory Location number, or you may have to press period, Memory Location number, and period again.

SHOW MEMORY LOCATIONS

The Show Memory Locations window is used to manage, edit, and delete Memory Locations and Markers. To open it, go **Windows → Show Memory Locations** or press ⌘**+5** (Ctrl+5).

Figure 20-16

All the Memory Locations you've created will be displayed here, and you can click on them to call them up. The little icons on the upper-left can be used to show and hide the various types of Memory Locations. *See Figure 20-17.*

The pop-up menu under the Name button can be used to set Memory Location options and access other functions.

Figure 20-17

Figure 20-18

At the top of the menu, you can Show Markers Only, which will show only location Markers. Show View Filter Icons shows and hides the little icons to the upper-left, and the corresponding icons beside each Memory Location. Show Main Counter and Show Sub Counter display columns with the time locations for Markers and Selection Markers.

You can choose to sort Markers by time; with this deselected, the Memory Locations will be listed in the order in which they were created.

Add Memory Location is another way to create a new Memory Location; Remove Memory Location deletes the current Marker, while Delete All erases all Memory Locations.

Default To Marker makes each Memory Location you create appear as a Marker; you can, of course, change the Marker to a Selection Range or "None" Memory Location. Auto-Name Memory Location assigns a generic numbered name to each new Memory Location, for example, "Marker 4," Marker 5," and so on.

Dropping In

If you want an easy way to enter Markers at locations in a song, you can do so during playback. For this to work Default To Marker and Auto-Name Memory Location must be selected in the Show Memory Locations pull-down menu.

Simply play the Session, and hit the **Enter** key on the numeric keypad where you want the Marker to land. Try it: Hit play, and add a few Markers during the Session by hitting **Enter**—try dropping one at the beginning of each measure.

Figure 20-19

twenty-one

PLUGGED IN

Plug-ins are one of the most important advances that digital audio workstations have introduced to the recording world. A plug-in is a small piece of software that runs inside another piece of software, called the "host"—Pro Tools, in this case.

RTAS FORMAT

We've already talked about AudioSuite plug-ins, which are non-real-time—they're used when Pro Tools isn't playing. And while AudioSuite plug-ins have a great deal to offer, the real magic resides in Pro Tools' RTAS (Real-time AudioSuite) plug-ins, which can be used to process tracks in real time, as the Session is playing.

There are two ways to use plug-ins; you can use them directly in a track's inserts to process the entire signal from the track. This is usually the way that "serial" processors are used: equalizers, compressors, gates, and the like. With this approach, a plug-in processes the signal passing through a single track, Aux Input, or Master Fader. (Keeping in mind that an Aux Input or Master Fader may be carrying a submix of signals from a bunch of other tracks—in that case, the plug-in will be applied to the submix as a whole.)

The second method for using plug-ins is in the insert of an Aux Input, which is fed by sends from the tracks. Usually effects such as reverb, and delay are used this way. With this approach, multiple tracks can be routed to and share a single plug-in.

One method isn't better than the other, they're simply different approaches. We'll learn how to do both in this chapter.

USING INSERT PLUG-INS

Open up the CD-ROM Session "Chapter 21." (It's the same Session we were working on in the last chapter.) First let's put a few plug-ins to work on channel inserts.

The Kick track could use a bit of EQ. We'll use a 1-band equalizer to punch up the sound. Go to the Kick track's inserts, and select 1-Band EQ II.

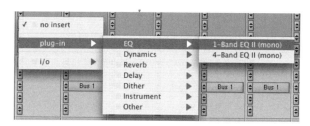

Figure 21-1

The plug-in window will open.

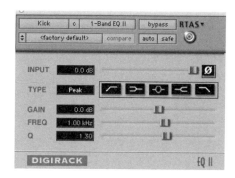

Figure 21-2

The Input level can stay at 0.0dB. Select a "peak" type EQ, and set its gain to 3.0dB, the frequency to 640Hz, and the Q (bandwidth) to 1.30. Play the track; hear the difference? Solo the track if you like, so you can hear more clearly.

TOURING THE RTAS PLUG-IN WINDOW

Most RTAS plug-ins have the same features in the top portion of their windows. The upper-left button pulls down to let you select the track you're looking at.

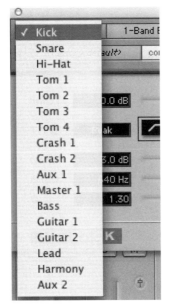

Figure 21-3

The small button next to the Track Selector is the Insert Selector; the five inserts for each track are labeled "A" through "E." I've inserted the EQ on the middle insert on the Kick track; insert "C."

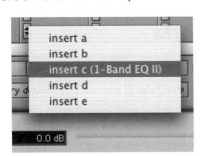

Figure 21-4

The next button allows you to change the plug-in assigned to the insert. *See Figure 21-5.*

The last button in the top row is the plug-in bypass button. The left-most button on the bottom row (the one with up/down arrows on it) is where you'll save, copy, delete, and otherwise manage presets for the plug-in—you can store and recall your settings, building up a library of your favorite settings for each plug-in.

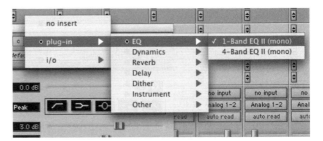

Figure 21-5

Figure 21-6

If there are presets stored for the plug-in, you can recall them from the next button, which pulls down the Librarian Menu. When you open a plug-in, this button will be labeled "<factory default>." Next to it is the Compare button, which allows you to switch between the plug-in's default setting (or the preset you've loaded) and the current state of the plug-in. So you can easily switch back and forth to compare the preset and whatever changes you've made. The Auto button opens up the Plug-In Automation window. In this window you set which parameters can be controlled by automation. There will be much more on this in the next chapter.

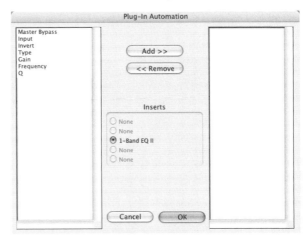

Figure 21-7

The Auto button locks existing automation to prevent it from being overwritten. Rounding out the common plug-in controls is the "target." As we learned in Chapter 9, The Mix Window, when the target is selected, the next plug-in window will open in place of the current one. With the target deselected, the next plug-in will open into a new window, leaving the current one open.

There are a few other things to do before we move on. Go to the Guitar 2 track. Add a 1-Band EQ II to this track as well—hey that's the beauty of plug-ins: With a hardware EQ, we would only be able to use it on one track. With a plug-in, we can have as many independent "instances" of the same plug-in inserted as our computer has power to run. We could put a 1-Band EQ II into every insert on every track if we wanted—and our computer had the power to run them all.

For this track, we want to pull some of the low end out of the rhythm guitar. Set the EQ for "HiPass" at 100Hz. The Input can stay at 0.0dB. To hear the difference, solo the track, then listen to it with the plug-in bypassed and active. Unsolo the track, and listen to the mix.

One more: let's tighten up the bass guitar, and even out its level a bit. For this, we'll use a compressor plug-in; insert the Compressor on the Bass track.

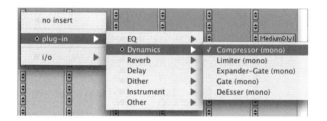

Figure 21-8

Using the Librarian Menu, call up the "Basic Bass" preset.

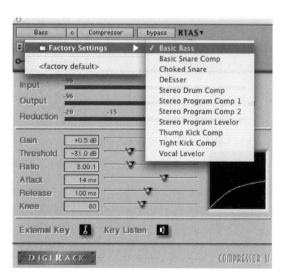

Figure 21-9

While you could use this preset as is, we'll get better results by modifying it a bit—we don't want to squash the bass, just even it out a bit. (Most of the time, the presets that come with plug-ins are

designed to demo its capabilities or to get you started; don't rely on them too much, as they often won't apply well to the specific situations you're facing.) Raise the gain to +1.6dB. Set the threshold to -25.0dB. The rest of the controls can stay as is.

Do I Have To Stop?

You don't have to stop playback to insert or remove a plug-in—you can plug-in while you're listening to the Session. There are a few limitations, but in many cases feel free to insert away.

USING PLUG-INS ON AUX INPUTS

The second way to use plug-ins is inserted on Aux Inputs and fed via sends from other channels. We'll start by putting a bit of reverb on some of the drums, to give our mix a sense of space. Begin by creating a mono Aux Input next to the Crash 2 track. Name it "Reverb." Insert the D-Verb plug-in. Note that this time you're given two choices: D-Verb (mono) and D-Verb (mono/stereo). The first one is a mono in/mono out plug-in. The second is a mono in, but stereo out version—the reverb effect will be in stereo. Choose the mono/stereo version to give the reverb more width and space.

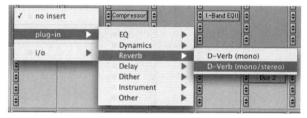

Figure 21-10

Notice that since the plug-in has a stereo output, the Aux Input it's inserted on automatically becomes stereo to support it. We want to get input into this Aux Input (and therefore into the D-Verb plug-in) from other channels, so we'll feed it with a bus. Select Bus 1 as the input for the Aux Input.

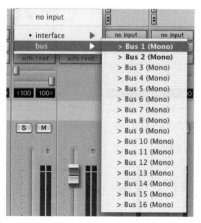

Figure 21-11

Begin by feeding the Snare track to the Reverb Aux Input: Go to the Snare track's sends, and assign Send C (the middle one) to Bus 1.

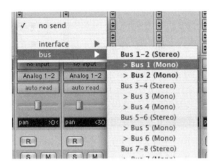

Figure 21-12

The plug-in send window will open when you assign the send. Turn up the Send level to 0.0dB.

Figure 21-13

Go back to the Reverb Aux Input, and turn up its level to 0.0dB. Now solo the Snare track and Reverb Aux Input. Play the Session. When the Snare begins playing in the second measure, you should hear reverb along with it—more than we want, actually. Let's make some adjustments. Click on the D-Verb plug-in insert to open its window. Change the algorithm to Room 2. Set the Decay to 500ms. Make sure the Mix control is set to 100% so that we get only reverb on the Aux Input. Leave everything else as is. *See Figure 21-14.*

Close the plug-in window. Unsolo the Snare track and Reverb Aux Input. Listen to the Session, focusing on the amount of reverb. We're probably overdoing it a bit; let's pull the Reverb Aux Input level down to -6.5dB. Listen again...much better!

Now that we've got reverb on the Snare track, the four Tom tracks are sounding sort of dry. Add a Bus 1 send to each one, turning each send level up to 0.0dB. *See Figure 21-15.*

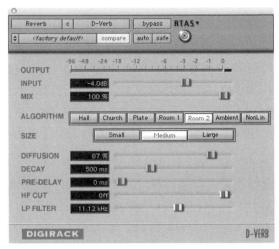

Figure 21-14

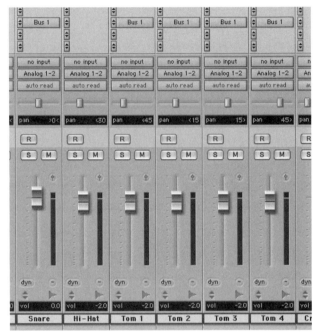

Figure 21-15

Now all five tracks will be sent to the reverb. Give the Session a listen.

Pre-fader Versus Post-fader Sends

Pro Tools Sends can be configured to be either pre-fader or post-fader. When the send is pre-fader, if you change the position of the track's volume fader, the send will be unaffected. This is what you want when, for example, you're using the send as a headphone feed for a musician.

A post-fader send, on the other hand, follows the track's volume fader. Pull down the volume fader, and the send will come down. This is what you want when using a send to feed a reverb, echo, or other effect. Otherwise, when you turn down the fader, you'll still hear the processed output of the track being sent to the effect.

Figure 21-16

You set whether a send is pre- or post-fader by clicking the "Pre" button on the Send Output window. With "Pre" selected, the send will be Pre-fader; with it unselected, the send will be post-fader—post-fader is the way a Send defaults when you create a new one.

The Lead track is sounding dry as well. Rather than adding more reverb to the mix, let's add a short echo. Create another mono Aux Input; label it Delay. Insert the mono Medium Delay II plug-in.

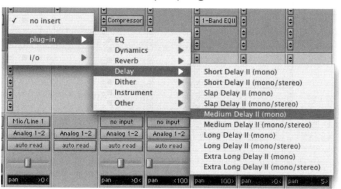

Figure 21-17

Make sure Mix is set to 100%. Set the Delay to 125ms. Leave everything else at the default.

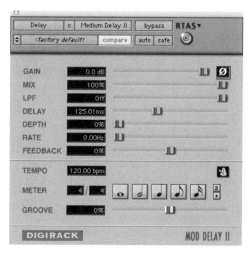

Figure 21-18

To keep things cleaner, pan the Delay Aux Input to the left (try <30). We need to feed the Delay Aux Input from the Lead channel. Assign a Send on the Lead channel to Bus 2. (Bus 1 is already in use by the

Reverb.) Turn up the send level to 0.0dB. Set the input for Delay Aux Input to Bus 2. Turn up the Delay Aux Input level to 0.0dB.

Play the Session. Whoa—too much delay! Try turning it down to -12.0dB. Solo the Lead track, then solo and unsolo the Delay Aux Input to hear what we've done. When you're finished, unsolo everything and listen to the entire mix with plug-ins. Feel free to adjust levels, settings, and panning.

MULTI-CHANNEL VERSUS MULTI-MONO PLUG-INS

You can also insert plug-ins on stereo channels, whether Audio tracks, Aux Inputs, or Master Faders. There are two types of stereo plug-ins: Multi-channel and Multi-mono.

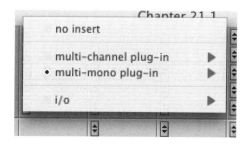

Figure 21-19

Multi-channel stereo plug-ins work just like mono plug-ins; both the right and left sides of the plug-ins work together, and are controlled by one set of controls.

A multi-mono stereo plug-in, on the other hand, is like two mono plug-ins bundled into one window. Here's the Limiter multi-mono stereo plug-in inserted on the Master Fader in our Session, for example.

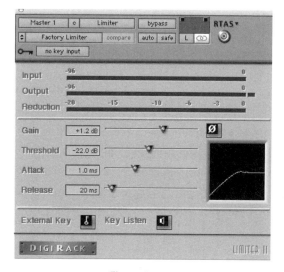

Figure 21-20

The difference is in the upper-right part of the plug-in window.

Figure 21-21

Using the Link/Relink button (the one with the two intersecting circles) you can set up the plug-in so both sides are controlled by one set of controls, or with it deselected, each side can be controlled separately. You choose which side you're working on using the "L" button to choose the Left or Right channel.

BYPASSING PLUG-INS AND MAKING INSERTS INACTIVE

You can bypass a plug-in using the Bypass button in its window. You can also bypass a plug-in by ⌘-**clicking** (Ctrl-clicking) its insert slot. When you do so, the insert slot will turn blue.

Figure 21-22

You can also make a plug-in inactive by **Ctrl+⌘-clicking** (Ctrl+Start-clicking) it.

Figure 21-23

The advantage to making a plug-in inactive versus bypassing it is that inactive plug-ins consume no computer resources, making more available for other plug-ins to use. Bypassed plug-ins still use computer power.

MOVING AND DUPLICATING PLUG-INS

You can move a plug-in to another track or to another insert slot on the same track by simply dragging it. You can duplicate a plug-in by **Option-dragging** (Alt-dragging) it to another insert slot. The duplicate plug-in will have the same settings as the original.

OPENING MULTIPLE PLUG-IN WINDOWS

Normally one plug-in window opens at a time; when you open another, the first closes. You can open multiple plug-in windows at the same time using the

target as described above, or by ↑+**clicking** on the inserts to open the desired plug-in windows.

REMOVING PLUG-INS

Remove a plug-in from a track or Aux Input in similar fashion to the way you insert it: Pull down the insert and select "No Insert."

Figure 21-24

MULTIPLE PLUG-INS ON THE SAME TRACK

You can have up to five plug-ins inserted (or "instantiated") on a track, using any of the five track inserts.

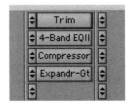

Figure 21-25

System Usage Window

Want to keep track of how much computer power all those plug-ins are using up? Pro Tools has a window that will show you what's going on with your system. To open it, go **Windows → Show System Usage.**

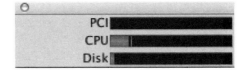

Figure 21-26

The window has three meters, two of which are important to us: CPU and Disk. CPU shows how much any active plug-ins and tracks are loading down your computer's brain. Disk shows how heavily playing your tracks is taxing your hard drive.

Some plug-ins, such as reverbs, will put heavy demands on your computer. Others, such as equalizers, won't drag things down as much. When you're first using Pro Tools LE, keep an eye on these meters to get an idea of what your computer is capable of, and what kind of power each plug-in requires.

twenty-two

AUTOMATION

Time to take complete control over Pro Tools and our mixes. How to do this? Hey, you made a big step in the right direction by working your way through this book! To go the rest of the way, you need to learn to use Pro Tools' automation features.

Automation allows Pro Tools to remember and play back changes made to most controls in the Pro Tools mixer or plug-ins. You can enter automation in real time by moving the faders and controls on the mixer or on a hardware control surface; Pro Tools will record those moves. Or you can use the Pencil tool to draw automation in the tracks of the Edit window.

Automation can be edited just like anything else in Pro Tools. You can cut, copy, and paste it, delete it, move it around. You can make the automation exactly the way you want it, and therefore tweak your mixes so they're exactly the way you want them.

SHOW AUTOMATION ENABLE

In order to automate a type of parameter, first make sure that it is enabled (highlighted) in the Show Automation Enable window. Open this window by going **Window → Show Automation Enable** or by typing ⌘**+4** (Ctrl+4).

Figure 22-1

RECORDING AUTOMATION

Recording automation into a track is straightforward. Open the CD-ROM Session "Chapter 22." At it's most basic, here's how easy it is to record automation: Go to the Guitar 1 track; pull down its Automation Mode Selector and set it to Auto Write.

Figure 22-2

The Automation Mode Selector will flash. *See Figure 22-3.*

Now play Pro Tools—you don't even have to go into Record—and move one of the track's controls. Try grabbing the track's volume fader with your mouse and moving it up and down. When you're finished, stop playback. The Automation Mode

Selector will change to Auto Touch. *See Figure 22-4.*

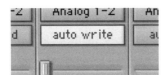

Figure 22-3

Figure 22-4

Now play the Session again. The fader will move exactly the way you moved it while recording the automation.

You can continue writing other types of automation as well: mute buttons and pan controls are two likely candidates. The Lead and Harmony tracks, for example, have quite a bit of noise before the instruments begin playing. You could edit this out of the audio regions. Or you could use mute automation to mute the track until just before each guitar starts playing.

AUTOMATION MODES

There are five automation modes in Pro Tools. We've already encountered two: Write and Touch. Let's dig deeper and learn more.

Auto Off

No surprises here; this mode is fairly self-explanatory. When Auto Off mode is selected for a track, all automation data for that track will be ignored.

Auto Read

Another mode with few surprises: In Auto Read mode, any automation data on the track will be played back.

Auto Write

As we saw earlier, Auto Write is the mode you'll use when you want to record automation data into a track. Auto Write is always destructive; each successive pass of writing automation erases the previous pass (although you can undo). When you finish a pass of writing automation, Pro Tools will automatically switch the track to Auto Touch mode.

Auto Touch

Auto Touch is the mode you'll use when you want to re-write a passage of automation on a track. In Auto Touch mode, as long as you are "touching" (or clicking/dragging with your mouse) a control, new automation will be written over whatever automation was there previously. When you release the control (going out of Auto Touch mode), it moves to the position of the previous automation.

Auto Latch

Auto Latch mode is very similar to Auto Touch, with one big difference: When you release the control, it will stay at the current position, not revert to the previous automation position. This mode is best for overwriting pan and certain types of plug-in automation where you want the control to remain where you set it.

USING CONTROL SURFACES

If you have a Digi 002, or a compatible Digidesign control surface such as the Control 24 or Command 8, or a third-party MIDI control surface such as the Mackie HUI, you can use the hardware faders and other controls to write and edit automation data. The automation modes work the same way as they do when you are entering automation by clicking and dragging controls with the mouse.

DRAWING AUTOMATION

"Playing" automation from a control surface works pretty well, but I've never been a fan of trying to use the mouse to click and drag faders or turn knobs. For me, if I'm not using a control surface, I often find it easier to draw in automation using the Pencil tool.

In the Chapter 22 Session, go to the Edit window. Make the Guitar 2 track Large. Change so that you're viewing Volume.

Figure 22-5

Choose the Pencil tool. Now draw in the Guitar 2 track.

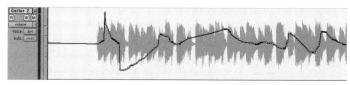

Figure 22-6

Switch to the Mix window and play the Session. The Guitar 2 fader will move in response to the automation you drew in the Edit window. The Pencil tool can draw in your choice of five modes; switch among the modes by clicking and holding the Pencil button or by repeatedly selecting the Pencil tool.

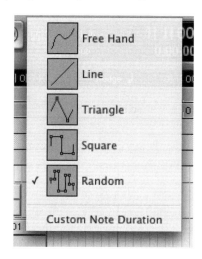

Figure 22-7

Freehand

The Pencil tool defaults to Freehand mode, where you can draw whatever curves and lines you want—it's the mode you just used to draw automation into the Guitar 2 track.

Line

In Line mode, the Pencil is constrained to drawing straight lines: vertical, horizontal, or at angles.

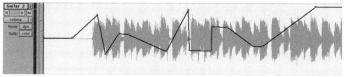

Figure 22-8

Triangle

When you use the Pencil in Triangle mode, you'll get a repeating triangle pattern of automation; the width of the triangles is determined by the Grid setting. The height of the triangles is set by how tall you draw with the pencil.

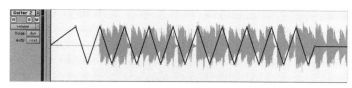

Figure 22-9

Square

Square mode works the same way as Triangle, except that (surprise) squares are drawn.

Figure 22-10

Random

The Random Pencil mode works much like Square mode, except that the height of the squares is set at random by Pro Tools.

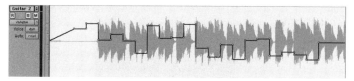

Figure 22-11

EDITING AUTOMATION

There are a number of ways to edit automation data in Pro Tools. Which one you use will depend on what you want to accomplish.

REDRAWING AUTOMATION

The fastest way to graphically edit automation is simply to draw over the old automation with the pencil. In this case, I've used the Pencil in Freehand mode to draw over the Random automation I did above.

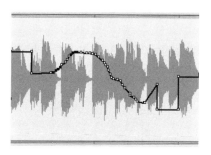

Figure 22-12

MOVING, ADDING, AND DELETING BREAKPOINTS

You can use the Grabber tool to select and drag a "breakpoint"—a junction in the automation line.

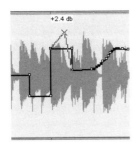

Figure 22-13

If you click with the Grabber or Pencil, you can add a new breakpoint. If you **Option-click** (Alt-click) with the Grabber or the Pencil, you can delete a breakpoint.

USING EDIT MENU COMMANDS

The Edit menu commands can be used to Cut, Copy, and Paste automation data on the same track or across to other tracks. Duplicate, Shift, and Repeat also work; in this case I've selected a range of automation using the Selector tool and repeated it four times.

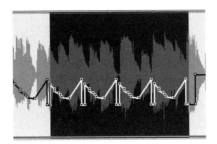

Figure 22-14

THINNING AUTOMATION

When you draw Freehand or write automation using a controller, Pro Tools may generate more automation data than it probably needs; each breakpoint sucks up some of the computer's memory and brain power, so it makes sense to use as few as possible. Often you can thin down the number of breakpoints in a curve without changing the response of the automation audibly. To do this, select the automation you want to thin out.

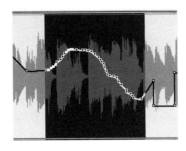

Figure 22-15

Go **Edit** → **Thin Automation,** or type **Option+ ⌘+T** (Alt+Ctrl+T). Pro Tools will remove a certain number of breakpoints, thinning out the automation density.

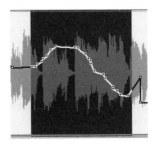

Figure 22-16

TRIMMING AUTOMATION

If you choose the Trimmer tool, you can use it to adjust automation data, but it doesn't shorten or lengthen the region the way it does with audio. Rather, the Trimmer can be used to raise or lower the level of a selected region of automation. Simply click and drag up or down with the Trimmer tool in your selection.

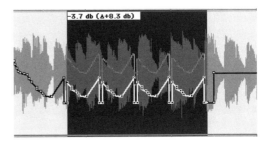

Figure 22-17

AUTOMATION AND GROUPED TRACKS

So what happens when you have tracks grouped, and you want to automate them? If there's existing automation when you create the group, that automation will remain in effect for each track. But if you create automation after the tracks are grouped, the same automation will be applied to all the tracks in the group. Hold down the **Ctrl** (Start) key to edit the automation on one grouped track without affecting the others in the group.

AUTOMATING SENDS

Automating send controls works the same as other track controls—the only difference is that you have to open the Send Output window for the send you want to automate. Then simply put the track into Auto Write (either on the track controls or on the Send window), press play, and move the send control you want to automate.

Try it: Add a Bus 1 send to the Snare track. The Send Output window will open. Select Auto Write on the Send Output window's automation selector.

Figure 22-18

Press play, and move the Send Output window's level fader. When you're finished, stop playback. Play the Session to see the automation work.

Once you have added a send to a track, its parameters will also show up in the Edit window, where you can draw and edit its automation data.

Figure 22-19

AUTOMATING PLUG-IN CONTROLS

Plug-in controls can be automated just like mix or send controls. But you have to enable the parameter you want to automate first. On the Tom 4 track, open the Long Delay II (mono) plug-in.

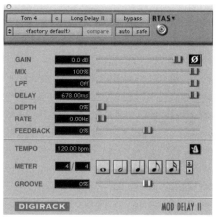

Figure 22-20

Click the "Auto" button to open the Plug-in Automation window.

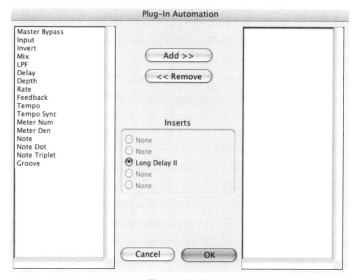

Figure 22-21

Choose "Delay" in the left-hand column, then click Add>> to move it to the right-hand column—any parameters you move to the right will be available for automating. Click OK. Put the track into Auto Write mode, press Play, and move the Delay control on the plug-in window using your mouse.

As with Sends, any parameters you have enabled for automating will show up in the Edit window, where you can draw or edit them.

Figure 22-22

PLUG-IN AUTOMATION SAFE

You can "lock" plug-in automation so that you don't accidentally overwrite it. This is done using the "Safe" button on the plug-in window. Note that Safe only protects the automation from being recorded over; you can still edit and delete the automation in the Edit window.

SUSPENDING AUTOMATION

You can globally suspend the ability of Pro Tools to write a type of automation data using the Show Automation Enable window. Simply de-select the type of automation you don't want written.

Figure 22-23

You can also suspend writing and playback for individual parameters in the Edit window. **⌘-click** (Ctrl-click) on the parameter name in the Track View to disable it. ↑**+⌘-click** (↑+Ctrl-click) to suspend all controls. **Option+⌘-click** (Alt+Ctrl-click) to suspend a type of control on all tracks.

DELETING AUTOMATION

To delete automation you can delete one breakpoint at a time, as described earlier. Or you can use the Edit menu Cut or Clear commands to delete a selection. To delete the automation for an entire track, select the entire track using the Selector tool, then press **Delete.**

twenty-three

MIXDOWN

There's only one thing left to do in our voyage through the audio portion of Pro Tools LE: final mixdown. Once the audio is recorded, edited, processed, mixed, and automated perfectly, we need to get it into a format that we can distribute to listeners, whether on CD, over the Internet, or by some other means. The format we need is final stereo audio. There are several ways we can accomplish this.

MIXING TO AN EXTERNAL RECORDER

If you have an external recorder, you can simply play the audio out of your Pro Tools interface into an external hardware recorder. You'll get best results if you use a digital recorder, connected digitally.

RECORDING TO UNUSED TRACKS

Another method for obtaining a final stereo mix is to record back into a stereo track in your Pro Tools Session. Open the CD-ROM Session "Chapter 23." *See Figure 23-1.*

Listen to the mix; it's the same excerpt we've been working on, fully automated and with plug-ins added—ready to mix down to stereo. To do this, create a new stereo track. Name it "MIX."

Assign the outputs of all the tracks to Bus 3-4. You can do this painfully, track by track, or to do it in one step, hold the **Option** (Alt) key and change any track's output to Bus 3-4; the rest of the tracks will change as well. In order to monitor, we'll listen to the output of the MIX audio track. Assign it to Analog 1-2, or whatever outputs are connected to your

speakers. Assign the Mix audio track input to Bus 3-4. *See Figure 23-2.*

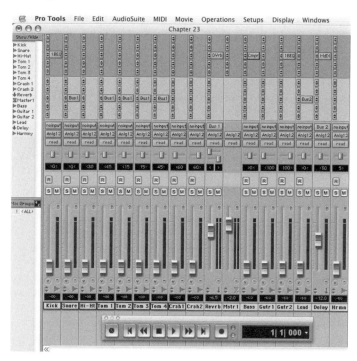

Figure 23-1

Figure 23-2

Record-enable the MIX track. Hit Record and Play; the mix will be recorded to the stereo MIX track. Be sure you let the track record for a few seconds after the music ends to allow time for the reverb tail to ring off.

When you're finished, switch over to the Edit window, and look at the results.

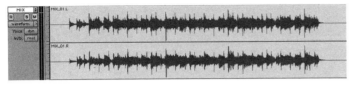

Figure 23-3

Solo the MIX track to listen to the results. Make sure that there is no distortion and that the reverb at the end isn't chopped off. The final stereo track is now ready to be loaded into a CD burning program, or to be ripped to MP3.

BOUNCE TO DISK

Before we begin the next method of doing final mixdown, go **File → Revert To Saved;** click "revert." This will take the Session back to the way it was when you first opened it.

The last method for creating a final mixdown is called Bounce to Disk. When you Bounce to Disk, the audio output from Pro Tools is recorded directly to a new audio file on the hard drive. To Bounce to Disk, go **File → Bounce to Disk...**

Figure 23-4

The Bounce to Disk window will open.

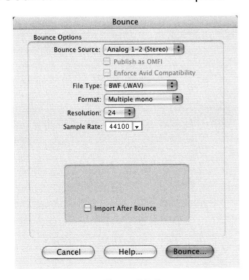

Figure 23-5

There are several parameters that need to be set here—although most of them will default to the correct settings.

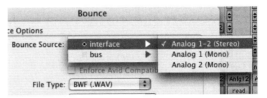

Figure 23-6

The Bounce Source menu sets where the signal that will be bounced comes from; generally you'll want this set to the hardware outputs that you are listening to.

Next, choose the File Type that you want the bounced file to use.

Figure 23-7

The Format menu sets how the bounced file will be saved; as a single mono file (not the way to go if you're bouncing a stereo mix), as two separate mono files (one for each side of the stereo pair), or as one stereo file. Choose the format type that's compatible with your CD burning software or your MP3 ripper.

Figure 23-8

Now set the resolution for your bounced file. If your file will ultimately end up on a CD, choose 16-bit, since that's the resolution for that medium.

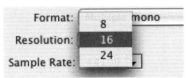

Figure 23-9

Dither

When you change the resolution of audio, say, from 24 to 16 bits, those extra eight bits are truncated—chopped off. This can sometimes result in audible degradation of the sound quality, depending on the type of material you're working with.

Generally, you're best off to insert a dither plug-in on the Pro Tools mixer output (the Master Fader, in this case) to help maintain the best audio quality. Dither is very low-level random noise that helps cover up the digital problems that can result when converting from 24- to 16-bit—or any time you're going from higher to lower resolution.

Pro Tools LE includes two dither plug-ins: Dither and POWr Dither.

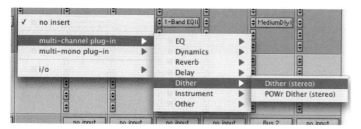

Figure 23-10

There are only two controls on a Dither plug-in: Bit resolution and noise-shaping.

Figure 23-11

Noise-shaping is filtering that can help make the dither process less audible. I recommend experi-menting with the Dither plug-ins to see which one, and which noise-shaping settings, you prefer.

Set the sample rate next. For CD, choose 44.1kHz.

Figure 23-12

If you've elected to change the resolution of your file—say from 24-bit to 16-bit for use on CD, or if you're changing the sample rate of your file, you'll be given the option to make the change either during the bounce or after the bounce is completed. Converting after the bounce is the best sounding option, but if you're in a hurry, you can choose to convert during the bounce.

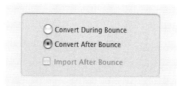

Figure 23-13

If you're converting the sample rate of your session as part of your bounce, another option will appear that offers varying conversion quality. Higher quality takes longer, but sounds noticeably better.

Figure 23-14

If you're not converting sample rate or resolution during the bounce, you'll be given the option to automatically import the audio files resulting from the bounce back into the Session so that you can listen to them immediately.

Figure 23-15

If you're completely confused, there's a Help button at the bottom of the window that will open a screen describing the Bounce to Disk features. Otherwise, once you're ready, click Bounce...

The "Save" window will open. Name the file, and choose where you want Pro Tools to store it.

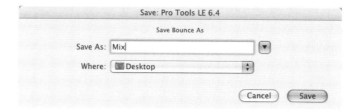

Figure 23-16

The Session will play, and a progress box will open, counting down as the bounce is being accom-plished. If for some reason you want to stop the bounce process, type ⌘+. (Ctrl+.) or hit the **Escape** key. *See Figure 23-17.*

When the bounce is finished, the resulting audio file(s) will appear where you directed that they be saved. You can now import them into your CD burning program, rip them to MP3, or import them back into Pro Tools. *See Figure 23-18.*

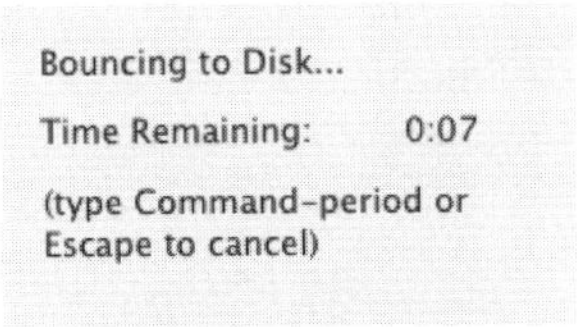

Figure 23-17

Mix.R.wav

Figure 23-18

to Disk, you probably noticed that the reverb tail was chopped off. To allow time for the reverb tail, use the Selector to make a selection that extends past the end of the longest track by enough time to let the tail ring out.

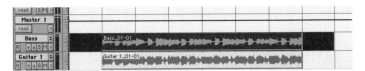

Figure 23-19

ALLOWING FOR REVERB

Normally the bounced audio that results from Bounce to Disk is as long as the longest track in the Session. Often, however, reverb or some other sound will ring on past the end of the longest track—and that's the case with our Session here. If you listened to the bounced audio that resulted from our Bounce

USING BOUNCE TO DISK TO SUBMIX

The Bounce to Disk command can also be used to create a submix. You create the submix in exactly the same way; just mute the tracks that you don't want to be part of the submix. To submix just part of a track by bouncing, select the area you want bounced with the Selector tool, then Bounce to Disk

PART SEVEN

MIDI to the Max

twenty-four

MIDI TRACKS

So you've made it through six parts of this book—feeling pretty good about yourself? You should—we've covered a ton of ground, working our way through many of Pro Tools LE's audio recording, editing, and mixing features. Now we're ready to embark on the last part of our journey to Pro Tools mastery: MIDI.

Far from a topic of deepest mystery, MIDI (Musical Instrument Digital Interface) is a tool that we can use to take our songs beyond where they can go through recording and editing of acoustic sounds. We had a short introduction to MIDI in Chapter Three—Basic Pro Tools Concepts.

MIDI is a communication standard. It allows various kinds of devices to talk to one another. For example, one keyboard can be used to play the sounds in another keyboard. You can use controls—such as a pitchbend wheel or volume knob—in one keyboard to change the sound in another. You can call up presets on one effects box from the front panel of a second.

The cool part is that Pro Tools LE can record MIDI messages in regions on MIDI tracks and play them back—and it can edit them in a variety of ways. This process is called "sequencing." You can enter notes using the Pencil tool, cut/copy/paste them, shift them in time or pitch, correct their rhythms (quantize), and more.

The Key to MIDI
There is one thing that you must remember when dealing with MIDI: MIDI is not audio. MIDI is instructions that tell a synthesizer or sampler what audio to play. So a MIDI cable or MIDI track does not carry audio. It carries messages that tell an instrument what notes to play.

GETTING STARTED

We hooked up our MIDI equipment back in Chapter 7, Making Connections. Remember that you must connect both the audio and MIDI connections from your keyboards and modules in order to hear them.

Create a new Session called "MIDI Recording." On the Mac, even though the wires are all connected properly, you still have to let your computer and Pro Tools know what you have connected. Under OS X, this is done using the AudioMIDI Setup utility. You can access this from within Pro Tools by going **Setups → Edit MIDI Studio Setup...**

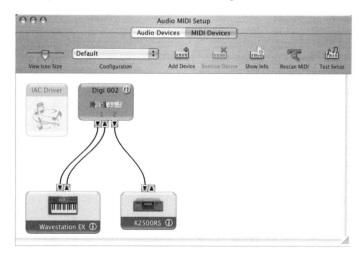

Figure 24-1

On the Mac, you also must make sure that the inputs are enabled in Pro Tools LE. You can do this by going **MIDI → Input Devices…,** then making sure that there is a check beside your input device's name. In my case, the Wavestation EX is my MIDI input device.

The other four inputs, Pro Tools Input 1-4, are "virtual" software inputs that can be used to receive MIDI messages from other music software running on your computer. (We'll learn more about these inputs in Chapter 27, Going Soft.)

Figure 24-2

Under Windows XP, the MIDI drivers will show up in the right place and Pro Tools will know what it is doing. You don't have to configure anything.

One last thing to set up before we get started: If your MIDI keyboard has built-in sounds, you'll want to set it up so that those sounds are only triggered via MIDI, not from the keyboard itself. To do this, look for a way to set "Local Off" in your keyboard (if you can't find this setting, consult the keyboard's manual). Once you have your keyboard set for local off, then select **MIDI → MIDI Thru…** in Pro Tools.

With MIDI Thru set to "on," MIDI messages will come out of your keyboard, go through Pro Tools, come back out, and be fed to your keyboard to play its sounds. If local off isn't set in your keyboard, its sounds will be played twice: once by the keyboard, once via MIDI—this can create some problems. With local off set, and MIDI Thru selected, the sounds will only be played via MIDI.

There are a couple of optional settings you can make; Pro Tools has a powerful input filter that can prevent unnecessary information from being recorded. Go **MIDI → Input Filter…** to open the window for this function.

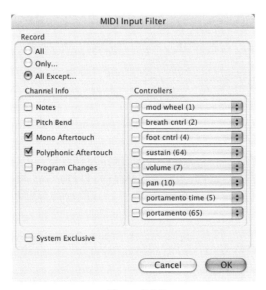

Figure 24-3

With this window, you can choose which types of MIDI messages will be recorded in Pro Tools, and which will be filtered out. Unless you have a specific reason for filtering a type of message, the default settings should be fine.

You can also quantize MIDI notes—correct the rhythm of the notes—as they're being recorded. Go **MIDI → Input Quantize…** to open the Input Quantize dialog.

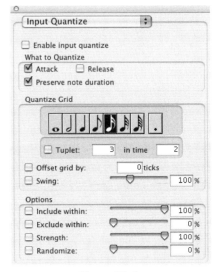

Figure 24-4

In most cases, you're better off to quantize after the fact—after the MIDI tracks are recorded. This is because Input Quantization is a destructive process: Once you've input-quantized your playing, you can't go back. (Okay, there is a sneaky way to go back, which we'll learn next chapter.) Regular (after the fact) quantizing is non-destructive, so generally it's a safer way to work. We'll cover the various quantization parameters and settings in the next chapter, Chapter 25, MIDI Editing. The parameters and settings are the same for both input and regular quantizing.

SETTING UP MIDI TRACKS

Working with MIDI tracks is similar to working with audio tracks. Begin by creating a new track: go **File →New Track...**or type ⇧+⌘+**N**(⇧+Ctrl+N). Set the dialog for one new MIDI track.

Figure 24-5

Click Create. A new MIDI track will appear in the Session. Rename it if you like. As with Audio Tracks, the track name will be given to any regions that are recorded on that track.

ASSIGNING INPUTS

Just as with an audio track, you must set the input source for your MIDI track before you can record on it. The track will default to "All" inputs, which should work fine for most things. If you do need to set the track to a specific input source, pull down the input selector, and choose the one you want.

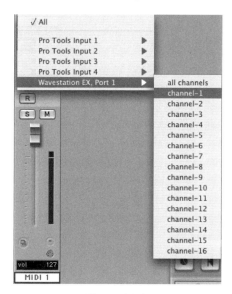

Figure 24-6

ASSIGNING OUTPUTS

You'll also need to set the MIDI output that the track will be feeding. Pull down the output selector and choose the device/port and channel you want to send MIDI to.

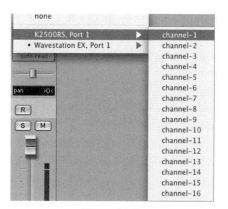

Figure 24-7

If you want the track to feed more than one channel, **Ctrl-click** (Start-click) the MIDI Output Selector and choose additional devices/channels. This is an easy way to layer together MIDI instruments, should you need to do so.

BRINGING MIDI DEVICES INTO PRO TOOLS

Depending on your audio interface and how you have things set up, you may want to monitor your keyboards/synths/samplers through Pro Tools. If you're just going to be monitoring the instruments without recording them to audio tracks, you can use Aux Inputs. Otherwise, if you want to record the output of the MIDI gear, route them into audio tracks.

I've got two MIDI instruments connected to my Digi 002, a Korg Wavestation and a Kurzweil K2500 module. In order to monitor them, I set up two stereo Aux Inputs that match the hardware inputs that they're connected to.

Figure 24-8

If you decide to monitor your MIDI gear through Pro Tools in this fashion, I highly recommend turning on low-latency monitoring. (Unless you're on an Mbox, which doesn't support low-latency monitoring. On Mbox, use the front-panel Mix knob to set up delay-free monitoring.) Go **Operations → Low Latency Monitoring** to turn on this function. (Remember that you can't use the Click—or any other plug-ins—while in Low Latency Mode.)

RECORDING A TRACK

Recording a MIDI track is done in the same way as recording an Audio track. Set up a click if you want. Record-enable (arm) the track.

Figure 24-9

Once the track is armed, you'll be able to play your MIDI keyboard; the device/channel that's selected as the MIDI output for the track will sound, and you should see activity on the MIDI channel's meter.

When you're ready, put Pro Tools into record, just as you did with audio tracks: click Record and Play, hit ⌘+spacebar (Ctrl+spacebar), or press F12.

As with audio tracks, you can undo a MIDI recording, or discard the take completely by typing ⌘+. (Ctrl+.) to stop recording and delete the recorded region. In the Edit window, MIDI regions appear in the MIDI Regions List, at the lower right of the window.

Anatomy of a MIDI Note

After recording a MIDI track, switch to the Edit window.

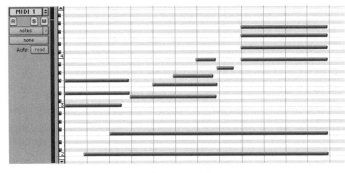

Figure 24-10

Each MIDI note that you record appears as a bar stretching across the track. The length of the bar indicates the duration of the note. The pitch of the note is shown by the bar's vertical position relative to the little keyboard to the right of the track. Stacked bars indicate chords.

Switch to velocity view for the track.

Figure 24-11

You'll be able to see how hard each key was pressed. The taller the "stem" from the beginning of each note, the harded it was played. More than one diamond on a stem indicates a chord where notes were played simultaneously.

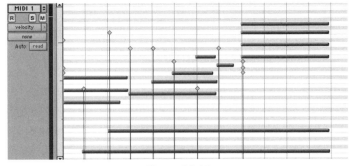

Figure 24-12

Switch the track back to notes view when you're finished checking out the velocities.

WAIT FOR NOTE

If you're recording yourself, Pro Tools' "Wait for Note" function can come in very handy. Turn this feature on by clicking the button with the MIDI connector/pause icon on it, at the upper left of the MIDI controls on the Transport window.

Figure 24-13

When you press Record and Play, Pro Tools will go into record-ready—the record button will flash, the click will sound—but won't actually begin recording until the first MIDI note is received. Any countoff or pre-roll you have set up will be disabled when you use Wait for Note.

MIDI MERGE

There are two modes for recording MIDI. These are

selected using the MIDI Merge button on the Transport window.

Figure 24-14

When the MIDI Merge button isn't selected (not highlighted), MIDI data recorded to a track will replace any existing MIDI data on the track. With MIDI Merge selected (highlighted), incoming MIDI data will be mixed with any existing MIDI data on the track. This allows you to easily overdub more MIDI information on the same track.

PUNCH IN/OUT

You can punch in on MIDI tracks, just as with audio tracks. There's no need for QuickPunch, since you can drop in and out of record on a MIDI track at any time, without selecting a region. (You can still make a selection to create a range to punch in on if you like, with pre-roll and post-roll, just as with audio tracks.)

If MIDI Merge isn't selected, the new punched-in data will replace the existing data. If MIDI Merge is selected, the new data will be mixed with the old at the point of the punch.

LOOP RECORDING

There are two modes for loop recording: With MIDI Merge unselected, loop recording works in exactly the fashion it does with audio tracks. Each pass through the loop range is recorded to a separate region, resulting in multiple takes. As with audio loop recording, you can switch among the takes by ⌘-**clicking** (Ctrl+clicking) with the Selector tool at the beginning of the loop selection.

With the MIDI Merge button selected, loop recording works "drum machine" style, where each pass through the loop range is mixed in on top of the previous passes. The end result is one single region containing the data from all the passes.

This is similar to how a drum machine works, where recording cycles through a drum pattern. On the first pass through, kick drum might be recorded. On the second pass, snare drum. On the third, hi-hat, and so on, until the drum pattern is complete.

ART LESSONS

There's another way to enter MIDI notes into a track:

You can draw them in using the Pencil tool. Switch to the Edit window. Create a MIDI track—make it Large or Jumbo in height, and zoom in so that the screen shows a couple of measures. Select the Pencil tool.

If you click in the track and immediately release, a note will appear, at the length set by the Grid menu. So if the Grid is set for quarter-notes, clicking will place notes that are a quarter note in length.

If you click and drag, the note length will be set by how far you drag in the track (either longer or shorter than the Grid length works). You can also determine the note length by holding down the Pencil button, and selecting "Custom Note Duration."

Figure 24-15

A button with a note icon will appear below the Pencil tool selector. If you click and hold this button, you can select rhythmic values for the notes you draw.

Figure 24-16

When using Custom Note Durations, clicking and releasing will result in notes of the length set by the Custom Note Duration. Clicking and dragging allows you to individually set the length of each note.

How the notes are placed depends on the Edit Mode you're in. Using Shuffle, Slip, or Spot Mode, you can place a note wherever you like. In Grid Mode, notes will begin at grid points, and extend for as long as is set in the Custom Note Duration or the Grid menu, if you're not using Custom Note Durations.

You can scroll to higher and lower pitches using the small arrows at the top of the track's keyboard.

IMPORTING

Don't play keyboards and can't draw to save your life? No worries, you can still get MIDI into Pro Tools—by importing it. Pro Tools supports Standard MIDI Files, a.k.a. SMFs. This file format is a standardized way to save a MIDI sequence so that it can be imported and opened in almost any MIDI-capable computer-sequencing program.

There are two ways to import Standard MIDI Files into Pro Tools. The first uses the MIDI Regions List in the Edit window. Create a new Session in Pro Tools, title it "MIDI File Import."

In the Edit window, go **MIDI Regions List → Import MIDI...** or type **Option+⌘+I** (Ctrl+Alt+I)

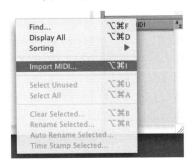

Figure 24-17

Find and open the file "Chapter 24.mid" from the CD-ROM. (Standard MIDI Files can be identified by their .mid extension.) The tracks within the file will appear as regions in the MIDI Regions List.

Figure 24-18

Create three new MIDI tracks named "Drums," "Bass," and "Organ." Drag the matching regions into those tracks. You may need to scroll the track pitches up or down and zoom in to see the notes on the tracks. To play the tracks, you'll need to assign their outputs to MIDI instruments set for sounds that match the track names.

There is a second way to import MIDI tracks into Pro Tools. Close the MIDI Import Session you created—save it first, if you like. Create a new Session, titled, "MIDI Import #2." Go **File → Import MIDI to Track...** Navigate to the "Chapter 24.mid" file we loaded above.

Figure 24-19

This time we also have to tell Pro Tools whether it should take the tempo from the Standard MIDI File or use the tempo that is set in the Session. If you're importing the MIDI tracks into an existing Session that already has a specific tempo, select "use Existing Tempo from Session." If you've created a new Session that you're importing to, and don't have a tempo set yet, select "Import Tempo from MIDI File." Since we're creating a new Session, select "Import Tempo from MIDI File."

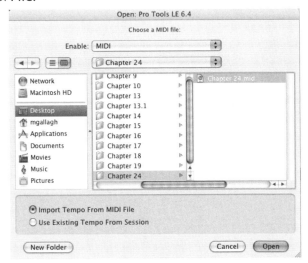

Figure 24-20

Click Open. The Standard MIDI File tracks will be imported as regions to the MIDI Regions List, and tracks with those regions already in place will be automatically created—pretty cool! All you have to do is assign the MIDI track outputs to the instruments of your choice, and you're rockin'.

EXPORTING

You can also export the MIDI tracks you create in Pro Tools as a Standard MIDI File for use in another program. To do so, go **File → Export MIDI...** A dialog will open where you can name the file, choose where it will be saved, and select either Type 0—where all MIDI channels are stored in one track—or Type 1—where each channel has its own track—format for the Standard MIDI File. Either type is generally acceptable, I usually use Type 1, just to keep the tracks separated. Pro Tools can import either format.

Figure 24-21

Click Save, and the file will be created at the location you specified.

Figure 24-22

The Standard MIDI File can now be opened in whatever application you choose to use.

twenty-five

MIDI EDITING

Now that we've learned how to get MIDI information into Pro Tools, let's learn how to slice, dice, and otherwise bend the data to our wills. Open up the CD-ROM Session "Chapter 25." You'll need to assign the track outputs to a MIDI instrument/port/channel in order to see and hear the Session play.

BEEN THERE, DONE THAT

A lot of what we need to learn is already residing comfortably in our brains: Most of the commands from the Edit menu we discussed in Chapter 19, Going Deeper can be applied to MIDI regions. Select the Drums region.

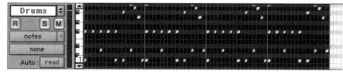

Figure 25-1

If you pull down the Edit menu, you'll see that most of the commands can be used: Cut, Copy, Clear, Duplicate, Repeat, Shift, Capture Region, Separate Region, Heal Separation, Quantize Regions, Mute/Unmute Region, Lock/Unlock Region, Consolidate Selection, Identify Sync Point, Identify Beat, Insert Silence, all work the same on MIDI regions as they do on audio regions.

Paste works the same as with audio; the newly pasted MIDI notes replace the old. There's also a second kind of paste function: Merge Paste. Using this command, the pasted MIDI data is mixed in with the existing MIDI data. Try it: Using the Selector tool, select the third measure of the Bass track.

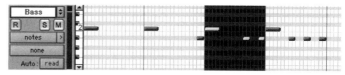

Figure 25-2

Copy the selection. Select the second measure of the Drums track, and go **Edit → Merge Paste,** or type **Option+M** (Start+M). The copied notes from the Bass track will be mixed in with the Drums notes. (The newly merge-pasted notes will play on whatever instrument is assigned to the track they're pasted to, in this case drums.)

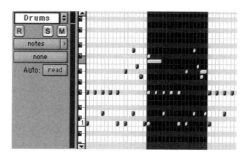

Figure 25-3

THE EDIT TOOLS

So we already know quite a bit about editing MIDI information. But remember that MIDI is simply information: notes and automation, not actually audio. That means that it's more malleable than audio. The tools can all be used; with the Zoomer you can zoom in, of course, both vertically and horizontally.

You can use the Trim tool to change the length of the note—either at the beginning or end of the note.

The Selector tool can be used to select a range of notes (but you already knew that).

The Grabber tool can be used to drag a vertical and/or horizontal selection around notes. If you position the Grabber over a note, it will change to a hand with a finger extended. You can use this hand to drag notes vertically to change their pitch or horizontally to change their position in time on the track.

MOVING RIGHT ALONG

There's even more that we can do with MIDI editing—in fact, there's an entire Pro Tools menu devoted to specialized MIDI editing functions.

QUANTIZE

One of the most powerful tools for MIDI editing is quantizing, or rhythmically correcting note positions in a selection. Note that MIDI Quantize isn't quite the same as Quantize Regions in the Edit menu. Quantize Regions moves the start or sync point of a region to a grid point; the relative rhythmic relationships of the notes within the region remain the same. With MIDI Quantize, individual notes are adjusted to correct their timing or to achieve a particular rhythmic feel.

Zoom in on the Organ track. Switch to Grid mode. You'll see that many of the notes on the track are slightly out of time.

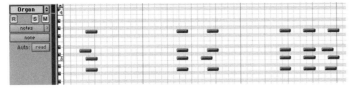

Figure 25-4

Using the Selector or Grabber tool, select the notes on the Organ track. Go **MIDI → Quantize...** or press **Option+0** (Start+0)—that's a zero, not an "O." The Quantize window will open. *See Figure 25-5.*

In the top of the window is the section where you set what will be quantized; you can affect the attack time of notes, the release time of notes, the duration of the notes, or all three. Most often you'll be quantizing the attacks and note durations, but you may find instances where you want to fix the release times of notes.

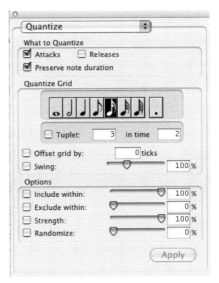

Figure 25-5

Below this is the Quantize Grid, which sets the rhythmic grid that the notes will be corrected to; you can use straight rhythmic values, tuplets, or offset, which slips the grid over by a number of ticks. (A "tick" is the smallest MIDI rhythmic value; analogous to a sample in audio timing. In Pro Tools, a quarter note is equal to 960 ticks.)

Swing can also be added; this simulates the human ability to "swing" a rhythm. At 0%, no swing is added. 100% swing will result in triplets.

There are four other options at the bottom of the window. When you select "Include Within," only notes that fall within a certain area around the Quantize Grid will be quantized. Anything too far away will be ignored. The percentage control determines how wide the inclusion range is. "Exclude Within" works the opposite way. Notes within a certain range of the grid aren't affected while those outside the range will be quantized.

"Strength" determines how much the notes will be quantized. At 100%, the notes will be shifted all the way to the nearest grid point. At lower strengths, notes will only be moved partway, preserving some of the feel of the original performance.

"Randomize" moves notes forward or backward in time by a random amount. While in some cases this can result in more natural feel, other times it simply loosens the feel of the passage.

For our example here, set the window so attacks and durations are quantized to 16th-notes. Nothing else should be selected. When you're ready, click Apply. The rhythm for the notes will be corrected to the nearest 16th-note.

Figure 25-6

A word to the wise: Too much quantizing will result in a rigid, mechanical feel. To preserve the feel of a performance while correcting the rhythm, use Exclude Within and Include Within, and especially the Strength function to selectively tighten things up.

When you're finished quantizing our example, undo to return the track to its original state. If you've gone too far to undo, go **File → Revert to Saved...** to return the file to where it was when it was opened.

GROOVE QUANTIZE

Quantization allows you to correct the timing of a performance, and even add swing, but it can't do much to enhance the "feel" of a MIDI passage. Groove Quantize, on the other hand, is all about feel. A groove template, which contains the rhythmic feel extracted from a recorded performance, is applied to your MIDI notes—think of it as a map for the feel of a performance that can be applied to another performance.

Select the notes in the Drums track. Open the Groove Quantize window by going **MIDI → Groove Quantize...**

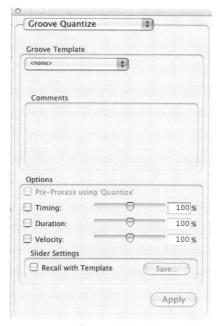

Figure 25-7

You'll need to pull down the Groove Template menu to select a Groove Template. Go **Groove Template → Feel Injector Templates → 11 FeelInjector_16thTrShfl** to pull up a 16th-note triplet shuffle template.

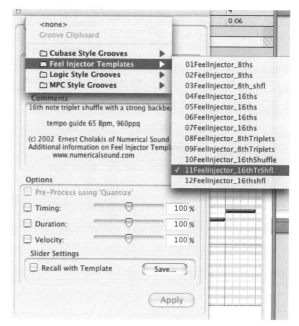

Figure 25-8

You can apply the template to quantize note timing, duration, velocity, or a combination of those parameters. 0% on the sliders makes for no change in these parameters, 100% applies the template full strength, and 200% doubles the strength of the template.

To apply the template to our drum track, select Timing; set the percentage slider to 100%. Click Apply.

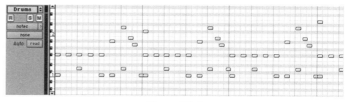

Figure 25-9

You'll see that some notes are moved slightly earlier in time, others are shifted a bit later—Groove Quantize is changing our notes to match the feel of the template.

RESTORE PERFORMANCE

This function puts the selected MIDI notes back to their original positions—where they were when they were recorded or entered with the Pencil. You can restore a note's original timing, duration, velocity, or pitch. Select the drum notes you just processed with Groove Quantize. Go **MIDI → Restore Performance...**

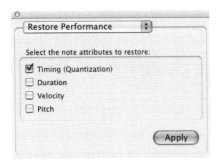

Figure 25-10

Select Timing (Quantization) and click Apply. The notes will return to their original positions. Restore Performance can also be used to remove Input Quantization—this is the only way that a performance recorded with Input Quantization can be returned to the way it was originally played.

FLATTEN PERFORMANCE
The Flatten Performance function creates a new point that the "Restore Performance" command will return the selection to—it establishes the current state as the "original" state for the data. Go **MIDI** → **Flatten Performance...** to apply this command.

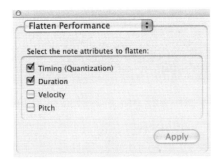

Figure 25-11

As with Restore Performance, you can choose to "flatten" timing, duration, velocity, pitch, or any combination of those parameters. Be absolutely sure before you use it—there's no undo for this one!

CHANGE VELOCITY
The cleverly named "Change Velocity" function processes the velocity of MIDI notes in various ways. Select the notes on the Bass track. Change the track so that you're viewing velocities.

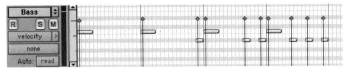

Figure 25-12

Go **MIDI** → **Change Velocity...** to open the Change Velocity window.

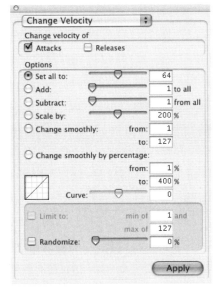

Figure 25-13

You can process the velocities of the selected notes in several ways. Click "Set all to" and move the slider to or enter 50 in the value field. Click Apply. The Bass track's velocities will all change to the same value: 50 (the velocity stems in the track will become shorter).

Select "Add" and move the slider or set the value to 40. Click Apply. 40 will be added to all the notes' velocities. (The stems will get taller.)

Select "Subtract" enter 40 and click Apply. The stems will all drop by 40.

Select "Scale by." Set it to 150% and click Apply. The velocities will all be multiplied by 150%. Multiply by less than 100%, and the velocities will be scaled down by that amount. Scaling is useful if you want to preserve the relative relationship of velocity values between notes.

Select "Change Smoothly." Make the "from" value 20, the "to" value 100. Click Apply. The velocities of the notes will change linearly from 20 to 100 over the course of the selection. You can also make a downward slope by making the "from" value greater than the "to" value.

"Change Smoothly by Percentage" applies a curve to the note velocities. Before you try this, go back and use the "Set all to" command to make all the velocities equal to 50, just to give us room to work. Now select "Change smoothly by percentage." Set "from" to 50%, "to" to 200%; make the curve equal to 50. Click Apply to process the velocities with the curve. Using Change Smoothly by Percentage, the velocity values will change in a concave or convex curve, depending on whether the curve value is a positive or negative number.

You can set limits on the softest and hardest values when using any of the above methods for processing velocity. You can randomize the values as well. The higher the randomize percentage, the more randomize will affect the values. For example, go back and set up "Set all to" to 50 again. This time, select Randomize, and enter a value of 15%. Instead of velocities of 50 across the board, you'll get random deviations of up to 15% from 50 for the track's velocity values.

CHANGE DURATION

To activate the Change Duration function, go **MIDI → Change Duration...**

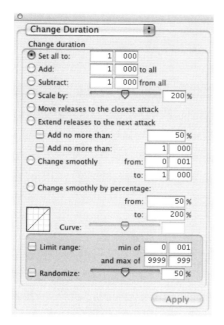

Figure 25-14

Looks very similar to the Change Velocity window, doesn't it? This time we're processing the length of notes. You can set all durations to the same length, add to or subtract from all the durations, scale, change smoothly, change smoothly by percentage, limit durations, and randomize them.

Two other processes are new in this window: "Move releases to the closest attack" moves the ends of notes to the nearest note beginning

"Extend releases to the next attack" extends the notes' duration to the beginning (attack) of the next note. You can specify the maximum amount that is added to the notes, in percentages or exact lengths.

TRANSPOSE

For changing the pitch of an entire track or a large selection of notes, Pro Tools' Transpose function is the way to go. To open the Transpose window, go **MIDI → Transpose...** or press **Option+T** (Alt+T).

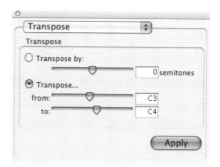

Figure 25-15

You can choose to transpose by adding or subtracting semitones from each pitch—for example, add two semitones to each pitch—or you can transpose up or down by interval. You set the interval by specifying a base (from) note, then the "to" note above or below that defines the interval.

For example, if the "from" note is *C3*, and the "to" note is *A3*, the interval will be a major 6th up—each pitch will be raised by that interval. If the "to" note was an *A2*, on the other hand, the interval would be a minor 3rd down; each note would be transposed down by that amount. Try it; transpose the Bass track down by a major 4th. (Hint: *C3* to *G2* is a major 4th interval down.)

Another way to think of this is transposing to a new key; say from A to D. Whatever "from" note you enter is the original key, the "to" note is the destination key.

SELECT NOTES

You can use the Selector and Grabber tools to select MIDI notes on a track—works fine. But if you want to select a specific note or range of notes, the "Select Notes" function is the one you want. Let's try an example. First you have to select a range of notes or a region. Go to the Drums track, and use the Selector tool to select all its notes.

Go **MIDI → Select Notes...** or type **Option+P** (Alt+P).

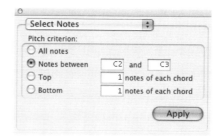

Figure 25-16

We're going to select just the closed hi-hat note,

which is *Fs1*. In the Select Notes window, click "Notes between." Enter *F1* and *G1*. (You could actually enter *Fs1* and *Fs1* to select just that one pitch.) Click Apply. All the notes outside the range you entered will be deselected. Just the *Fs1* notes will be left selected. You can now choose another MIDI editing process, such as Transpose, Change Velocity, or whatever, and apply it to the hi-hat notes.

Other options in the Select Notes window allow you to choose all notes, or to just select the bottom or top notes in each chord.

SPLIT NOTES

The Split Notes function works exactly the same as Select Notes, but with a twist: Cutting or copying the selected notes. Select all the notes on the Drums track again. Go **MIDI → Split Notes...** or type **Option+Y** (Alt+Y).

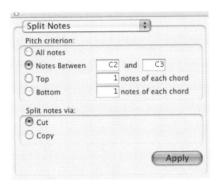

Figure 25-17

Set the window up the same as you did the Select Notes window: Select "Notes between" and enter *F1* and *G1*. (Again you could enter *Fs1* and *Fs1* to select just that one pitch.) Select Cut, then click Apply. This time, instead of selecting the hi-hat note, the hi-hat note *(Fs1)* will be cut. You could now paste or merge paste the hi-hat notes at a different time in this track, or onto a completely different track.

THE MIDI EVENT LIST

If you want to get exact in your work on MIDI data, then Pro Tools LE has a window you should check out: The MIDI Event List. To open the MIDI Event List, go **Windows → Show MIDI Event List** or type **Option+=** (Alt+=). If you have a specific track that you want to examine, **Ctrl+double-click** (Start+ double-click) on the track name. The track you click on will open in the MIDI Event List window. *See Figure 25-18.*

The menu at the upper left selects that track

you're viewing. Pull it down to choose the Bass track. *See Figure 25-19.*

Figure 25-18

Figure 25-19

The columns in the main part of the window show the MIDI events—in this case, all we have are notes, but if there were pitchbend, mod wheel, sustain pedal, or any other events, they'd all show up here.

The Start column shows when the event begins—how it reads depends on what the Main Counter is set to show: Bars:beats, Min:Secs, or Samples.

The Event column displays the types of events (in this case, the little note symbol indicates a MIDI note), to the right is the pitch of the note, then the velocity, and release velocity—not many synths or samplers support release velocity, but it is recorded and displayed nonetheless.

The Length/Info column shows the duration for the note.

If you play the track with the MIDI Event List open, a blue arrow will indicate the current event.

Start	Event			length/info
0:00.000	♩ C2	80	64	0:00.500
→ 0:02.000	♩ C2	80	64	0:00.500
0:03.750	♩ Bb1	80	64	0:00.250
0:04.000	♩ C2	80	64	0:00.500

Figure 25-20

You can click, drag, and shift-click to select events in the List. *See Figure 25-21.*

Once the events are selected you can edit and

process them using the functions in the Edit and MIDI menus—cut/copy/paste, transpose, etc. You can also double-click a value in a column to edit it directly; you can type in a new value or drag the mouse to change the value. *See Figure 25-22.*

	0:02.000	♩	C2	80	64	0:00.500
→	0:03.750	♩	Bb1	80	64	0:00.250
	0:04.000	♩	C2	80	64	0:00.500
	0:05.250	♩	Bb1	80	64	0:00.250
	0:05.750	♩	Bb1	80	64	0:00.250
	0:06.000	♩	C2	80	64	0:00.500
	0:06.750	♩	Bb1	80	64	0:00.250

Figure 25-21

	0:05.250	♩	Bb1	80	64	0:00.250
→	0:05.750	♩	Bb1	80	64	0:00.250
	0:06.000	♩	C2	80	64	0:00.500
	0:06.750	♩	Bb1	80	64	0:00.250
	0:07.250	♩	Bb1	80	64	0:00.250

Figure 25-22

OPTIONS

Back at the top of the window, the Options menu lets you change a variety of settings.

Figure 25-23

If you go **Options** → **Show Sub Counter** a second time column will appear under Start; this column shows the time relative to the Sub Counter.

Figure 25-24

If you go **Options** → **Go To...** or type ⌘+G (Ctrl+G), the Go To Dialog window will open.

Figure 25-25

Enter a time in the field and click OK. The cursor/current event will jump to the time you entered—if you hit Play, that's where Pro Tools will start playback.

The next three items set how the MIDI Event List scrolls; generally you'll want Page Scroll During Playback and Scroll During Edit Selection to be checked; that way, the Event List will keep current with the locations of playback and selections in the Edit window.

You can switch so that the Length/Info column displays note end times instead of duration.

The next three items have to do with where events will be inserted using the Insert menu—more on the Insert menu below. Events can be inserted at the Edit insertion point, at the playback location in realtime, or at the playback location using the grid. Generally you'll leave this set to Insert At Edit Location.

At the bottom of this menu is the MIDI Event List View Filter. Go **Options** → **View Filter...** or type ⌘+F (Ctrl+F).

Figure 25-26

The View Filter lets you decide what kinds of events will be displayed in the MIDI Event List. You can choose to view all types of events, only those selected in the lower part of the window, or all events except those selected in the window.

INSERTING EVENTS

The menu at the upper-right of the MIDI Event List allows you to insert MIDI events into the selected track. Pull down the menu.

Figure 25-27

You can insert notes, pitch bend messages, MIDI volume and pan, aftertouch, program changes, and controllers. Try it: Go **Insert** → **Note** or type ⌘+N (Ctrl+N).

Figure 25-28

A line for a new note will appear in the Event List; you set the location of the note, the pitch, the velocity and release velocity, and duration.

Once you've inserted an event type, you can go **Insert** → **Another [event type]** or type ⌘+M (Ctrl+M) to insert another event of the same type into the track.

twenty-six

TAKE CONTROL

There's more to MIDI than just MIDI notes and their velocities. MIDI channels in the Mix window can send volume and pan automation. Keyboards and other controllers can send other types of MIDI information, such as pitchbend, modulation wheel, aftertouch, sustain pedal, and more—you can also enter those types of data directly into the Edit window tracks. You can change the patch and patch banks on your MIDI gear from Pro Tools. And, of course, you can easily edit any of those kinds of data. In short, you can use MIDI via Pro Tools to take complete control over all your MIDI keyboards, modules, and MIDI-compatible effects processors, as well as hardware mixers, if they support MIDI automation (as many digital models do).

MIDI AUTOMATION

The simplest form of MIDI automation is to write automation for a MIDI track's volume fader, pan control, and mute button—this works almost exactly the same way as it does with audio tracks; the biggest difference is that the automation data you record is sent out via MIDI.

Open the CD-ROM Session "Chapter 26." Assign the MIDI output for the track "MIDI 1" to a MIDI device that's connected to your Pro Tools rig. Play the track; it's a simple major scale in C.

To automate the MIDI volume for the track, go to the Mix window, select Auto Write for the track, hit Play, and move the fader. (With MIDI, full volume is with the fader all the way to top, which sends a value

of 127.) Play the Session to see the results. Check it out in the Edit window, if you like, by choosing Volume in the track's View Selector.

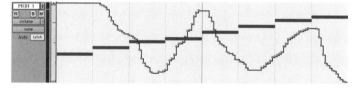

Figure 26-1

Back in the Mix window, try the same thing with MIDI pan. (Your MIDI keyboard or module may or may not support MIDI pan, but you can still write it into the track.) Leave the track in Auto Touch, or switch it to Auto Latch mode. Hit Play, move the pan control. When you stop and play back the Session, both the volume fader and the pan control should be moving. Check it out in the Edit window by choosing Pan in the View Selector.

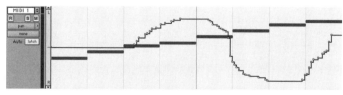

Figure 26-2

CONTINUOUS CONTROLLERS

MIDI Volume and Pan are examples of a type of MIDI message called a "continuous controller." The MIDI specification supports a total of 128 continuous controllers (numbered 0-127), which can be assigned to control parameters in MIDI gear. Some continuous controllers are by default assigned to things like volume, pan, and modulation wheel (although they can be re-assigned in your MIDI gear if you like). Others "float" and are used for whatever control applications are needed. Two other messages, pitchbend and aftertouch, technically aren't considered continuous controllers, although in practice they work in pretty much the same way. In Pro Tools we can record, insert, and edit any of these messages.

INSERTING CONTINUOUS CONTROLLERS

We can use the MIDI Event List to insert continuous controllers into a track. Open the MIDI Event List window; scroll down. You'll see MIDI notes, as well as the MIDI volume and pan that we recorded above.

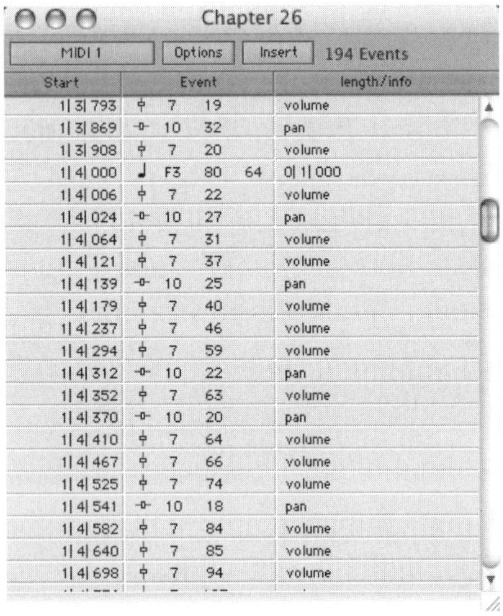

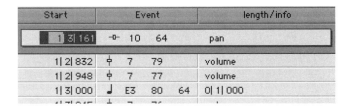

Figure 26-3

When you're looking at controllers in the Event List, on the left you'll see the time of the event. The little icon tells you the type of event. The next column shows the continuous controller number; volume happens to be 7, while pan is 10. Next up is the value of the controller from 0-127. How that value is interpreted depends on the type of controller. For example, with MIDI volume, 0 is all the way off, while 127 is all the way up. With Pan, 64 is center, 0 is full left, and 127 is full right.

You can change any of the values for an event by simply double-clicking on it and typing in the new value that you want. *See Figure 26-4.*

You can also insert new events into the list. Click the Event List window's Insert button, and choose Pan. *See Figure 26-5.*

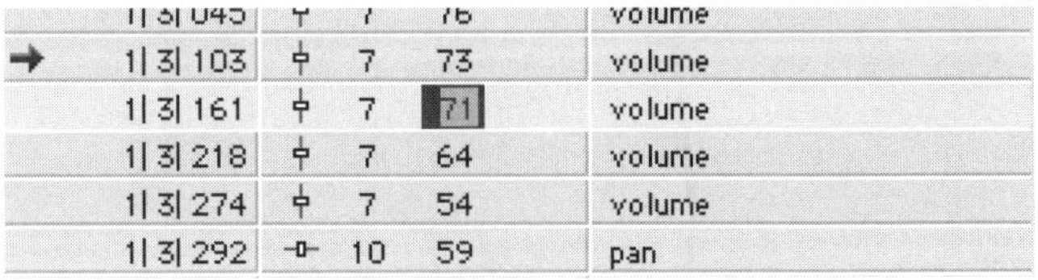

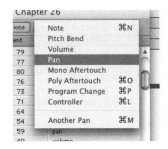

Figure 26-4

Figure 26-5

The new Pan event will appear at the top of the list. Now you can enter the time you want it to occur, as well as its value; click on the other value fields to change them. Hit the **Return** (Enter—the one on the alpha keys) key to accept the new event. Hit the **Enter** (Enter—the one on the numeric keypad) key to accept the event, and prepare to enter another one.

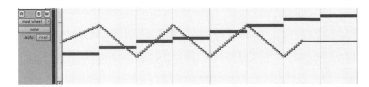

Figure 26-6

DRAWING CONTINUOUS CONTROLLERS

The Pencil tool can be used to draw in continuous controllers. Any of the Pencil modes (Freehand, Line, Triangle, Square, and Random) can be used.

Figure 26-7

Select the controller that you're drawing by choosing it in the track's View Selector. *See Figure 26-8.*

If you want to add a controller, and don't see it listed, choose Add/Remove Controller from the bottom of the list. *See Figure 26-9.*

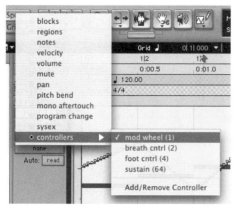

Figure 26-8

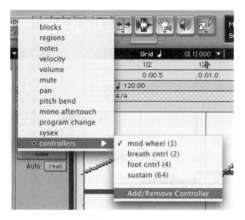

Figure 26-9

The Automated MIDI Controllers window will open.

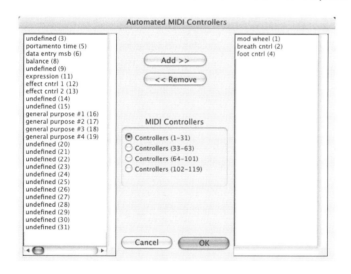

Figure 26-10

You can choose to add (or remove) any of the 128 MIDI continuous controllers to the list of those enabled for automation—except volume and pan, which are always in the list. Once the controller you want is enabled, you can choose it in the View Selector and draw it in using the Pencil tool.

EDITING CONTINUOUS CONTROLLERS

You can edit MIDI continuous controllers in the same

way that you can regular automation: Select a range with the Selector tool. The Edit menu commands will work, you can use the Trimmer tool, you can redraw with the Pencil, or you can simply hit Delete to erase unwanted events.

PATCH SELECT/BANK CHANGES

Each MIDI track can be set to send out a default MIDI program change message, which will call up a preset on the assigned MIDI device—you can call up patches on synths, samplers, or even on effects boxes and mixers that support MIDI patch changes.

MIDI allows for 128 patches; but many pieces of MIDI gear contain way more than that, usually organized into banks of 128 presets. To address the additional banks, a bank change message can be sent. There's no standard way to do this; some devices use continuous controller 0 messages for bank change, others use continuous controller 32 messages. (Check your MIDI device's manual to find out which type of bank change message it likes to see.) Pro Tools can send both types from its Patch Select window.

If you're on the Mac and your device is supported, you can choose the patch change you want by name. If you're on Windows XP or your device is unsupported, you'll have to do it the old-fashioned way: by number.

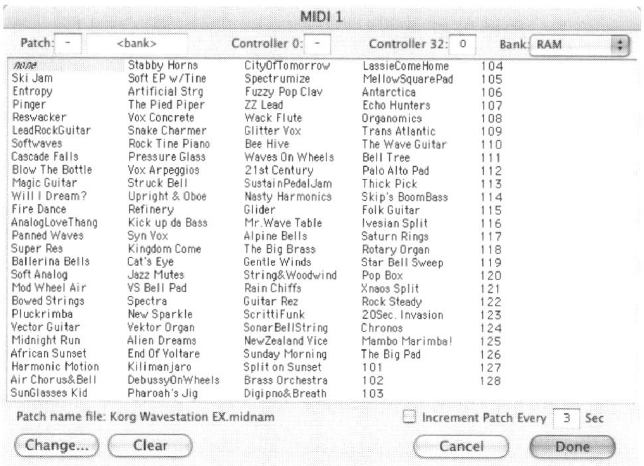

Figure 26-11

The default patch change you select will occur right at the beginning of the track. If you want the patch to change during the course of the track, you can enter additional patch change events anywhere you like. You can do this in the MIDI Event List window by choosing Program Change from the Insert menu, or by typing ⌘+P (Ctrl+P). *See Figure 26-12.*

The new event will be appear at the top of the list. You can now enter the time you want it to occur, as well as the patch you want. Click "none" under the Length/Info column to open the Patch Select window. *See Figure 26-13.*

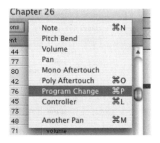

Figure 26-12

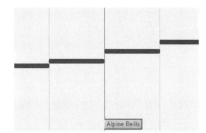

Figure 26-13

You can also enter program changes with the Pencil. Choose Program Change from the track's View Selector. Now click with the Pencil in the track where you want the change to occur. The Patch Select window will open. Choose the patch you want and click Done.

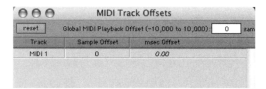

Figure 26-14

The program change event will appear in the track, with the patch name (if supported) displayed.

EDITING PATCH CHANGES

To edit a program change, double-click on it in the track using the Grabber or Pencil tool. The Patch Select window will open.

AUDITIONING PATCH CHANGES

The Patch Select window has a special feature that you can use if you're unsure what preset you want to use for a track: Audition Program. Select the checkbox next to "Increment Patch Every XX Sec," and Pro Tools will move through the available patches in the window, at a rate determined by the number of seconds you've set (the default is 3 seconds).

NOTE CHASING

Here's a problem that can happen if you don't start playing a MIDI track from the beginning: If the track has long notes playing that begin before the location where you start playback, those notes won't sound. A Pro Tools feature called "Note Chasing" fixes this. To enable Note Chasing, select it in the track's Playlist menu. (Note Chasing will automatically be turned on when the MIDI track is created.)

Figure 26-15

SYSTEM EXCLUSIVE

MIDI system exclusive messages are a type of data that is specific to only one MIDI device—examples include the patch memory for a keyboard or effects box and control changes that aren't supported by continuous controllers. Pro Tools can record this information, but can't edit it. You can move it around on the track, and cut/copy/paste or delete it.

OFFSETTING MIDI TRACKS

In some cases, you may find that your MIDI tracks sound like they're playing late compared to your audio tracks—this will mainly be an issue when you're monitoring your MIDI gear through your Pro Tools hardware. You may also run into this problem if you have a MIDI track that's layering or doubling an audio track. To fix it, go **Windows → Show MIDI Track Offsets.**

The MIDI Offset window will open. In this window you can set a global offset (which moves the MIDI tracks either earlier or later in time) that affects all MIDI tracks, or you can offset individual tracks by different amounts.

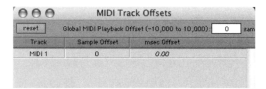

Figure 26-16

EMERGENCY!

It happens occasionally: A MIDI error occurs, and a note won't stop sounding. The brute force fix is to turn the offending MIDI box off and back on. A better

approach is to go **MIDI** → **All Notes Off** or type
↑+⌘+. (↑+Ctrl+.)

Figure 26-17

twenty-seven

GOING SOFT

Over the past few years a new category of instruments has appeared on the scene: virtual instruments, or software synthesizers—soft synths, for short. Recently a number of software samplers hit the market as well. Soft synths and samplers come in two flavors: plug-in and stand-alone.

A stand-alone soft synth works as a separate program running on your computer. If the program supports the ReWire protocol, the soft synth output can be routed right into the Pro Tools mixer. If the synth is available as an RTAS plug-in, you can use it as a plug-in right within Pro Tools. In either case, Pro Tools' MIDI tracks can be used to drive the synthesizer or sampler, just as if it were an external hardware box.

SYNTH PLUG-INS

There are many software instruments available as RTAS plug-ins. At the time of this writing, Pro Tools LE comes with one included for free: IK Multimedia's SampleTank LE. If SampleTank LE came with your Pro Tools package, install it following the manufacturer's instructions. (If you have some other RTAS-format soft synth, the following process will hold for most other manufacturers' soft synths and samplers, too.)

Create a new Session. Name it "Soft Synth." Switch to the Mix window.

Add a stereo Aux Input and a MIDI track. *See Figure 27-1.*

Insert SampleTank (or any other RTAS-format soft synth) into the Aux Input. *See Figure 27-2.*

Figure 27-1

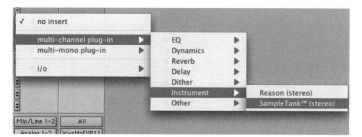

Figure 27-2

The synth's plug-in window will open. *See Figure 27-3.*

Once you have the plug-in inserted on the track, it will appear as an output option for the MIDI track. Assign it as the track's output. *See Figure 27-4.*

Figure 27-3

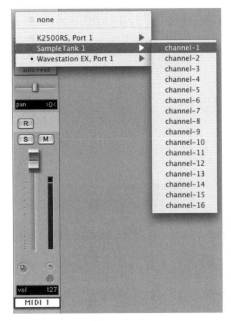

Figure 27-4

Turn up the Aux Input volume level, and arm the MIDI track to prepare to play the soft synth—depending on the instrument you're using, you may also have to select a patch for the soft synth or sampler. (You will have to load a patch for SampleTank LE.) If you don't have a MIDI keyboard to play the soft synth, you can use the Pencil to draw whatever notes you want played into the MIDI track.

Any MIDI information that can be sent to an external MIDI device can be routed to a soft synth or sampler: volume, pan, continuous controllers, pitchbend, aftertouch or anything else that the instrument supports. Simply play it in from a keyboard or enter it into the MIDI track in the Edit window.

ReWire

ReWire is a communication protocol developed by Propellerheads to facilitate sending MIDI and audio information between programs running on the same computer. Think of ReWire connections as virtual patch cables that can connect pieces of software together. Many standalone software synths and samplers can communicate via ReWire; Pro Tools LE includes a ReWire plug-in that can send and receive ReWire information.

As I'm writing this book, a free copy of Propellerheads' Reason Adapted virtual studio software is included with Pro Tools LE. Reason Adapted contains a variety of modules, including synthesizers, samplers, effects processors, and mixers. Audio from Reason Adapted can be sent into the Pro Tools mixer, and MIDI from Pro Tools can be sent into Reason to control the various modules.

If Reason Adapted came with your Pro Tools system, install it according to the manufacturer's instructions. Once it's installed, make sure that it works properly, then quit from the program. If you don't have Reason Adapted, use any other ReWire-compatible synth or sampler. (I'll be using the full version of Reason for these examples; functionally everything works the same as Reason Adapted, however it may look slightly different.)

To use Reason Adapted with Pro Tools, create a new Session. Name it "Never Been Any Reason." Add a stereo Aux Input to the Mix window.

Assign the Reason plug-in (which is actually a ReWire link to the Reason program) or the plug-in for whatever virtual instrument you're using, to any insert on the Aux Input. You can use either the multi-channel or multi-mono version of the Reason plug-in; in this case it doesn't matter which one.

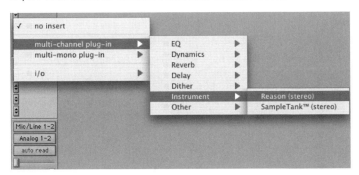

Figure 27-5

The Reason plug-in window will open. There's really only one parameter to set in this window: Which Reason outputs will be feeding the ReWire plug-in. It will default to the main left/right stereo out. *See Figure 27-6.*

Reason Adapted supports Auto-launch, so the program will start up as soon as you select the Reason ReWire plug-in. If you're using a software synth or sampler that doesn't support Auto-launch, start the program now. Reason Adapted will open up. *See Figure 27-7.*

Figure 27-6

Figure 27-7

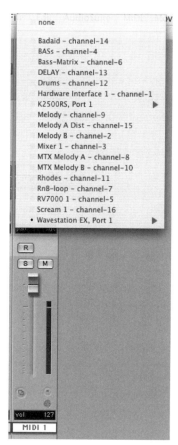

Figure 27-8

Reason's outputs will automatically be set to feed ReWire. Click back over to Pro Tools. Turn up the Aux Input track. Play the Pro Tools Session. Pro Tools will start playing, and simultaneously Reason will be playing locked rhythmically to Pro Tools. You can fast-forward, rewind, or locate in the Pro Tools Session, and Reason Adapted will follow right along. The audio output from Reason will be fed in the Aux Input to the Pro Tools' mixer.

REWIRE AND MIDI

You can also use ReWire to route MIDI out of Pro Tools and into your virtual instruments. Add a MIDI track to our Reason Adapted session. Click its Output Selector. You'll see that any of Reason Adapted's modules that can be addressed by MIDI will show up as an output option. (This example shows Reason, which may differ slightly from Reason Adapted.) If you're using a different ReWire-compatible virtual instrument, you'll see its MIDI connections instead of Reason's.

REWIRE TIPS AND TRICKS

Here are some suggestions for making ReWire work its best for you:

- With ReWire, you're running more than one application at once. This means that the memory demands placed on your computer have increased significantly. You may get better performance if you add more RAM to your computer.

- When it comes time to quit, shut down the ReWire "client" (the virtual instrument) first, then shut down the "host" (Pro Tools).

- If your computer seems to be struggling or having performance problems, choose **Setups→Playback Engine** in Pro Tools, and change the CPU Usage Limit. The ReWire client may also have a CPU usage setting that you can adjust. Experiment until you find the right balance between the two.

- ReWire supports up to 64 audio channels, so you have plenty of "wires" for getting various virtual instruments into Pro Tools. You could bring several separate virtual instruments into the Pro Tools mixer. Or you could bring multiple outputs from Reason in—Reason has up to 64 outputs. Just add more mono or stereo Reason ReWire plug-ins (each on their own Aux Input) to Pro Tools to bring in more outputs.

• While ReWire is normally used for virtual instruments, it could be used with another ReWire-compatible audio program, such as Ableton Live, a powerful audio looping program. A version of Live, called "Ableton Live Digidesign Edition" is included free with Pro Tools LE at the time of this writing. It is used in similar fashion to Reason Adapted; it can synchronize with Pro Tools, and its outputs can feed ReWire plug-ins on Pro Tools Aux Inputs.

Afterword

We've arrived at the end of our journey through this book—congratulations! But you've only just begun your journey to complete Pro Tools mastery. That can only come with lots of practice and continued study and learning. A book like this can introduce you to the basic concepts, and guide you through using the day-to-day techniques you'll need, but to become a true expert will require that you take the next steps of the journey on your own.

The good news is that you're now well prepared to venture out on your own. By working through this book, you've learned more than enough to make outstanding recordings using Pro Tools LE. You know how to record, overdub, edit, process, and mix audio, as well as how to use MIDI to enhance your productions. What's the next step? Get out there and make recordings! Push the Record and Play buttons as often as you can. The more you record, edit, and mix, the more your Pro Tools and recording and mixing skills will improve.

In the midst of all that learning and gaining of experience, don't forget the real reason you're doing this...not to become a Pro Tools expert (unless you're after a job as a Pro Tools operator), but to make great recordings of music that you can share with the world.

That's what it's ultimately all about—all the money spent on gear, the hours spent studying and practicing, the time spent becoming proficient with your computer and Pro Tools—it all comes down to just one thing: Making music. Keep that in mind as your goal, and your investment in Pro Tools LE will pay off in countless ways.

If I may, I'll leave you with one last vitally important Pro Tools LE tip: Have fun!